Public Administration

Third Edition

Public Administration

Social Change
and
Adaptive Management

Third Edition

N. Joseph Cayer
Arizona State University

David L. Baker
California State University, San Bernardino

Louis F. Weschler
Arizona State University (Emeritus)

Birkdale Publishers
San Diego

Front cover photograph of the Sumter Town Hall-Opera House courtesy of the South Carolina Department of Archives and History. In 1912, Sumter, South Carolina became the first city in the United States to adopt a charter incorporating the council-manager form of government.

Editor: Sidney Shiroma
Design Consultant: Steven Shultz
Copy Editor: Leonard Rosenbaum
Editorial Assistant: Ashton Penton

ISBN 978-0-9724419-5-7

Birkdale Publishers, Inc.
P.O. Box 270261
San Diego CA 92198-0261

www.BirkdalePublishers.com

Contents

Preface

Since the original publication of *Public Administration: Social Change and Adaptive Management* in 1988 and the second edition in 2003, many of the details of public administration theory and practice have changed. However, the basic interpretive themes we addressed from the first edition have remained amazingly resilient. Although they are reflected in different substantive concerns and in different ideas about how to conduct the activities of public administration, the administrative swamp metaphor still aptly captures the tension between the ideal of rational processes and the reality of the social and political world in which American public administration takes place.

In our democratic society, citizens expect government to pursue goals and to address problems with clear and successful measures. Public administration is traditionally viewed as the application of rational processes to the accomplishment of governmental agency missions. In reality, however, complex forces make the rational pursuit of goals difficult. Many public problems are intractable. The competing interests and forces surrounding public agencies make administrative life uncertain. Consequently, public agencies and administrators find themselves in the administrative swamp. Management of public agencies is a high-risk endeavor. This book deals with the reality of public administration and contrasts it with the unreal expectations that American society often has of public organizations.

American public administration is practiced in a complex social, economic, and political environment. The constraining effects of the environment, along with limits on human rationality, lead the practice of public administration to be more fluid than concrete. Public administration and administrators need to be inventive, flexible, and adaptive. Planning, resource allocation, and people management rely more upon intuitive and contingent approaches than traditional public administration theory postulates. Public administration is a living experience in which constant personal and organizational adjustments are made as public policy is implemented in a changing and unsure setting.

Public administration has also come to be increasingly important in the general governance of our society. In many respects, the manager, who is at the center of the policy process and at the service delivery level, is the final decision-maker and interpreter of policy. In short, public administrators often determine what the policy actually means. We also recognize that public agencies and administrators increasingly work in partnership with others in achieving their goals. Governance involves private sector organizations, nonprofits, and governmental agencies working together to deliver the services the public expects.

In attempting to capture the reality of public administration, this book examines the context, major actors, activities, and issues that surround the field. In the first two chapters, we address the context of public administration. Chapter 1 looks at the field of public administration and the way people have conceptualized it, with an emphasis on the need for collective human effort to accomplish the objectives of administration. Chapter 2 examines the specific American political context. The effects of imperfect political pluralism and the political aspects of administration are used to contrast public administration with administration in general.

Chapters 3 and 4 turn to the organizations and people doing the work of public administration. Chapter 3 focuses on bureaucracy, the dominant form of organization in public administration. Bureaucracy as an ideal, rational form of organization for accomplishing any goal is contrasted with the reality of bureaucratic behavior. Criticisms of bureaucracy and suggestions for reform are examined to provide an understanding of the prospects for success. Chapter 4 deals with the individual members of the bureaucracy and the factors that motivates them. Theories of organization, from the perspective of the role of the individual in organizations, are used to illustrate problems in organizational behavior.

Chapter 5 examines the major activities of bureaucracies in applying and managing resources in the execution of their responsibilities. In particular, we look at the ways bureaucracies use planning, budgeting, and evaluation to facilitate administration. Various approaches to each of these activities are examined, as are the problems associated with the idea of rational conduct in carrying out these activities.

Chapter 6 considers managerial work under risky conditions. Various roles and functions of the top-level public manager are examined in the context of limited resources and the uncertainty of the environment in which public administration occurs. We emphasize the need for a strategic approach to leading organizations through the swamp.

Chapter 7 addresses recent trends in public administration that provide both opportunities and constraints for improving practice. It also suggests the challenges that lie ahead for public administration.

The third edition continues the second edition's inclusion of review and study questions as well as suggested exercises for use with the book. The exercises vary in complexity and time involved. Although some of the exercises may exceed the needs of a given course, we feel that it is useful to include the many exercises that the authors have used successfully in their courses. We like to get students into the field to make reflective observations. Instructors may pick and choose which to use in consideration of the way they organize their courses and the time available to the students. Some of the exercises build on others or are compatible with others. These may be used as semester-long projects, with applications made to each of the chapters.

We hope the study questions will stimulate students to think about the field of public administration and the challenges that confront anyone who enters it. They also may be used as guides to review and critique the major ideas of each chapter.

In addition to updating the references, we include Web sites the authors find helpful for the subject matter of each of the chapters. The Web sites listed include those of government agencies, nonprofits, professional associations, and research centers. There are, of course, thousands of potentially useful Web sites. Students and instructors are certain to find their own.

The third edition brings on David Baker of California State University at San Bernardino as an author. His extensive experience in local government management, particularly county management, brings added perspective to the endeavor.

In writing this book, many individuals have provided help, many too many to list here. Nonetheless, we thank our colleagues, our students, and others who have challenged our thoughts and led us to a better understanding of the field. We owe a special debt to Robert Biller, retired Executive Vice Provost of the University of Southern California, for his early formulations on the contrast between the swamp and bedrock in the conduct of public administration. We also appreciate the help of the publisher, Sidney Shiroma, throughout the process. His thoughtful suggestions and questions, along with support, made the creation of the third edition a smooth one. Thank you also to the copy editor, Leonard Rosenbaum.

Despite the help of many people, there are sure to be shortcomings. We accept responsibility for them.

N. Joseph Cayer
Mesa, AZ

David L. Baker
San Bernardino, CA

Louis F. Weschler
Tempe, AZ

Public Administration

Third Edition

1

Public Administration

Public administration has been compared to life in the swamp (Biller, 1978, 1979; Luthans & Steward, 1977) because of the uncertainty it faces. In the swamp, footing is uncertain, the path is unclear, the terrain keeps shifting, and the alligators are mean and hungry. In such a risky setting, a person is hard-pressed to survive. Some also argue that the swamp provides an environment for symbiotic relationships and for some creatures to prosper and grow (Liggett, 2005).

Public administrators must conduct their activities in a much more unstable environment than business administrators. They are affected by politics, changing political power relationships, economic swings, and volatile social issues. Business administrators are accountable for the bottom line and have relatively clear lines of authority to follow. Public agencies seldom have a bottom line, and public administrators are accountable to numerous authorities including politically elected officials and the general public. Their accountability includes requirements to use financial resources responsibly and to be responsive to the democratic values of the governmental system. They operate in a fishbowl environment, observable by everyone. In such an environment, it is difficult to know which path to take, whether one will be on solid ground, or where the mean and hungry alligators are lurking. Public administrators are fortunate if they can maintain the status quo, let alone get on with major programmatic goals, whereas, in the business sector, planning and achieving programmatic goals are part of the bottom line.

The administrative swamp is inhabited by changing political forces, changing economic conditions, the media spotlight, interest groups, and citizen demands. Additionally, internal forces such as employee concerns, interagency conflict, and bureaucratic routines lie in wait for the manager who attempts to drain the swamp and establish firm ground on which to work. Having to worry about all these alligators in the swamp, public administrators are not able to pursue the goals of the organization with undivided attention. Instead, each of these forces affects the resources available to administrators and the way they might utilize those resources. The forces in the swamp environment also have many impacts on public organizations, including constant change through reform, re-organization, re-engineering, and re-invention especially arising from efforts to make them accountable (Burke, 2009; Denhardt & Denhardt, 2007; Lynn, 2001; Riccucci, 2001; Rosenbloom, 2001; Williams, 2000).

The unpredictable environment of the administrative swamp can also stimulate public administrators to innovate and try new approaches. Tensions and conflict may lead to creative ideas on how to change policies or implement strategies. Alligators challenge public administrators to find ways to survive in the swamp with both positive and negative effects.

In addition to having an uncertain environment in which to operate, public administration is difficult to define because its boundaries are unclear. Government is involved in almost everything people do because it is the ultimate provider of services that keep society together and the final arbiter that ensures that the activities of one person are not detrimental to others. Counter to the swamp, government tries to stabilize the environment and maintain social cohesion and tranquility. It creates the structure for civility and civil order (Cochran, 1982; Putnam, 2000). As government gets involved, agencies are created with administrators to see that government policy is implemented. In policy implementation, administrators also become policy formulators as they develop expertise in what should be done or what will work best in any given situation. Administrators are in a good position to shape the future development of policy through their recommendations to policy-making bodies. At the same time, they make policy by interpreting and applying elected officials' general policies to specific situations.

Today's governance means that government works in concert with many other entities to achieve public goals. The nongovernmental nonprofit sector represents one of the most important of such entities. Many nongovernmental organizations receive public funding and serve the public interest by providing public goods and services similar to governmental services. The trend in the United States since the 1970s has been to shift much of the responsibility for the delivery of social services to the private nonprofit sector. Operating with a public trust, they are subject to governmentally imposed rules and regulations and operate in the public spotlight. Such organizations include the United Way, Red Cross, and cultural agencies such as museums and symphonies. Government also contracts with many for-profit organizations. They include vendors for various health services as well as hospitals and private colleges that serve the public interest.

Some public interest groups such as the National League of Cities and the Council of State Governments, as well as professional associations such as the International Public Management Association for Human Resources (IPMA-HR) and the International City/County Management Association (ICMA), are part of the nonprofit sector. Since the 1980s, homeowners' associations (HOAs) and neighborhood associations have become important actors in managing local affairs. These organizations are subject to many of the same concerns as government agencies and are considered part of public administration in the broad sense that they work in the public interest. Nonetheless, this book concentrates primarily on governmental organizations in examining public administration.

Another factor helping to create the administrative swamp is the fact that government is often asked to deal with intractable problems, sometimes referred to as *wicked problems* (Rittel & Webber, 1973: Weber & Khademian, 2008). Wicked problems are those that often have no agreed upon definition such as unemployment and poverty. Consequently, it is impossible to know when the problem is solved or what will solve it. As long as people disagree on what poverty means, for example, who can tell when it is solved? Wicked problems also involve those issues where emotional, religious, or ideological perspectives allow for no compromise thus the problems are not solvable by government. For example, the issue of abortion is one that government can never solve because no "solution" will ever be acceptable to all sides of the issue. Cloning of human cells is another example where deep-seated values make compromise virtually impossible.

In order to understand public administration, it is necessary to understand the changing environment and the political relationships among actors in that environment. We must also understand the individuals who make up public organizations and the values that shape their behavior and the behavior of organizations. Superimposed on these issues are efforts to develop rational processes and organizational structures to insure proper implementation of public policy. The issues outlined below are recurring themes throughout the book as we attempt to explain public administration as adaptive management in an ever-changing society.

Public Administration as Collective Human Endeavor

All administration, including public administration, depends upon the cooperative effort of the individuals who make up the administrative organization. In order to accomplish most objectives, the organization needs to attract members and gain their cooperation. Securing the compliance and support of members requires that they interact with and adjust to each other. Therefore, administration is affected by the complexities of human nature. In public administration, administrators deal not only with those people who make up the organization but also with interested members of the political environment including elected political leaders, citizens, interest groups, and clients of the organization. These elements of the political environment affect the ability of the organization to accomplish its mission. Along with the internal human interactions, these external elements create an ever-changing, often perplexing, setting for public administration.

Internal Dynamics

The ability of organizations to accomplish their objectives is greatly affected by the people within the organization and the way they interact. Managers and employees of the organization may operate on the basis of different needs and perhaps, conflicting expectations; therefore, their behavior may differ (Tullock, 1965). An organization's managers usually feel the necessity of pleasing elected public officials and thus attempt to control the activities of employees so as not to alienate those external superiors. Managers are interested in appearing to be as competent as possible to their superiors and in having their departments run as smoothly as possible. Their own careers depend upon how well they are perceived to be doing their jobs; hence, they normally want their subordinates to do their work with a minimum of trouble. In order to maintain the image they want, managers often attempt to control information provided outside the organization as well as the external flow of information into the organization.

Employees may have other concerns. Among them are earning or collecting a paycheck, pleasing the manager, obtaining a good annual performance review, and getting along with others in the organization. Ralph Hummel (2008) indicates that bureaucrats adapt to a set of norms that permits them to accomplish their tasks without getting fully involved in the human aspects of the work. They operate under guidelines developed by managers or others and accommodate themselves to those guidelines. By accepting the ways of doing things as a requirement of the job, they do not have to deal with justifying their actions by their own values. These characteristics are typical of members of large, complex organizations in the private sector as well as in government. Essentially, organization members displace their own personal values in favor of organizational norms.

The bureaucrats' personal values often differ from what is required in their roles or positions. As a result, there may be tension between the requirements of the job and the personal concerns of the employee. If those tensions become too strong, the employee is likely to engage in dysfunctional behavior that is in conflict with the interests of the organization and higher-level management. An example of such a situation might be an employee in a public health agency who has strong feelings against abortion. If that employee's agency funds family planning clinics or works with clients in all forms of family planning, including abortion, it is possible that the employee could make it difficult for those clinics performing or clients seeking abortions. The same conflicts could be felt by an employee who strongly supports abortion as a choice having to deal with clinics or clients with opposing views. The effect on the organization may be interference with its ability to get its work done effectively.

These value conflicts often result in ethical dilemmas and issues for employees (Svara, 2007; Traaen, 2000; Van Wart, 1998). If the organization requires the employee to violate a strongly held value or to do something the employee believes to be wrong, the employee has to make an ethical choice. The converse is the problem of employees imposing their ethical values on the organization and everyone in it.

Employees have other personal interests and concerns that affect their work activity. Their economic security as well as emotional and psychological well-being affect their performance in the organization. If they perceive managerial directions to be inconsistent with their own self-interests, it is possible that they may act in ways that are dysfunctional to the organization. Managers may attempt to impose control, but conflicts are likely to develop between employees and managers, further diminishing the effectiveness of the organization.

External Factors

Public administrators work in an environment in which they have to respond to a variety of outside forces. Public servants have many superiors who often have differing and even conflicting expectations of the public agency, thus destabilizing the foundation on which they work. Elected public officials usually have agendas they wish the administrators to pursue. Many of the agendas take the form of public policy adopted by legislative bodies or directives of chief executives. However, many times the newly elected officials expect the administrative agencies to fall in line with their policy preferences even if they are in conflict with formally established policy. The primary concern of many elected public officials appears to be control over the activities of public agencies. In particular, they do not want public administrators to embarrass them or to do things that are contrary to their policy preferences. They claim that they were elected to run things.

When George W. Bush became president, for example, he and his administration reversed policy on levels of arsenic in the drinking water without consultation with others involved in the issue. Also during the Bush administration, the attorney general reinterpreted the Second Amendment to the Constitution stating that it guarantees individuals' rights to guns, thus reversing consistent interpretation of it as referring only to the right to bear arms as a collective right for purposes of defense. Similarly, the Obama administration revised the Bush administration policy that placed a strategic missile defense system in Poland and the Czech Republic over the objections of many in the military, Congress, and the public. In Arizona and many other states, the state legislature consistently raids education funds to bail out state budget deficits. These actions place personal policy preferences of public officials as the formal public policy without reference to the will of the people or majorities that put the original policies in place.

Problems emerge for public employees when different elected officials have conflicting expectations and demand different results from the same agencies. Additionally, public agencies often get caught in the middle of conflicts between elected executive officers and legislative bodies. Each of these actors may have a different agenda and goal, yet the public agency must serve and attempt to satisfy both. In addition to having differing agendas and goals, executive and legislative officials may interpret the same policy in differing ways, thus increasing the difficulty for public administrators in finding clear paths and firm terrain.

Theoretically, public administrators exist to serve citizens. It is impossible to satisfy the desires of every individual in all ways; thus, some calculation of the "public interest" occurs. This estimation is inexact, does not result from any particular system of rational understanding and often depends upon impressions. Further, the public interest is often defined outside the agency by elected policy-making bodies or the courts, and the administrator must interpret and adjust this abstraction to practice.

An important fact for the administrator is that individual citizens expect responsiveness to their private wants. When they perceive that administrators are not responsive to their needs, they complain. It is not easy for a public servant to explain that the interests of the general public come before those of any one individual. The public administrator is put in the position of attempting to follow agency guidelines and general public policy while satisfying elected officials and individual citizens at the same time. These are inevitable conflicts that the administrator must juggle in order to survive in the administrative swamp.

The public interest is often defined by interest groups that have the resources to gain access to administrative agencies. In the absence of a clearly defined public interest, administrators react to those who make claims in the public interest. Interest groups have their own stakes in the activities of agencies. They pressure agencies to interpret and implement policy according to their best interests, again putting public administrators in the position of mediating conflicting demands.

Clients of the organization are most directly affected by the actions of public agencies. Agencies created to serve a particular clientele are often hampered in doing so because laws or administrative regulations limit the flexibility of the administrator to act. For example, the law or regulation may require that families be residents of the state or locality for a specified period of time before they are eligible for services. Consequently, a family with no money or food just arriving in the locality may not be eligible for food assistance. The administrator who has to deny the assistance is perceived as being cold and impersonal. Yet the administrator has little flexibility to change the rule. The policy to provide food represents one value of society, whereas the rule regarding eligibility represents another. The power to resolve the conflict between the two values may or may not be within the discretion of the street-level public administrator.

These elements of the external environment constrain administrative options and influence agency actions that produce outcomes. Conflicting external signals and expectations lead administrators to act in ways that maximize the ability of the organization to survive. Often they react by attempting to routinize activities in such a way so as to insulate themselves from as much pressure as possible. They fall back upon bureaucratic rules and procedures when pressed and pulled into situations that appear to threaten the agency.

Faithful Execution of the Public Trust

The bureaucratic response of falling back on rules and procedures when faced with threats begs the question of doing the right thing. We expect public administrators to do the right thing. Often they do. Nonetheless, public administrators in the swamp are vexed by ethics. Finding the right path often is not easy in a rule-bound world.

Public administrators, like all public officers in the United States, affirm or swear to an oath of office that binds them to the faithful execution of the laws. Faithful execution of the laws, including the national and state constitutions, constitutes a public trust. The public expects that public administrators will behave in a legal and moral manner in carrying out the duties of the office that they have sworn that they will execute to the best of their abilities. Constitutional government expects no less of its public servants (Rohr, 1999). Not all public officials, of course, actually behave in legal and moral ways in their public actions. More frequently than one would like, public officials cut corners or take the easy road, and betray their public trust. Nonetheless, the record of public administrators faithfully executing their public trust is remarkably good in this country. Public ethics, however, continues as a major concern in education for public administration, in-service training of agency personnel, and guiding the actions of officials. Ethical training currently constitutes a kind of consultants' cottage industry.

Part of the reason for a resurgence of ethical concerns in recent times is unhappiness with the version of utilitarianism that dominates American public administration. *Utilitarianism* is an approach to morality that makes human satisfaction the primary element in judging the moral acceptability of a given action. The shorthand form is "the greatest good for the greatest number," in which good is defined as meeting the demands (utilities) of the public. Ironically, the actual outcome of administrative action is often not the measure of utility or goodness. Administrative agencies, as rule-bound organizations, take and defend actions not solely because of the instrumental good the actions produce, but also because the action is done in accordance with the rules. This "rule-consequentialism" permits public agencies to pursue the public good through strict adherence to the agency rules rather than the actual consequences of the actions (Honderich, 1995, p. 890)

Rule-consequentialism, coupled with growing political pressures to meet the specific demands of interest groups, put individual public administrators and agencies in a double moral bind. It is tempting for them to continue to treat each new event as a call for simple application of the rules. It is also tempting to bend the rules in the face of strong political pressure. In the swamp, where risk abounds, the administrator may commit moral errors in overzealous rule-bound behavior or in over-flexibility in the interpretation of laws and rules.

The responsible administrator (Cooper, 2006) must avoid both errors. Rather, the administrator must find the path that permits a balance of good substance and correct procedure. Aristotle's doctrine of the golden mean offers guidance. The virtuous administrator is not overly responsive to any particular impulse, pressure, or rule, but rather to each to the right extent. A responsive, virtuous administrator chooses to act as a matter of self-conscious, educated judgment. What is right in a given instance cannot be derived from a neat formula. It must result from mature judgment in response to a wide range of circumstances in which an action is required. The responsive and responsible administrator is self-aware, introspective, prudent, and confident in facing the challenges of the swamp.

Public Administration as Art, Science, and Craft

The nature of public administration has been subject to debate for as long as it has been studied. People argue over whether it is an art, craft, science, profession, field of study, or discipline (Berkley, 2008; Lynn, 1996). Although there has been a great deal of debate over these issues, there are few definitive agreements or answers to the debates. In reality, public administration is each of these things to some degree, although individuals may differ on how they view it. The most long-standing debate has centered around whether public administration is considered an art or craft on the one hand, or a profession or science on the other.

As Dwight Waldo (1977) indicates, the scientific management movement crystallized the debate by attempting to establish public administration as a science with universal laws or tendencies that could be applied in any situation. Humans are viewed as malleable, to be shaped to the needs of the organization. Once the general laws are codified, people may be taught to apply them in any given situation.

Challenges to this approach suggested that management is a practical skill based upon highly variable personal characteristics and abilities. These skills and abilities can be acquired and honed through training or may be a part of one's personality. The skills and abilities also vary according to the situation or environment in which they are used.

Experience suggests that many of the accepted principles and practices of scientific management do not endure societal changes or transfer to other societies. Therefore, they are suspect as science. Nonetheless, the scientific method can be used in many management situations and can be useful in decision-making processes. Science as a method of inquiry and a body of knowledge may be used to inform managers and estimate the possible consequences of actions. Science, however, is a tool with considerable limits in management. Because management depends upon the coordination of human beings, nothing is totally predictable or certain. Thus, public administration is part of the social sciences, which are inexact as measured by the standards of the life or physical sciences. That caveat does not mean that public administration should not strive for as much certainty as possible. Rather, scientific approaches are incorporated as appropriate while public administrators understand that much of their success depends upon adaptation to ever-changing circumstances. Much of their adaptiveness flows from intuition and feelings rather than from facts. Some scholars suggest that rather than using the positivist, rational approaches, public administration would be better served by a postmodern approach that emphasizes discourse and collaboration among citizens, administrators, and public officials (Box, Marshall, Reed, & Reed, 2002; King & Stivers, 1998; Miller & Fox, 2006; Schachter, 1997).

Those who perceive that public administration should aspire to be a practical science believe that political values can be separated from the administrative process. Values are represented by the policymakers who are separate from the administrators. Thus, the policy/administration or politics/administration dichotomy evolves from the effort to establish public administration as a separate entity. Woodrow Wilson's essay, "The Study of Administration" (1887), gave intellectual legitimacy to the concept of separating politics and administration. This approach to the field has been remarkably durable (Cook, 2007; Overeem, 2008; Stivers, 2008; Svara, 2008). Although the separation is continually challenged and public administration now eschews the reality of the separation, it is an important analytical distinction for understanding many aspects of public administration. Until the late 1950s and 1960s, the separation of policy and administration was accepted virtually as a given in the field.

The development of the council-manager form of municipal government, which began in 1908, is perhaps the most dramatic symbol of the policy/administration dichotomy. The plan, which separates the policy function (council) from professional scientific management (manager) is used by approximately half of the cities in the U.S. with a population over 2,500. The approach is mirrored in school districts in which boards of education are the policymakers and the superintendent and other professional staff are managers.

In the post-World War II era, scholars began to challenge the purported scientific nature of the scientific management school. Herbert Simon (1997) characterized the principles of administration advocated by the Scientific Management School as proverbs that often conflicted with one another or proverbs whose opposites were just as plausible. Simon favored attempting to develop a truly scientific approach to administration but also developed a fact–value distinction as a guide to the new science. The fact–value distinction led to a renewed interest in the policy/administration dichotomy. The major impact of Simon's work was to stimulate an interest in more scientific approaches to analyzing public administration. Much of the quantitative study of public administration owes its start to Simon's challenge. Of course, quantification is not synonymous with science, although many treat it as such.

As public administration achieved an identity and attempted to utilize the methods of science, it also began to assume some of the characteristics of a profession. The organization of several associations of public administration such as the International City Manager's Association (later to become the International City/County Management Association) in 1914, and the New York Bureau of Municipal Research (renamed the Institute of Public Administration) in 1906, signaled the legitimacy of public administration as a field of study and practice. Several other associations, particularly the American Society for Public Administration (ASPA), established in 1939, helped to foster a sense of professionalism. As Chester Newland (1984) notes, these events symbolized the maturing of public administration, and the leadership of the emerging field had the prestige to have significant impact on public policy.

As professionalism developed in the field of public administration, new debates over whether it was really a profession also emerged. During the 1940s, a debate raged between Herman Finer (1941) and Carl Friedrich (1940) and their respective followers. Finer saw responsibility in public administration requiring responsiveness to elected officials and adaptation to changing environmental forces. Friedrich took the position that administrators must answer to scientific standards represented by their expertise and fellowship of science as represented by professional organization standards and accepted practice. The debate over responsiveness and accountability had implications for the "science" vs. "craft" debate about public administration as well as for its development as a profession. Those who wish to ascribe strict professional standards to public administration reflect Friedrich's perspective, whereas those who are more concerned with it as a craft and practice are likely to feel more comfortable with the Finer perspective.

The controversy over whether public administration is a profession often devolves to a disagreement on semantics. Frederick Mosher (1982) attempted to address the issue by distinguishing between the established and emerging professions. The established professions would be those, such as medicine, that already have a well-ordered system of standards of conduct and a method for enforcing them. The debate over whether public administration is a profession and, how strict the definition must be emerges regularly in the literature (Garvey, 1996; Kline, 1981; Stewart, 1985). There seems to be growing consensus that public administration is a profession in a general sense but that the rigid standards by which many professions are judged are impractical for it. Nevertheless, attempts to establish more conventional professional criteria are made as in the American Society for Public Administration's 1984 adoption of a code of ethics for public administrators (revised in 1994). A major problem with development of such standards is in their implementation. A very small proportion of the people who work in public organizations actually belong to ASPA or other associations. It very well may be impossible to impose codes of conduct on people who do not first accept a specific professional association as the legitimate developer of standards.

Along with the development of public administration as a profession, a field of study emerged. Wilson's essay in 1887, in addition to legitimizing the politics/administration dichotomy, has served as a major intellectual beginning for American academic public administration. During the 1930s and 1940s, the literature on public administration as an academic field of study burgeoned, and many academics were brought into administrative positions in government. The administration of Franklin D. Roosevelt, in particular, included many of the leading academics in public administration. Leonard White's introductory text, first published in 1926, set an agenda for the field of study that was to endure through the early 1960s. Chester Newland (1984) characterizes the 1930s–1950s as the Golden Era of public administration. It was an era of optimism about the impact the field could have on improving government along with a strong sense of community among the scholars and practitioners in the field. Simon's work and the rise of "scientific" political science in the 1950s began to draw a wedge between the academic and practitioner perspective. As with many other parts of society, during the 1960s, the sense of community and innocence of the field were severely challenged. The challenge led to a loss of the unity of feeling that had characterized the Golden Era. Today there is much more diversity in the field with numerous areas of specialization that have developed their own professional identities and ways of approaching the study and profession of public administration.

Currently, there is much less cohesion in the scholarship of public administration than there appeared to be during the Golden Era referred to by Newland (1984). The positivists of the 1960s and 1970s have given way to a variety of approaches including the postmodernists, reinvention advocates, new public administration advocates, proponents of the new public management, and advocates of the new public service perspective, among other variations on the theme.

In addition to the difference about what public administration is, there is a natural conflict between the study and the practice of it. The practice of public administration was firmly established before its identity as a specialized field of study was fully developed. Although a few professional programs of public administration were established in the 1920s, most academic institutions eschewed separate professional studies programs; thus, the field of public administration long existed as a subfield of political science in most colleges and universities. During the 1950s and 1960s, the opposition to professional degree programs in public administration subsided and programs proliferated. With this proliferation, there also came much diversity of research and study. Many practitioners felt that university programs were too theoretical and not relevant to their interests and concerns. A common theme of most public administration academic programs and conferences is the effort to bridge the divide between the academic and practitioner worlds. The result has been a much closer relationship of scholarship to practice, especially in independent schools and departments of public administration that have more flexibility to reward faculty members for applied work.

The diversity of research interests has also resulted in a diversity in approaches to the study of the field as represented by new public administration, new public management, new public service, postmodernism, etc. The variety of journals in the field representing different approaches and specializations also reflects diversity. Accordingly, there are journals for every subfield within public administration, such as *Review of Public Personnel Administration, Public Budgeting and Finance Journal, The Journal of Arts Management, Law,* and *Society, and Public Integrity,* among many. There also are journals that cut across the field, such as *Public Administration Review, Administration and Society, Administrative Theory and Praxis, American Review of Public Administration, Journal of Public Affairs Education,* and *Journal of Public Administration Research and Theory.*

Rationality in Public Administration

As Morstein Marx (1957) indicates, public bureaucracies are created with a sense of purpose and are expected to apply specified means to accomplish specified goals or objectives. In other words, public administrators are supposed to be rational in focusing on the goals for which their organization was created. They must find the most efficient and effective ways of achieving those goals and objectives. The creation of public agencies implies this rational process or behavior. This form of rationality may be referred to as institutional or procedural rationality and is at the foundation of traditional public administration theory.

This ideal of rationality is often not achievable, however, because of the swampy conditions under which public sector organizations operate. Foremost among the problems is the fact that most organizations actually have multiple goals and the goals are usually ill-defined. Also, as time passes, new goals may develop. The result is that the organization can simultaneously pursue incompatible or conflicting goals. Such behavior is substantively rational, although it may not be procedurally rational. What is rational then depends upon which goal the evaluator expects the organization to pursue. The Immigration and Naturalization Service (INS), for example, was expected to both enforce laws regarding all types of immigrants (including illegal immigrants) and provide services to assist legal immigrants. The goals of enforcement and service are sometimes in conflict, and some might consider the conflicting aims and activities to be irrational. Subunits within the INS pursue the two different major goals. From the perspective of each subunit, it is acting rationally given the goals it has to pursue. What is rational to one subunit may be in conflict with the goal of the other. In 2002, these conflicting goals led to some embarrassing lapses for the agency and to the reorganization of the agency with the creation of the Immigration and Customs Enforcement and the Bureau of Customs and Border Protection.

Subunits of organizations may diverge in other ways in their pursuit of organizational goals. Subunits develop their own norms and ways of doing things that may or may not be consistent with the needs of the organization as a whole. The resulting dissonance may impede rational pursuit of the overall goal.

Along with conflicting goals, public organizations often find that their rational pursuit of a particular goal may be interrupted by changing goals. New administrations may bring new goals with them, and organizations find that their activities suddenly conflict with the goals of their political superiors. For example, when the George W. Bush administration came to office in 2001, many environmental policies were deemphasized or opposed by the administration. After many years of developing rules and regulations and means to implement numerous environmental policies, many of the agencies were asked to abandon or reverse their efforts. For many state and local governments, which had spent time and money complying with a growing list of national government rules and requirements on environmental issues, the switch seemed irrational in that it either negated expensive actions already undertaken or led them to put plans on hold until policy was clarified. When Barack Obama became president in 2009, many of the Bush administration environmental rules were reversed, thus changing goals once again. Changing goals make it difficult for agencies to behave consistently, as the ground upon which they base their activities is unstable.

Public agencies also find that differing publics may interpret their purposes differently. Even members of legislative bodies that create agencies disagree on what an agency should be attempting to accomplish. The alligators—interest groups, clientele, citizens, and elected political leaders—may also differ on what the agency should be doing and usually attempt to influence the agency. As political power shifts among these competing groups, agency agendas also often shift.

Even assuming that there is agreement on the goals of the organization, there are still many limits to rational action by the agency. Individual rationality traditionally comes into conflict with organizational rationality. Individual employees come to the organization with differing assumptions, norms, and values. Each employee has the potential of having interests that are incompatible with those of the organization. One objective of an organization is to get the employees to temper their incompatible interests and values so as to work in concert with the organization. Given that organizations are made up of many individuals, it is not surprising that many conflicts develop. Employees accommodate the conflicts in many ways, ranging from suppressing their own interests to sabotaging the organization. In the vast majority of cases, individuals are able to reconcile their own needs with those of the organization.

In addition to the conflicts between individual and organizational rationality and among subunits, many other factors affect the capacity of an organization to pursue its ends in a rational manner. Complete operational rationality requires perfect information, unlimited time, and slack resources. In real life, it is almost impossible to have complete information. Given limits in time and other resources, organizations have to act on the basis of partial information. Although the decision or action may be rational in terms of the information available, it is not rational in the comprehensive sense. Especially in the public sector, time may be an important factor. Because of political factors, agencies may make decisions or take actions that they otherwise would not. Even if decisions are made on the basis of complete rationality, there are always some critics regardless of what is done.

In 1986, the Challenger space shuttle accident in which seven crew members died illustrates the point. There were charges that NASA went ahead with an unsafe launch despite warnings by engineers that malfunctions would occur if the temperature were below a certain point. Critics of the decision to go ahead charge that NASA was under pressure from the administration and the media for a success. Additionally, it was suggested that NASA was concerned that its forthcoming calendar of launches would be detrimentally affected by another delay. The Challenger was launched with tragic results. Political and time constraints may have affected NASA's willingness to fully consider all the information it had. There were political goals that may have overridden scientific goals in the decision to launch the shuttle. In most such decisions, money is not available to collect and analyze complete information. Agencies act on the basis of partial information.

Although it is assumed that organizations proceed rationally, it is impossible for them to be perfectly rational in their actions. With the incredible variety of pressures under which public agencies operate, it is difficult for them to know what they are or should be doing. Therefore, it is difficult to measure how rational they are. For example, every decision to locate a freeway, create an agricultural program, protect an endangered species, or prevent global warming, or whether to do any of them at all is subject to multiple and conflicting pressures from groups supporting or opposing the prospective decision. Once the decision is made, disagreement often remains on what the decision actually means and how it is to be implemented.

Governance by Bureaucracy

Modern bureaucracy arose from efforts to make administration more productive, neutral, legal, and rational. Max Weber's ideal construct of bureaucracy (Weber, 1968) as the most efficient method of organizing activity conformed to traditional public administration theory and practice. In a positive sense, bureaucracy is viewed as the most rational way of accomplishing any activity and is an inevitable part of our society. Basically, bureaucracy is a form of organization that is hierarchical, impersonal, formal, and based on specialization, rules, and merit. Whereas Weber believed that in its ideal construct, bureaucracy was the most rational and efficient way of organizing, others focused on the dysfunctional and nonrational aspects of bureaucracy (Blau & Meyer, 1987; Argyris, 1960). For example, paying doctors in a public hospital according to the number of patients they see may be dysfunctional to the overall goals of the hospital. Doctors may be inclined to see as many patients as possible and not take as much care as they should in diagnosing problems. The result is likely to be poorer health care than intended. The behavior is dysfunctional to the goal of providing the best possible care. The resulting behavior may be rational from the perspective of the individual doctor's goals but nonrational from the perspective of attaining the goals of the hospital. Weber, himself, had doubts about some of the same issues and utilized the ideal type as an intellectual construct to analyze elements of reality rather than as an accurate description of reality (Weber, 1968).

Whether people believe that bureaucracy is the best alternative for organizing or believe that it is dysfunctional, complex modern society is dominated by it. Bureaucracy is a logical result of the positivist reaction to industrial society, which called for expansion of government into virtually all activities of society (Weiss, 1979). Though it is popular to denounce bureaucracy as incompetent, inefficient, and too large, people also expect government to perform services for them. Even if they favor reductions in services, they want cuts in services that *other* people use. Governmental bureaucracy is the result of these expectations of government. Individualistic action of choice is impractical for accomplishing the tasks of government.

There is extensive use of bureaucratic organizations in the public sector, and bureaucratic government has many implications for self-governance. As David Nachmias and David Rosenbloom (1980) note, there are inevitable conflicts between bureaucracy and democracy. Democracy presumes plurality and diversity, whereas bureaucracy requires unity. Dispersion of power and equal access are essential to democracy, whereas bureaucracy demands a hierarchy of authority. Command and control are integral to bureaucracy, but democracy requires liberty and freedom. Officials of bureaucracy are appointed and enjoy long tenure, whereas democracy is characterized by the election of officials with relatively short terms and potentially frequent turnover. In a democracy, everyone has the opportunity to participate in the process whereas in a bureaucracy, participation is limited by one's place in the hierarchy of authority. Finally, democracy cannot exist without openness, whereas bureaucracy thrives with secrecy and control over information.

These conflicts between democracy and bureaucracy lead to tensions between citizens and public agencies as well as between elected officials and bureaucracies. The tensions often result in the disparaging view people have of government as citizens come to feel that there is little efficacy in participating because they feel helpless in the face of powerful bureaucratic organizations. Nachmias and Rosenbloom (1980) believe that the dominance of bureaucracy and its increasing power give rise to a crisis of legitimacy in United States government because people are discouraged from participating.

Eugene Lewis (1988), on the other hand, believes that bureaucracies have displaced legislative and other elected officials as representatives of constituents, and George Frederickson (1997) notes the traditional role of administrators as representatives of citizens. Although Lewis is critical of the effects of bureaucracy, he suggests that individuals and groups have access and notes that some groups view specific bureaucracies as their particular representative organizations in government. He uses the example of the Department of Agriculture as an advocate for farmers, with various parts of the department representing differing farming interests. The same could be said of the Departments of Labor and Commerce. Labor organizations view the Department of Labor as their representative, whereas the business world looks to the Department of Commerce to represent its interests. Whenever anyone suggests combining the two into one department, each constituent group reacts negatively.

Whereas Lewis sees bureaucracy playing the role of representation, he also believes that it makes victims of people. The large and complex bureaucracies in government and society in general do not have the time or resources to pay attention to all members of society. Some get lost and become victims by inattention to their problems. The homeless and the hungry are examples of those who suffer from inattention. In many cases, the policymakers have not provided programs for them. In others, agencies have to develop criteria to distribute the limited resources they have. Some people get left out. Others are victims by virtue of the fact that some decisions and actions of bureaucracy have detrimental effects for some individuals. For example, although there may be many beneficiaries of a new light rail system, those who lose their homes or businesses to the path of the light rail tracks may not view it as beneficial. Instead, they may be victims because they lose the only home and security they may have known. Their psychological and emotional security may be irreparably damaged. The need of complex society to act bureaucratically leaves little room for consideration of an individual whose interests may be different from the interests of the majority.

Bureaucracies supposedly operate to serve the needs of society in general, but they may also be captured by special interests or the self-interest of the individuals who make them up. Vincent Ostrom (1974) notes that individual bureaucrats develop their own missions, especially the protection of their own self-interests, and thus may lose sight of the purposes for which they are employed in the first place. It is difficult for elected politicians and citizens to maintain control over the missions of bureaucracies. It is also possible that bureaucracies develop alliances with their clientele or those they regulate and then pursue interests benefiting those groups rather than the general public. Given that the public interest is difficult to define, it is difficult to control bureaucracy in the public interest. Some even suggest that bureaucracy represents a stable and continuing bias in favor of dominant interests. Edward Greenberg (1974), for example, argues that the positive state represented by big government/big bureaucracy is really based on the protection of economically powerful interests. Thus, organized groups—big business, big labor, big agriculture—dominate to the detriment of the interest of individual citizens.

Although bureaucracy implies many challenges for democratic government, it is difficult to imagine government functioning without it. Recognition of its effectiveness leads to its continuing use. Discovery of its negative implications can provide the basis for developing methods of mitigating them. Bureaucracy is going to be a part of our modern society for the foreseeable future. Learning to live with it and harness it to our needs may be our only option.

The next chapter examines the political context of public administration. It shows how American political institutions and practices result in an unstable and uncertain political environment that challenges the efforts of public administrators and agencies to systematically serve the public interest.

Review and Study Questions

1. How is public administration like life in a swamp and how does its environment differ from those of private and non-profit organizations?

2. Why are the values, wants, and needs of persons who work in public organizations often the source of conflict?

3. Why do tensions often develop between elected officials and appointed administrators?

4. Why is defining the "public interest" operationally a difficult task? In developing your answer, select two varieties of street-level public administrator—for example, a fire fighter, teacher, park ranger, building inspector, military pilot, solid-waste collector, librarian, social welfare case worker, mail clerk, receptionist, judge, CIA field operative—and compare and contrast how each of them might define "public interest" in their day-to-day work.

5. Why do public agencies pay so much attention to their clients? Why do clients and client groups pay so much attention to "their" public agency?

6. What is the role of science in public administration? Why do conflicts develop about its proper role?

7. What are the main differences between public administration as a field of study and public administration as a field of practice?

8. Why is it probable that most public agencies cannot be fully "rational" and must opt for actions that will be "suboptimal"?

9. What are some of the consequences for popular government in America given the fact that bureaucracy in its nature is not a democratic form of governance?

Exercises

1. Think about some recent local public issue that seems insolvable. Find out from newspaper and TV sources what the major points of contention are and which community leaders are supporting the different sides. Does there seem to be an overriding public interest in this issue? To what degree are the various leaders and sides addressing the public interest, and to what degree are they addressing their private interests? Do they appear to see any difference between their private interests and the public interest?

2. Find some research-based information on global warming from the Internet, national newspapers, and the public document section of your college or university library. What seems to be the predominant scientific understanding of global warming? Given this, why is there still debate about whether it should be addressed as a policy issue and how it should be addressed?

3. Think about your own recent personal experiences with street-level public administrators. Collect your impressions of instances when you found the interaction satisfactory and the services useful. Collect your impressions of instances when you found the interaction unsatisfactory and the services not useful. Based on your personal recollections, did you think public agencies are basically effective or ineffective in meeting individual needs? Explain why.

4. Find out the name and telephone number of some local public professional organization such as the local chapter of the American Society for Public Administration, American Planning Association, International City/County Management Association, etc. Call to see if students may attend a local lunch meeting, and attend the meeting. What went on? What seemed to be the most important things that the members were doing at that meeting? Why do you think members of the professions go to such luncheons? What did you learn about the profession from that meeting?

5. Attend a city council meeting. How is business conducted?
    Does the process seem very democratic, and does it allow for
    input by all who are interested in providing input? Do you
    see any evidence of the administrative swamp in the delib-
    erations?

References

Argyris, C. (1960). *Understanding organizational behavior.*
Homewood, IL: Dorsey.

Berkley, G. E. (2008). The craft of public administration (10th
ed.). Boston: McGraw-Hill.

Biller, R. P. (1978). Public policy and public administration: Implications for the future of cross-cultural research and practice. *Korea Observer, 9,* 253-84.

Biller, R. P. (1979). Toward public administrations rather than
an administration of publics: Strategies of accountable disag-
gregation to active human scale and efficacy and live within
the natural limits of intelligence and other scarce resources.
In R. Clayton & W. B. Strom (Eds.), *Agenda for public administration* (pp.151-178). Los Angeles: School of Public Administration, University of Southern California.

Blau, P., & Meyer, M. (1987). Bureaucracy in modern society (3rd
ed.). Boston: McGraw-Hill.

Box, R. C., Marshall, G. S., Reed, B.J., & Reed, C. M. (2002). New
Public Management and substantive democracy. *Public Administration Review, 61,* 608-619

Burke, J. P. (2009). Advice for a new president: From inside and
out. *Public Administration Review, 69,* 976-978.

Cook, B. J. (2007). *Democracy and administration: Woodrow Wilson's ideas and the challenges of public management.* Baltimore, MD: Johns Hopkins University Press.

Cooper, T. L. (2006). The responsible administrator: An approach to ethics for the administrative role (5th ed.). New York: Wiley.

Cochran, C. E. (1982). *Character, community and politics*. Tuscaloosa: University of Alabama Press.

Denhardt, J. V., & Denhardt, R. B. (2007). *The New Public Service: Serving not steering*. Armonk, NY: M.E. Sharpe.

Finer, H. (1941). Administrative responsibility in democratic government. *Public Administration Review, 1,* 335-350.

Frederickson, H. G. (1997). *The spirit of public administration*. San Francisco: Jossey-Bass.

Friedrich, C. J. (1940). Public policy and the nature of administrative responsibility. *Public Policy, 1,* 3-24.

Garvey, G. (1996). *Public administration: Profession and practice: A case study approach*. Florence, KY: Cengage.

Greenberg, E. S. (1974). *Serving the few: Corporate capitalism and the bias of government policy*. New York: Wiley.

Honderich, T. (1995). *The Oxford companion to philosophy*. Oxford: Oxford University Press.

Hummel, R. T. (2008). *The bureaucratic experience: The postmodern experience* (5th ed.). Armonk, NY: M.E. Sharpe.

King, C. S. & Stivers, C. (1998). *Government is us: Public administration in an anti-government era*. Thousand Oaks, CA: Sage.

Kline, E. H. (1981). To be a professional. *Southern Review of Public Administration, 5,* 258-281.

Lewis, E. (1988). *American politics in a bureaucratic age: Citizens, constituents, clients and victims* (reprint ed.). Lanham, MD: University Press of America.

Liggett, B. S. (2005). Want effective public administration? Know the setting and have the right competencies. *American Review of Public Administration, 35,* 94-97.

Luthans, F., & Steward, T. (1977). A general contingency theory of management. *Academy of Management Review, 2,* 181-195.

Lynn, L. E., Jr. (2001). The myth of the bureaucratic paradigm: What traditional public administration really stood for. *Public Administration Review, 61,* 144-160.

Lynn, L. E., Jr. (1996). *Public management as art, science and profession.* New York: Chatham House.

Miller, H. T. & Fox, C. J. (2006). *Postmodern public administration: Toward discourse* (rev. ed.). Armonk, NY: Sharpe Reference.

Marx, F. M. (1957). *The administrative state: An introduction to bureaucracy.* Chicago: University of Chicago Press.

Mosher, F. C. (1982). *Democracy and the public service* (2nd ed.). New York: Oxford University Press.

Nachmias, D., & Rosenbloom, D. H. (1980). *Bureaucratic government USA.* New York: St. Martin's Press.

Newland, C. A. (1984). *Public administration and community: Realism in the practice of ideals.* McLean, VA: Public Administration Service.

Ostrom, V. (1989). *The intellectual crisis in American public administration* (2nd ed.). Tuscaloosa: University of Alabama Press.

Overeem, P. (2008). Beyond heterodoxy: Dwight Waldo and the politics-administration dichotomy. *Public Administration Review, 68,* 36-45.

Putnam, R. D. (2000). *Bowling alone: The collapse and revival of American community.* New York: Simon & Schuster.

Riccucci, N. M. (2001). The "Old' Public Management versus the "New" Public Management: Where does public administration fit in? *Public Administration Review, 61,* 172-175.

Rittel, H.W. J., & Webber, M. (1973). Dilemmas in a general theory of planning. *Policy Sciences, 4,* 155-169.

Rohr, J. A. (1999). *Public service, ethics, and constitutional prac-*

tice. Lawrence, KS: University Press of Kansas.

Rosenbloom, D. H. (2001). History lessons for reinventors. *Public Administration Review, 61,* 161-165.

Schachter, H. L. (1997). *Reinventing government or reinventing ourselves: The role of citizen owners in making a better government.* Albany: State University of New York Press.

Simon, H. A. (1997). *Administrative behavior: A study of decision-making processes in administrative organizations* (4th ed.). New York: Free Press.

Stewart, D. W. (1985). Professionalism vs. democracy–Friedrich vs. Finer revisited. *Public Administration Quarterly, 9,* 13-25.

Stivers, C. (2008). The significance of the Administrative State. *Public Administration Review, 68,* 53-60.

Svara, J. H. (2008). Beyond dichotomy: Dwight Waldo and the intertwined politics-administration relationship. *Public Administration Review, 68,* 46-52.

Svara, J. H. (2007). *The ethics primer for public administrators in government and nonprofit organizations.* Sudbury, MA: Jones & Bartlett.

Traaen, T. J. (2000). *A matter of ethics: Facing the fear of doing the right thing.* Stamford, CT: JAI Press.

Tullock, G. (1987). *The politics of bureaucracy.* Lanham, MD: University Press of America.

Van Wart, M. (1998). *Changing public sector values.* New York: Garland.

Waldo, D. (1977). The prospects of public organizations. *The Bureaucrat, 6,* 101-113.

Weber, E., & Khademian, A.M. (2008). Wicked problems, knowledge challenges, and collaborative capacity builders in network settings. *Public Administration Review, 68,* 334-349.

Weber, M. (1968). Economy and society: an outline of interpretive sociology. G. Roth & C. Wittich (Eds.). Ephraim Fischoff et al., (Trans.). Vol. I, Ch 3. New York: Bedminster Press.

Weiss, C. H. (1980). Efforts at bureaucratic reform: What have we learned? In C. Weiss & A. H. Barton (Eds.), *Making bureaucracy work* (pp. 7-26). Beverly Hills, CA: Sage.

White, L. D. (1926). *Introduction to the study of public administration.* New York: Macmillan.

Williams, D. W. (2000). Reinventing the proverbs of government. *Public Administration Review, 60* (November/December), 522-534.

Wilson, W. (1887). The study of administration. *Political Science Quarterly, 2,* 197-222.

Selected Web Sites

American Society for Public Administration (Membership organization for public administration professionals, academics, and students.)
http://www.aspanet.org

Council of State Governments (National organization of state officials and organizations.)
http://www.csg.org/

International City/County Management Association (Membership organization of city and county managers.)
http://www.icma.org

Internet Nonprofit Center (Information center for and about nonprofits.)
http://www.nonprofits.org

National Association of Counties (Membership organization of county governments.)
http://www.naco.org

National League of Cities (Membership organization of city and town governments.)
http://www.nlc.org

2

The American Political Context

The political context of American public administration constantly changes. The 21st century offers an ever-expanding menu of value-laden local, state, national and international political discord. Continuous political conflict about such matters as reproductive rights, Middle East violence, international terrorism, energy policy, environmental issues, health care, immigration, same-sex marriage, and local taxes contribute considerably to the uncertain terrain of the administrative swamp.

Elected officials, lobbyists, pressure groups, mass media, and citizens interact in the American political system at all levels in such a way that public administrators often are hard pressed to find an effective way to carry out their agencies' missions and, at the same time, survive in the turbulent political setting. Contradictory requests, conflicting messages, demands for political accountability, loss of trust in public bureaucracy, diminished resources, and confined choices all make it increasingly difficult for administrators to select carefully crafted responses to life in the swamp.

Public administration, as an integral part of public life, is a value-based human endeavor (Fischer, 1980; Van Wart, 1998). It requires people to act out values within a larger political context which itself is value laden (Benveniste, 1981). This condition of values within values has long plagued American public administration. In the face of open political corruption and favoritism, reformers in the late 19th and early 20th centuries tried to neutralize administration and promote professional public management by reducing its political vulnerability and culpability. Efforts ranging from the passage of civil service laws to the adoption of professional codes of conduct are institutional and behavioral attempts to separate administration from politics. Commentators often have noted that it is not really possible to completely separate administration from politics. Nonetheless, this conceptual division has served as a guiding ideal of the American administrative tradition (Overeem, 2008; Svara, 2008). Elected officials during the past thirty years, especially at the national level, have tried to repoliticalize administration (Bowman & West, 2009; Hall, 2002; Shenkman, 1999). The ideal of a politically neutral public service barely survives.

Democracy makes it especially difficult to develop a politically neutral public service. Much of the political life of a democracy concerns the resolution of value conflicts. Public managers and agencies, as key participants and arenas in democratic processes, must deal with political values. For example, after September 11, 2001, career attorneys in the U.S. Department of Justice found themselves at odds with others in the administration in dealing with suspected terrorists. The controversy concerned the extent to which members of the department could constrain the civil liberties and legal rights of suspects by recording conversations between attorneys and the persons suspected of terrorist activities. Similarly, from 2003-2008, the FBI, CIA, and the Department of Justice, with prodding from political officials, authorized or engaged in the torture of detainees and other extraordinary activities against the advice of career Justice Department lawyers and career military personnel. The tension between high-profile, politically-oriented administration officials and process oriented members of the career service created extensive media attention and promoted political discomfort for the administration as well as damage to the image of the United States. The continuing struggle, as this example demonstrates, has been to satisfy the requirements of popular governance, changing political environments, and resolution of value conflict on the one hand and the desire for a professional system of public management expertise free of partisanship on the other.

The concern is rather basic. As Herbert Simon (1997) reminded us some time ago, all human decisions are composed of *factual* (scientifically warranted) and *value* (preference) components. A decision is always a mixture of and a trade-off among value and factual aspects of the same issue. Simon's characterization of a fact–value dichotomy has been disputed philosophically, empirically, and practically, but the essence of this characterization remains: decisions are mixtures of objective (factual) and subjective (value) considerations.

A good example of this conflict between and mixture of facts and values is speed limits. In 1984 the national government in coordination with the states mandated a fifty-five mile per hour speed limit for freeways and the interstate highway system (Highway Safety Amendments of 1984). Concerns for safety and fuel economy prompted this change. Not all states agreed with this change, and some state governments openly opposed what they saw as unneeded federal intervention. Lives were saved and fuel was conserved in the states where the speed limits were enforced. Yet, strong opposition from the trucking industry, some state governments, the mass media in some areas, automobile associations, drivers, and conservative think tanks led to the rescinding of the federal speed standards and regulations in 1995 (Moore, 1999). The scientific evidence supported the lower speed limit. Values of individualism, free enterprise, freedom of choice, and love of speed did not. Now we find that most states are hard pressed to enforce the nominal seventy-five mile an hour limit on the rural sections of the interstate highways. Similarly, many state and local governments installed cameras to catch speeders and red light violators based on evidence that cameras reduce speeding and save lives. Nonetheless, many oppose the cameras on the same grounds that they opposed the 55 mph limits and on privacy grounds.

Simon had a preference for basing decisions as much as possible on factual statements, but he saw that all decision-makers are constrained and influenced by a myriad of personal, group, organizational, and societal values. It is useful to remember that one of the basic dilemmas of management is the melding and balancing of the objective and subjective aspects of a given choice situation (Stone, 2002).

Since values remain forever a part of decision making, it follows that politics, as a system of dealing with values, remains an essential part of the context of administration as well as a part of the administrative process itself. Successful public managers are adept at politics (Moore, 1995).

Private and Public in American Politics

American government and politics have their roots in liberalism. Anglo-American liberalism developed in the political writings and practices of seventeenth- and eighteenth-century England. We now consider many of its tenets—free market economics, protection of property rights, political individualism, and limited government—as conservative. Yet the political doctrines formulated by such theorists as Thomas Hobbes, Adam Smith, and John Locke were not only radical for their time, but also laid the foundation for much of the moral and philosophical foundations of the American experiment with self-government. For better or worse, we are all the children of these believers in secular government, science, humanism, and extreme individualism (Lowi, 1969).

There is an inherent tension and contradiction between the liberal notion of limited government and the practices of contemporary bureaucratic government. Although much of the tension is historical, the editorial pages of our daily newspapers, countless Web sites, radio talk shows, and TV news broadcasts amply illustrate continued debate about the appropriate role of government in the daily life of Americans. Not only is the doctrine of limited government current, but bureaucrat bashing is a refined tool of political communication (Hall, 2002). Policy debates about such diverse issues as the effects of second-hand cigarette smoke or shortcomings of inner-city schools often become arenas for attacking the public manager rather than dealing with the underlying causes of the problem. Cries for reduced waste and increased accountability appeal to a public that perceives bureaucratic abuses as commonplace.

Public administration is in many ways the stepchild of liberalism. Although in current approaches to governance, many traditional services have been partially privatized—with an emphasis on market provision of services such as education, recreation, social welfare, and waste management—public administrators, particularly at the local level, still are asked to do more and more for people. They continue to provide health care, public safety, corrections, protective services, welfare, streets, parks, clean water, a more desirable physical setting, better public transit, housing, and education among other things within the context of a political ideology that stresses individual rights and private property above all other goods. Thus, we live a contradiction. We retain our allegiance to the central tenets of liberalism, while at the same time requiring our public administrators to continue to implement policies characteristic of the socialist democracies of Europe, such as Sweden, Denmark, Finland, and France.

The starting place of most public policy in the United States is the market (Lindblom, 1977). Even with the tremendous growth of American government since the 1950s, we still have a market-based economy. Private individuals and firms provide a majority of goods and services. The ethic of capitalism and the tenets of liberalism underpin the American economy. The stress on private ownership of the means of production, and an unregulated market in which individual sellers and buyers transact *business*, constitute a secular faith. Notwithstanding that we live in a regulated economy and society (Hughes, 1977; Wilson, 1980) and despite the massive government intervention to address the 2008-2009 recession and financial crisis, we continue to hold firm to the ideology of the free market and many of the practices of capitalism. The commitment to a free market fostered attempts in the 1990s and early 2000s to reduce the national government's myriad of regulations, especially in environmental quality, financial markets, and labor relations. The 2008-2009 recession created calls for renewed regulation of the economy.

Conservative and Liberal Interpretations of *Liberalism*

A division of opinion exists about the proper role of government in our society. Some people, usually called *conservatives*, favor limited government (Friedman, 1962; Kristol, 1978; Reich, 1983), and other people, now called *liberals*, support a more active, positive role for government (Burns, 1963; Carnoy & Shearer, 1980).

Conservatives have more faith in the private market and support policies that promote a free, minimally-regulated market system. The role of government, true to liberal roots and capitalist ethos, is to do those *few* things that the market cannot or will not do. Notwithstanding the fact that these *few* things have become an almost uncountable *many* things, conservatives tend to see government as doing the residual group of activities not done by the individual and the market.

In the contemporary conservative view, government and, by extension, public administration, are not essential, primary activities, but rather supplementary, secondary activities. It is more than mildly ironic that in our postindustrial society, where the public sector subsidizes and regulates private action heavily and provides a vast variety of goods and services to private firms, government is so poorly regarded.

Yet, presidents from Jimmy Carter to George W. Bush have all campaigned on the promise of reducing the size, complexity, and pervasiveness of government. The more conservative of them, Ronald Reagan and George W. Bush, sought more reduction in the size of bureaucracy and scope of regulations. Even the more liberal of them, Jimmy Carter and Bill Clinton, sought to simplify government and reduce its scope. When the Republican Party secured voting majorities in both houses of the Congress in 1994, their *Contract With America,* firmly based on traditional, historic liberalism, sought to dismantle as much of the regulatory and welfare state as possible. Although the Congressional Republican leadership was actually able to enact only small portions of their programs, they were the vanguard of a more conservative American government. Part of their failure was that President Clinton adopted many of their ideas and slogans. In a sense, a seemingly progressive president turned out to be more conservative than his opponents and supporters thought. George W. Bush promised to reduce the size and cost of government. Although his administration was successful in reducing taxes, especially on the wealthy, he and the Republican Congress increased costs leading to unprecedented deficit spending. As Barack Obama came to office in 2009, he inherited a huge debt amid a financial crisis and severe recession. He chose to support a $787 billion stimulus package that increased government's role and debt, at least in the short run. He supports an expanded role for government in many aspects of the economy and in social support programs.

Traditional liberalism took secular government as a given (Hamilton, Madison & Jay, 1961). Since the mid-1970s, leaders of many sorts have challenged the conventional secularism of American government and the principle of separation of church and state. Since the mid-1970s, a succession of presidential candidates and presidents have made much of their Christian beliefs. George W. Bush, some members of his administration, and some congressional leaders of both parties made fundamentalist religious values a key part of their public decision making and leadership.

The conventional liberal stance, often reflected by leftist Democratic candidates and officials, has been, until recently, very different. Although they may hold strong private religious convictions, they adhere to the notion of a secular government and strict separation of church and state. They believe that the role of government in religion is to make sure all belief systems have full legal and procedural protection. Barack Obama, while supporting the traditional separation of government and religion, embraced religion as part of this campaign and also called for tolerance for different religious beliefs. At the same time, his administration appears to support religious organizations as deliverers of social programs, something leftist Democrats usually find difficult to embrace.

Liberals also differ from conservatives about the fundamental role of government in the economy. Government is viewed as the friend and defender of ordinary people. The power of the state is to be used as a positive instrument to overcome the limits and biases of the market economy and the maldistribution of income resulting from unchecked capitalism. Individualism and freedom are values in their own right, but contemporary liberals feel that collective action is required to carry out the ideals of egalitarianism and democracy.

Proponents of a positive role for public authority see government as the ultimate arbiter and protector of those without other resources. The progressive policies of the New Deal and the War on Poverty and the Obama stimulus package were based on the idea that government and public administration are necessary instruments in the reorganization and reform of our economy and society. In this view of political life, administrators and agencies are agents of democracy in the pursuit of social justice.

For much of the last half of the 20th century, the differences between left and right about the foundations of American government were more a variation on a theme than a fundamental cleavage. These differences, however, seemed sharper in the first decade of the 21st century. America has become the world's major superpower. As it struggles with issues of peace and safety here and abroad, and tries to protect American interests throughout the world, the ideological split between left and right at home is more intense.

A shaky consensus based on our common historical and ideological bias toward individualism and privatism still underpins the basic political processes. The commitment to individualism has had a profound effect upon the way we conduct our politics. In the liberal tradition, the fountain of political interaction is *private* want (Arrow, 1951; Laver, 1981). Individual citizens are expected to express their demands for government action, and governments are expected to respond to these expressions. Notice the direct analogy to the way the market is supposed to work. Citizens, as consumers of publicly provided goods and services, *demand* of the government an array of these goods and services. Further, they are willing to *pay* for them through their tax contributions and their participation in politics. Government, in turn, *supplies* that array of goods and services demanded of it. This is a limited and simplistic archetype of governance as practiced in America, but it is a useful heuristic model of how things work (Laver, 1981; Wade & Curry, 1970).

Political Pluralism and the Group Theory of Politics

Despite the emphasis on individualism and democracy as ideals, the American political system is largely based on political interaction among associations of individuals rather than individual citizens. Long ago, observers saw that few ordinary citizens have access to the actual working of policy-making (Lasswell & Lerner, 1952). Instead, they saw a system in which interest groups and lobbyists rather than ordinary citizens dominate the demand function. These observations led to the development of the *Group Theory* of American politics.

A. F. Bentley (1908), David Truman (1951), Earl Latham (1952), E. E. Schattschneider (1960), and Robert Dahl (1966) developed a theory of interactive political groups that became the standard interpretation of how American politics works. Known as *pluralist democratic theory*, this body of normative and interpretive thought, conceptually derived from James Madison's *Federalist 10* (Hamilton, Madison, & Jay, 1961). Much of it is based on the empirical political science of the 1950s and 1960s, and postulates that the building blocks of American politics are interest groups. These interest groups are coalitions of persons sharing common values and wants organized for the express purpose of demanding that governments perform specific acts for the members of that group. These usually are *private* associations whose main purpose is the lobbying of government to secure their own private ends (Edelman, 1964; Key, 1967).

Government officials are *brokers* and *producers* in this model (Dahl & Lindblom, 1953). Governments, the public arenas in which interest groups play out their private demands, permit officials to broker among the various interests to achieve some sort of compromise and tradeoffs among competing interests. This puts government and especially the legislative function in a passive, though central stance and role in policy processes. The legislature and legislators receive and respond to demands made on them by lobbyists. Over time, initiative in the legislative function passed into the hands of the interest groups and the executive branch.

This shift of power altered the separation of powers and enhanced the power of the president and the agencies. The president and the executive office of the president slowly have come to constitute a kind of *imperial* function in which presidential leadership dominates much of the initiation of policy (Burns, 1965; Neustadt, 1991; Schlesinger, 2004; Spitzer, 1992). Many critics complained that the George W. Bush administration drove the imperial presidency to new heights, and at least one member of Congress pushed to investigate the accretion of power (U.S. House Committee on the Judiciary Majority Staff, 2009).

Over time, interest groups have come to be known as *pressure groups* and special interests. They put pressure on elected and appointed officials to get what they want. By the 1980s, various kinds of pressure groups, often acting through political action committees (PACs), had come to dominate the demand function of political communication and to provide major resources to the election and legislative processes. PACs provide support for or opposition to specific candidates for public office at all levels of government. PACs permit pressure groups to put large amounts of money into electoral campaigns and to avoid many of the restraints of state and national campaign finance control laws. During the period from 1980 to 2002, *soft money*—contributions to political parties rather than individual candidates—was used to circumvent campaign regulations on contributions to candidates. For example, both Presidents Bill Clinton and George W. Bush proved to be masters at raising soft money for their respective parties at the state and national levels. Notwithstanding reform legislation famously supported by Senators John McCain and Russ Feingold and passed into law in 2002, contributions via PACs and other organizations have become the main fiscal foundation for today's enormously expensive electoral campaigns (Maisel & Brewer, 2007). During the 2008 presidential campaign, both Barack Obama and John McCain made effective use of PACs.

Thus, we have come to have a kind of semi-democracy in which politically active groups rather than individual citizens are the key units of expression. Some commentators doubt that lobbyists and PACs actually represent the values of the members of the larger associations they claim to represent (Parenti, 1970; Rose, 1967; Schattschneider, 1960). This appears to make little difference. Decision-makers at all levels act as if these agents do in fact represent the *public* or *publics* they claim to. The *pluralism* in American politics is an artifact of the existence of many powerful groups competing for attention. At any level in any given arena, for any issue, and at a particular time, there may be several lobbyists and advocates seeking to get their message across to governmental brokers.

Critical reflection about this group-based explanation of American politics suggests that it is flawed and masks some important issues about our so-called *representative* democracy (Manley, 1983). First, not all citizens and interests secure effective representation. Many are not represented at all. The biased pressure-group system overrepresents the interests of the business community and the managers and owners of capital wealth (Campbell & Schoolman, 2008; Connolly, 1969, 2005; McQuaid, 1982).

Second, the degree of competition among groups is more apparent than real. Stable coalitions of interests and *logrolling* (the trading of support and votes in legislative processes) are common at all levels of our system (Buchanan & Tullock, 1962; McGann, 2006; Riker, 1962).

Third, administrative agencies often act as interest groups in their own right. This produces a conflict of interest between their *public* function of implementing policy and their *private* function of getting their fair share of the budget (Borchering, 1977; Meier & Bohte, 2006).

Fourth, executives at all levels have come to dominate the agenda setting process (Cleveland, 2000; Hawkins, Culison, & Karjala, 2004; Nalbandian, 1991; Shenkman, 1999). Getting ideas and policy proposals on the public agenda is a key step of the policy process throughout our government (Bachrach & Baratz, 1961; Kingdon, 2003). Although the mass media, lobbyists, agencies, and legislators all may set the agenda on a given issue, the executive—mayors, city managers, governors and presidents—frequently take office with a vision of how the world should be. The exercise of executive leadership brings many if not most of the issues regarding change in our polity to the decision system.

A new wrinkle in the political participation issue is the mobilization of people through electronic communication. President Obama used blogs, Web sites, and other methods effectively in mobilizing people for his campaign. To a lesser extent, he has also used these means to communicate with the public on issues of the day. At the same time, the alligator he let loose has come to bite him, as opponents on issues, especially health care reform, have appropriated his successful approach and used the tactics against him. The town halls used by Obama and members of Congress to get information out about health care reform have generated highly organized efforts by opponents to subvert the town halls. Opponents have been effective in using the traditional as well as new media to generate fear among citizens about the health care initiatives to the point that reasoned debate about the issue is almost impossible. Those holding town halls on the topic wade into a tangled, hostile swamp.

The Iron Triangle

Pressure group politics have led to the fusion of interest groups, legislative committees, and administrative agencies into stable alliances that may be characterized as *Iron Triangles* (Cater, 1964; Helco, 1978). These Iron Triangles are the natural consequence of pressure-group politics in which agencies, lobbyists, and legislators strive to develop their own political space and leverage. Agencies partake in Iron Triangles to reduce the amount of uncertainty in the political swamp. Becoming an intregal part of an informal and formal communication system among other policy area specialists permits agencies to use their intrinsic expertise to best advantage.

It is well known that Congress's major work is done in committees and subcommittees. Lobbyists spend considerable time cultivating both the legislative members of the committees and their staffs. Agencies and subagency components likewise specialize in subject matter and in linkages with legislative committees. Members of Congress and their staffs in turn demand and make use of specialized information provided by lobbyists and agencies. Thus, there are literally hundreds of the tight little systems of communication among legislative-interest group-agency actors. They constitute interdependent, *functional fiefdoms*.

Although the focus of most commentary on Iron Triangles is the U.S. Congress and the national policy system, such functional fiefdoms characterize state legislatures, county boards of supervisors, school boards, and city councils (Harrigan and Vogel 2002). Wherever elected officials try to legislate in the United States, stable communication systems among elected representatives, lobbyists, and agencies abound. City councils in small- and medium-sized cities, which often try to combine legislative, administrative, and executive functions, are especially interesting. Most elected council members are amateur part-time politicians. Except in the larger municipalities, council members lack professional staff support. They depend on information provided by mayors, city managers, municipal departments, and lobbyists. Coalitions of subject matter specialists—department members, lobbyists, and representatives of the mayor's or manager's office—tend to dominate the municipal decision processes.

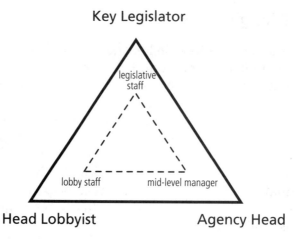

Figure 2.1: *The Iron Triangle*

There are triangles within triangles, as illustrated in Figure 2.1. The outer shell of the triangle is composed of the interest group, the legislative committee, and the agency. The person representing each of these units might be the head lobbyist of the pressure group, a key member of the legislative committee, (perhaps its chair), and the head of the agency. Inside of this outer shell is a more intimate, functionally more specialized, tighter triangle composed of a member of the legislative committee staff, a member of the lobby staff, and a middle-level member of the agency management. The inner group is likely to be the continuous operational communication network of the triangle.

Considerable day-to-day communication takes place among members of the inner-shell of the triangle. Middle-level managers, legislative staff personnel, and lobby staff members frequently meet to discuss common concerns. Equally important, they produce and manage much of the information used in the legislative process. They provide technical support for individual members of Congress as well as the committees. Finally, they are likely to be the persons who actually set up legislative hearings and agendas for the hearings.

Much communication takes place among the members of the outer shell but it is not as continuous and sustained as that in the inner shell. Together this communication binds the participants together tightly and overcomes some of the barriers set up by the constitutional systems of separation of powers and checks and balances. In a sense, the Iron Triangle promotes cohesion in the policy-making functions by pulling together decision making by the legislature with the information gathering and technical assistance activities of interest groups and agencies. Furthermore, it pulls the policy implementation activities of agencies into a network that provides informal feedback and oversight on the part of legislators, legislative staff members, and lobbyists. This interaction promotes a kind of team effort by participants as they try to adapt to the unsure, swampy world of legislative and mass media politics.

The Iron Triangle has worked well from time to time in some policy areas such as agriculture policy, environmental protection, resources management, weapons development, and space exploration. The National Aeronautics and Space Administration (NASA), though heavily supported by presidents since John Kennedy, owes much of its existence and successes to the interaction within and among triangles devoted to space exploration and weapons development. Not only have the particular interests of pressure groups—such as aerospace firms, U.S. military, and universities—been met, but also one can often see benefit for the general public (Cochran, Mayer, Carr, & Cayer, 2009).

Although Presidents Kennedy and Reagan had great successes in aerospace policy, governors and presidents generally find life outside of these triangles perplexing. Although nominally the head of administrative agencies in the state and national government, our elected executives must work especially hard to politically manage the agencies. President Reagan, for example, found it difficult to control managers in such agencies as the Environmental Protection Agency and the Department of Agriculture, both of which have richly developed Iron Triangle systems. Three recent presidents—Reagan, George H.W. Bush, and George W. Bush—unsuccessfully tried to secure relatively modest reforms in farm subsidies in the name of market efficiency. Coalitions of farm-state legislators, legislative staff, lobbyists, and U.S. Department of Agriculture administrators were not only able to blunt possible changes and reductions in farm support, they were able to increase farm subsidies for many crops. Predsident Obama faced the same challenges in pressing for cuts in farm subsidies.

Another concern is the impact of privatization on the relationships within the triangles. In privatization, private firms, through contract or other arrangements, produce and deliver goods and services in the name of the government using public resources. The balancing among the parties inside the triangle may be skewed as private firms fulfill some of the implementation functions traditionally done by public bureaucrats. Private concerns may displace the public concerns represented by public administrators. The sense of public purpose and responsibility may be eroded.

There are, however, limits to the overall effectiveness of these networks and questions about their propriety. A major concern is the narrow focus of the networks and their resistance to outside input. As highly specialized, functionally defined policy fiefdoms, the alliances of interests, legislatures, and agencies are closed and inaccessible to other values. This fragments policy between specialized areas and reduces the overall effectiveness of governmental efforts. Further, Iron Triangles protect established values, status quo groups, and established power relationships. They resist change and encourage incrementalism in policy and budgetary processes. Finally, they shield what should be public processes from public and media scrutiny. Sunshine laws, which require open meetings and public access to information, at all levels promote public exposure. Iron Triangles encourage covertness in government, not a healthy condition in a democracy.

Policy networks represent an alternative to the iron triangle conceptualization of the policy-making process (Considine, Lewis, & Alexander, 2009; Goldsmith & Eggers, 2004; Fischer, 1980; Hager & Wagenaar, 2003). The policy network approach suggests that the community of actors involved in any one policy decision is less constricted than in the iron triangle model. Instead, different groups engage in any given policy decision so that there is more fluidity in the collection of actors who influence any given policy. Given that modern governance involves private groups participating in and implementing public policies, the policy network approach adds to the understanding of how policies develop and operate.

Administrators and Agencies in Politics

Administrators often act as lobbyists and agencies as pressure groups (Freeman, 2005; Rourke, 1984). The U.S. Army Corps of Engineers, State Department, Federal Bureau of Investigation, Park Service, National Aeronautics and Space Administration, and Environmental Protection Agency are notable in this regard at the national level. Each has built strong client and support bases. Each has successfully lobbied Congress, often in the face of presidential opposition. Yet, administrative politics goes far beyond the role of advocacy in the legislative process. To a considerable extent, administrators are coming to be key linkages in the broader political processes of American governance (Moore, 1995; Huber, 2007)).

Some commentators see agencies as key actors in politics and especially in policymaking. as opposed to electoral politics, maybe as elitist organizations in their own right or as extensions of the general political elite (Bachrach & Baratz, 1961; Garventa, 1980). Some inquiry about the role and function of bureaucracy suggests, to the contrary, that administrators and agencies are steadily becoming *more* representative of their constituents than

are most legislative bodies (Lewis 1977). This observation begs
the question of how representative of the public the American
government actually is. It also suggests that as the public sector
has become the major employer in the nation, administrators are
the *most* represented class of the dominant political groups. Access and representation via bureaucracy is especially important
to groups generally underrepresented in government—women
and racial and ethnic minorities (Box, 2006).

In spite of the considerable efforts of reformers to depoliti-
calize administration and of practitioners to professionalize
management, public management is in the middle of politics.
Unanticipated by the founders of the good government and the
professionalization movements at the turn of the 20th century,
managers have, to some extent, become central participants in
the political process. Public managers abound in the 21st century political swamp.

Listing what administrators *may not do* politically is easier
than listing what they *actually do* in politics. In most jurisdictions, laws and professional codes of conduct such as the Hatch
Act and the Professional Code of the International City/County
Management Association specifically restrain most public administrators from actively engaging in partisan electoral politics. They may vote and belong to political parties, but they may
not openly and personally endorse candidates for elective office
nor use their position or public funds to support candidates. Further, they are circumscribed in the use of their public positions
and public funds for lobbying.

Nonetheless, even these limits are eroding. Public employees
often form collective bargaining units, associations, and groups,
which in turn have PACs that engage in partisan politics. Further, most local governments, state agencies, and federal bureaucracies conduct lobbying with the goal of promoting and protecting that organization's interests, especially in budget making.
Even more sophisticated political networking and communication frequently take place as administrators and agencies develop political support for their organizations and professions
in the policy process. Fostering continual political support now
is considered one of the hallmarks of successful public management (Svara, 1998, 1999).

Municipal police provide an interesting example. Reformers
expended considerable effort in the period between the 1920s

and 1970s to reduce corruption, develop well-trained, professional police forces, and remove the policing function from direct partisan influence. The net result has been the development of highly proficient, professional public safety systems in most states and cities throughout the country. All the effort toward reform, development of expertise, and professionalism has not, however, removed police administration from politics (Reiner, 2001; Wilson, 1968).

In most areas, we are past the days of massive corruption and favoritism. But in some ways, this has simply changed the quality of political communication. Successful police chiefs and departments are fully aware of the political functions of management. The modern police department, as in the case of other city departments in most municipalities, must engage in political communication and bargaining to do its job well.

Public administrators and agencies play a variety of important political roles and functions in the attempts of those in power to smooth out the vagaries of the political swamp. First, as noted in our discussion of Iron Triangles, top and middle managers often are in the position of advocating policies and expenditures to gain resources for their agencies and programs. They go to the mayor, city manager, governor, council, or legislature to promote policy recommendations, oppose undesirable legislation and policies, and protect budget shares. These efforts help them create predictable order in an otherwise confused, chaotic setting.

In a sense, civil servants are the only full-time lobbyists. They are continually defending their patch of turf. Such advocacy is so much part of their job that we often make such political communication activities part of the job description and expectations of top managers. Can you imagine a municipality hiring a police chief or a state selecting a doctor to head the health department who lacked the skills and experience to advocate well for their departments and to promote the city or state government in the larger community?

Moreover, managers frequently cultivate outside support for their agencies. Most agencies provide specific services to distinctive groups of users or relate to specific organizations in the larger society. Departments of fish and game, flood control agencies, school districts, universities, fire departments, and regulatory commissions all have target groups that often become *clientele* and *support* groups. Agencies work hard to meet the goals and expectations of their user groups. User groups, in turn, work hard to support the agencies and their staffs in the mass media, legislative process, and central administration.

Even administrative functions such as foreign aid and corrections that cannot easily develop tight clientele relationships with direct users also try to develop political support. All agencies try to cultivate friendly members in legislative staffs, support from good government organizations, and mutual support pacts with comparable agencies in other parts and levels of government. State-level natural resources and environmental quality agencies, for example, often cultivate support from federal agencies and local governments to facilitate smoother implementation of federal environmental mandates. Likewise, these state administrators try to develop a kind of *shadow user* support system from the very private firms and governmental agencies they regulate in the implementation of such laws as the Clean Air Act. Over time, state-level environmental managers have found that they need the active support of those they regulate as well as environmental groups. Ironically, these attempts to foster and balance support groups often lead state administrators into deeper political thickets and less firm terrain as they try to balance competing interests.

Consequently, agencies and agency personnel are frequently the targets of media campaigns, lobbying activities, and direct citizen inputs. At all levels, we experience the repoliticalization of the public bureaucracies. Most managers can testify to the hail of daily telephone calls, visits, and requests aimed at them, many of which deal with partisan rather than technical or administrative aspects of policy.

However, it is the street-level administrator—teacher, police officer, trash collector, postal deliverer, game warden, and employment clerk—who not only receives most of the complaints and hard looks, but also receives much of the political pressure from user groups, media, and elected officials. The street level tends to cope as well as it can and pass as much of the political pressure up as possible (Lipsky, 1976; Riccucci, 2005).

Managers at all levels of the organization find themselves in the midst of political communication with the outside world (Moore, 1995). Top managers bear most of the political pressure and much of the political communication. City mangers, for example, often try to *protect* department heads from political pressure by centralizing political communication through their office (Nalbandian, 1991). Yet it is often the middle manager who provides continuity in political communication. Remember the metaphor of the Iron Triangle. In the triangle, the middle manager often is in the midst of the lateral relationships that tie the organization with the other actors in the policy process. Middle managers link organizations both horizontally and vertically. This key functional position permits them to carry out much of both the external and internal political communication of the organization. The mundane "who do we see about this" political communication is the province of the middle manager. This concept of "manager in the middle" states well the idea of the middle manager caught in the middle of day-to-day politics of organizations.

Life in the Administrative Swamp

Administrators increasingly face an unstable environment. In the face of complexity, ambiguity, and rapid change, conventional methods of coping are not very useful. Increasingly, public managers must rely on a combination of strategic planning and contingency management to adapt to the unsure conditions they face. We shall turn to these topics in more detail later, but for now, remember that administrators need to become more strategic rather than tactical in dealing with the swamp. Managers often reactively respond to disturbances outside the organization through short-run tactics such as reinforcing top-down communication channels. They may be trying to protect the organization, but such short-sighted responses often make things worse. A less reactive and more anticipatory strategic stance in which managers expect and predict outside disturbances could move them toward increased lateral communication with outsiders under times of stress. This would improve the chances of weathering political storms in the swamp because the managers can call upon external resources and linkages to weather political conflicts. Managers need to be able to adapt to the swamp and cease trying to directly control the uncontrollable.

The observation that public administration takes place in an unsure setting is not new. At least since the 1920s, communicators have stressed the rapid change in the roles of government and nonprofit organizations, and the corresponding changes of setting in which public management takes place (Ogburn, 1922; White, 1926). Such factors as rapid urbanization, the rise in the international power of the United States, and resources development in the western states provided a heady, changing environment for public management in the first two decades of the 20th century. Several wars, depressions, and recessions later, in a vastly more urbanized society, in an internationalized economy with singular super power status, and inside a truly global communication system, today's managers face an even more unsure environment.

Problems and goals are not as clear as they once seemed. On the international level, we struggle with issues of terrorism, wars of liberation, global markets, and global energy and financial crises. On the national level, we continue to ponder the main direction and goals of our governments, but there is little agreement on objectives and little prospect of agreement in the near future. At the community level, there is often more agreement on goals, but not on how best to reach them or about who should provide the resources to pay for potential solutions to problems.

Public organizations and managers in the past thrived on more firmly established goals, known strategies, and sufficient resources. The prospects for this kind of firm terrain and strong support are not good. We find communities seriously examining under considerable conflict such basic questions as What is social equity? Can we afford high levels of public services? and Do we want to continue big government?

Traditional management practices not only require setting of common goals, but they also depend on the development of good, usable knowledge and information. Knowledge continues to expand. We live in an age of information in which all kinds of information and misinformation are instantaneously available over the Internet. Yet it is not clear that we have the applied knowledge and usable information we need to select promising solutions, design effective organizations, and monitor programs to see if things are working out well (Lindblom & Cohen, 1979; Schneider & Ingram, 1997). Our recent experience with international, national, and local issues suggests that we do indeed lack the fundamental understanding of how our policy options may or may not work.

Even local problems such as location of solid waste sites or inoculation of primary school children become more and more intractable. The amount we do not or cannot know and the paucity of usable information has transformed most public concerns into wicked problems. *Wicked problems* are not evil in the spiritual sense, but rather they are intractable problems whose dimensions are not easily grasped and whose solutions are problematic (Rittel & Webber, 1973).

During the last half of the 20th century, the usual response to continuing wicked problems such as drug abuse, school dropout rates, and poor air quality was to put a public boundary around them and to charge some public organization with taming them (Harmon, 1994). This strategy permits holding some organization and some group of people—DEA and its agents, a school district and its teachers, or a state-level environmental agency and its auto-emissions inspectors—responsible for *solving an unsolvable problem* and then chastising them soundly for failure to do their job well.

If wicked problems were not enough to drive one mad, public managers more often than not find that they lack adequate financial and human resources to meet their mandated objectives and levels of services. For example, all public components of the state and local justice system—police, courts, judges, prosecuting attorneys, public defenders, probation officers, and corrections officials—lack sufficient resources and have case loads exceeding those mandated by law.

Cutback management, reduction in force, cost savings, and service reductions are all too familiar to public officials, especially at the state and local levels. Under these conditions, public managers face a double bind. There is diminishing tolerance for error and fewer resources available to use in recovery from error. The probability of error, however, increases under conditions of increased risk. Selection of a wrong solution or practice is likely when faced with wicked problems and high uncertainty.

In this book, we characterize this unsure, rapidly changing environment of public management as *life in the administrative swamp*. Administrators frequently do not know the most promising path through the murky, unsafe surroundings. Danger abounds and there are few reliable clues to guide one to safety.

Managers may well select a bad path and sink into the marsh or be eaten by alligators. "Sink or swim" has much too much real meaning in these uncertain days.

One common response is to duck down, cover one's head and hope that the bad things go away. This is, however, a time for uncommon behavior. What can a reasonable, professionally dedicated manager do when faced with the swamp? Change the basic approach to problem resolution.

Managers are on their way toward the development of new ways of management based on dealing with uncertainty and limited resources. American public administration still faces wicked problems, but managers are becoming more and more sensitive to their political environments and are developing more flexible approaches with multiple ways of reaching proximate solutions to the problems thrust upon them by a more active and vocal public.

Along with the changing political context in which they operate, public agencies and managers face alligators and snakes from within. In the next chapter, we examine the culture of bureaucratic organizations. This culture, characteristic of most private, nonprofit, and public organizations, is as problematic and threatening as the rapidly changing external political environment.

Review and Study Questions

1. What are some of the recent major factors that have made the political environment of American public administration more swampy?

2. What are some of the main differences between conservative and liberal views of the role of government in the United States?

3. What are some of the limits and flaws of the group theory of pluralist democracy?

4. Who do pressure groups pressure?

5. What special advantages and resources do administrative agencies use in lobbying?

6. What is the Iron Triangle, and why is it so important in the political life of public agencies?

7. What are wicked problems, and why are they important in the political life of public agencies? Explain through the use of an example.

8. Why do successful administrators spend so much time cultivating external political support?

9. What are the special functions of middle managers in external and internal political communication?

10. Why have most attempts to insulate public administrators and public agencies from politics failed?

Exercises

1. Attend one or two meetings of a nearby city council. Try to find out which persons and groups dominate the agenda-setting process for that body.

2. Select a policy area and topic of personal interest such as charter schools, capital punishment, equal employment opportunity, water quality, immigration, homeland security, etc. Do a search about this topic on the Internet. Find three kinds of sites: (1) a public agency dealing with the topic, (2) a think tank doing research on it, and (3) an interest/pressure group taking a position on it. Compare the value premises and the quality of information provided by each. Which site provided the most balanced information? Why?

3. View the nightly news on FOX, NBC, CBS, or ABC for one week. On alternative nights also view the news broadcast on CNN and your local PBS station. Do these broadcasts reflect a liberal or conservative bias? Are there ideological differences between the various stations? Which is most conservative? Which is most liberal? Which is most balanced?

4. Read the Sunday editions of a local, regional and national newspaper one weekend. Try to find at least two good examples of lobbying and other political actions by public administrators. Do these actions support the contention that managers actively engage in political communication? If so, in what ways?

5. Select a policy issue and public agency responsible for it. Go to the agency Web site and identify its interaction with a legislative committee and interest/clientele groups on the issue. Does there appear to be an Iron Triangle or a Policy Network around the issue? Explain.

References

Arrow, K. (1951). *Social choice and individual values*. New York: Wiley.

Bachrach, P., & Baratz, M. S. (1961). Two faces of power. *American Political Science Review, 56*, 947-52.

Bentley, A. F. (1908). *The process of government*. Evanston, IL: Principia Press.

Benveniste, G. (1981). *Regulation and planning, the case of environmental politics*. San Francisco: Boyd and Fraser.

Borchering, T. (Ed.). (1977). *Budgets and bureaucracy, the source of governmental growth*. Durham, NC: Duke University Press.

Box, R. D. (Ed.). (2006). *Democracy and public administration*. Armonk, NY: M.E. Sharpe.

Bowman, J. S. & West, J. P. (2009). To 'Re-Hatch' public employees or not? An ethical analysis of the relaxation of restrictions on political activities in civil service. *Public Administration Review, 69*(January/February), 52-63.

Buchanan, J. & Tullock, G. (1962). *The calculus of consent*. Ann Arbor, MI: University of Michigan Press.

Burns, J. M. (1963). *The deadlock of democracy*. Englewood Cliffs, NJ: Prentice-Hall.

Burns, J. M. (1965). *Presidential government*. Boston: Houghton Mifflin.

Campbell, D. & Schoolman, M. (Eds.). (2008). *The new pluralism: William Connolly and the contemporary global condition*. Durham, NC: Duke University Press.

Carnoy, M. & Shearer, D. (1980). *Economic democracy: The challenge of the 1980s*. White Plains, NY: M.E. Sharpe.

Cater, D. (1964). *Power in Washington*. New York: Vintage.

Cleveland, J. Y. (2000). *Changing role of the city manager*. (Unpublished doctoral dissertation). Arizona State University, Tempe, AZ.

Cochran, C. E., Mayer, L. C., Carr, T. R., &. Cayer, N. J. (2009). *American public policy: An introduction* (9th ed.). Boston: Wadsworth Cengage.

Connolly, W. E. (2005). *Pluralism*. Durham, NC: Duke University Press.

Connolly, W. E. (Ed.). (1969). *The bias of pluralism.* New York: Atherton.

Considine, M., Lewis, J., & Alexander, D. (2009). *Networks, innovation and public policy: Politicians, bureaucrats and the pathways to change inside government.* New York: Palgrave Macmillan.

Dahl, R. (1966). *Pluralist democracy in America.* Chicago: Rand McNally.

Dahl, R., & Lindblom, C. E. (1953). *Politics, economics and welfare.* New York: Harper.

Edelman, M. (1964). *The symbolic use of politics.* Chicago: University of Chicago Press.

Fischer, F. (1980). *Politics, values and public policy.* Boulder, CO: Westview.

Freeman, J. (2005). Public agencies as lobbyists. *bepress Legal Services.* Working Paper 550. http://law.bepress.com/expresso/eps/550.

Friedman, M. (1962). *Capitalism and freedom.* Chicago: University of Chicago Press.

Garventa, J. (1980). *Power and powerlessness.* Urbana, IL: University of Illinois Press.

Goldsmith, S. & Eggers, W. (2004). *Governing by network: The new shape of the public sector.* Washington, DC: Brookings Institution Press.

Hager, M. A., & Wagenaar, H. (2003). *Deliberative policy analysis: Understanding governance in the network society.* New York: Cambridge University Press.

Hall, T. (2002). Live bureaucrats and dead public servants: How people in government are discussed on the floor of the House. *Public Administration Review, 62*(March/April), 242-251.

Hamilton, A., Madison, J. & Jay, J. (1961). *The federalist papers.* NewYork: New American Library.

Harmon, M. M. (1994). *Organization theory for public adminis-tration*. Burke, VA: Chatelaine Press.

Harrigan, J. J., & Vogel. R. K. 2002. *Political change in the me-tropolis* (7th ed.). New York: Longman.

Hawkins, L.A., Cullison, C., & Karjala, A. (2004, May). *Presiden-tial agenda setting: Richard Nixon, Bill Clinton and welfare reform*. Paper presented at the annual meeting of The Mid-west Political Science Association. http://www.allacademic.com/meta/p83204_index.html

Heclo, H. (1978). Issue networks and the executive establish-ment. In A. King (Ed.), *The new political system* (pp. 87-124). Washington, DC: American Enterprise Institute.

Highway Safety Act Amendments of 1984. Pub. L. 98-363 (1984).

Huber, G. A. (2007). *The craft of bureaucratic neutrality: Inter-est and influence in governmental regulation of occupational safety*. New York: Cambridge University Press.

Hughes, J. R. T. (1977). *The governmental habit*. New York: Basic Books.

Key, V. O., Jr. (1967). *Politics, parties and pressure groups*. New York: Crowell.

Kingdon J. (2003). *Agendas, alternatives and public policies*. New York: Longman.

Kristol, I. (1978). *Two cheers for capitalism*. New York: Basic Books.

Lasswell, H., & Lerner, D. (1952). *The comparative study of elites*. Palo Alto, CA: Stanford University Press.

Latham, E. (1952). *The group basis of politics*. Ithaca, NY: Cor-nell University Press.

Laver, M. (1981). *The politics of private desires*. Middlesex, Eng-land: Penguin Books.

Lewis, E. (1977). *American politics in a bureaucratic age: citizen, constituents, clients and victims.* Cambridge, MA: Winthrop.

Lindblom, C. E. (1977). *Politics and markets: The world's political and economic systems.* New York: Basic Books.

Lindblom, C. E., & Cohen, D. K. (1979. *Usable knowledge: Social science and social problem solving.* New Haven, CT: Yale University Press.

Lipsky, Michael. (1976). Toward a theory of street level bureaucracy. In W. D. Hawley (Ed.), *Theoretical perspectives on urban politics* (pp. 196-213). Englewood Cliffs, NJ: Prentice Hall.

Lowi, T. (1969). *The end of liberalism.* New York: Norton.

McGann, A. (2006). *The logic of democracy: Reconciling equality, deliberation and minority protection.* Ann Arbor: University of Michigan Press.

McQuaid, K. (1982). *Big business and presidential power: From FDR to Reagan.* New York: Morrow.

Maisel, L. S., & Brewer, M. D. (2007). *Parties and elections in America* (5th ed.). Lanham, MD: Rowman & Littlefield.

Manley, J. F. (1983). Neo-pluralism: a class analysis of pluralism I and pluralism II. *American Political Science Review, 77,* 370-89.

Meier, K. J., & Bohte, J. (2006). *Politics and the bureaucracy.* Boston: Cengage.

Moore, M. (1995). *Creating public value.* Cambridge, MA: Harvard University Press.

Moore, S. (1999). *Speed doesn't kill, the repeal of the 55-MPH speed limit.* Cato Policy Analysis No. 346, May 31. Available at http: www/cato.org/pubs/pas/pa-346es.html

Nalbandian, J. (1991). *Professionalism in local government: Transformations in the roles, responsibilities, and values of city managers.* San Francisco: Jossey-Bass.

Neustadt, R. E. (1991). *Presidential power and the modern presidents: The politics of leadership from Roosevelt to Reagan.* New York: Simon & Schuster.

Ogburn, W. F. (1922). *Social change.* New York: Viking Press.

Overeem, P. (2008). Beyond heterodoxy: Dwight Waldo and the politics-administration dicholtomy. *Public Administration Review, 68*(January/February), 36-45.

Parenti, M. (1970). Pluralism, a view from the bottom. *Journal of Politics, 32,* 501-530.

Reich, R. B. (1983). *The next American frontier.* New York: Times Books.

Reiner, R. (2001). *The politics of the police.* New York: Oxford Univesity Press.

Riccucci, N. M. (2005). *How management matters: Street-level bureaucrats and welfare reform.* Washington, DC: Georgetown University Press.

Riker, William. (1962). *The theory of political coalitions.* New Haven, CT: Yale University Press.

Rittel, H. W. & Webber, M. (1973). Dilemmas in a general theory of planning. *Policy Sciences, 4,* 155-69.

Rose, A. (1967). *The power structure.* New York: Oxford University Press.

Rourke, F. E. (1984). *Bureaucracy, politics and public policy* (3rd ed.). Boston: Little, Brown & Co..

Schattschneider. E. E. (1960). *The semi-sovereign people, a realist's view of democracy.* New York: Holt.

Schlesinger, A. M., Jr. (2004). *The Imperial presidency.* Boston: Houghton Mifflin Harcourt.

Schneider, A. L., & Ingram, H. (1997). *Policy design for democracy.* Lawrence: University of Kansas Press.

Shenkman, R. (1999). *Presidential ambition*. New York: Harper-Collins.

Simon, H. A. (1997). *Administrative behavior: A study of decision-making processes in administrative organizations* (4th ed.). New York: Free Press.

Spitzer, R. J. (1992). *President and Congress*. Philadelphia: Temple University Press.

Stone, D. A. (2002). *Policy paradox and political reason*. New York: Norton.

Svara, J. H. (2008). Beyond dichotomy: Dwight Waldo and the intertwined politics-administration relationship. *Public Administration Review, 68*(January/February), 46-52.

Svara, J. H. (1998). The politics-administration dichotomy model as aberration. *Public Administration Review, 58*, 51-58.

Svara, J. H. (1999). The shifting boundary between elected official and city managers in large council manager cities. *Public Administration Review, 59*, 44-53.

Truman, D. B. (1951). *The governmental process*. New York: Knopf.

U.S. House Committee on the Judiciary Majority Staff, *Reining in the imperial presidency: Lessons and recommendations relating to the presidency of George W. Bush*. http://www.cfr.org/publication/18227/house_of_representatives_report.html, accessed July 6, 2009.

Van Wart, M. (1998). *Changing public sector values*. New York: Garland.

Wade, L. L., & Curry, R. L. (1970). *A logic of public policy: Aspects of political economy*. Belmont, CA: Wadsworth.

White, L. D. (1926). *Introduction to the study of public administration*. New York: Macmillan.

Wilson, J. Q. (1968). *Varieties of police behavior*. Cambridge, MA: Harvard University Press.

Wilson, J. Q. (Ed.). (1980). *The politics of regulation.* New York: Basic Books.

Selected Web Sites

American Enterprise Institute. (National think tank focusing on the private sector and public policies affecting private property and private enterprise.)
http://www.aei.org

Brookings Institution. (National think tank focusing on social and economic policy issues.)
http://www.brookings.edu

The Council of State Governments. (National organization on state governance and politics.)
http://www.csg.org/

Eagleton Institute of Politics (Nationally recognized education, research, and public service unit of Rutgers University; one focus is practical politics.)
http://www.eagleton.rutgers.edu/

Hudson Institute. (National thinktank and forecasting center; one focus is election laws and campaign reform.)
http://www.hudson.org

International City/County Management Association. (The professional and educational organization for chief appointed managers, administrators, and assistants in cities, towns, counties, and regional entities throughout the world.)
http://icma.org

National Association of Counties. (National organization on county governance.)
http://www.naco.org

National League of Cities. (National organization on municipal issues and governance.)
http://www.nlc.org

Rand Corporation. (Consulting firm and think tank on public policy.)
http://www.rand.org

Roper Center for Public Opinion Research. (National center for public opinion research including election and political issues.)
http://www.ropercenter.uconn.edu/

Thomas Legislative Information on the Internet (Library of Congress site on legislative information on the Internet.)
http://thomas.loc.gov/

Urban Institute. (National think tank and policy center on urban issues and social policy.)
http://www.urban.org

3

Bureaucracy: Promise, Pathology, and Reform

Public policies are mainly administered by public organizations, the dominant form of which is bureaucracy. Public bureaucracies are expected to accomplish their tasks effectively and in ways that are responsive to the desires of the public or elected officials representing the public. Although this statement of objectives seems simple on the surface, it is subject to widely varying interpretations in practice. The issues are murky because agreement about the meaning of effectiveness and responsiveness is difficult to achieve. Lack of agreement on their meanings allows bureaucracies discretion about the way they carry out and assess their activities. With discretion there is always the potential for abuse.

Virtually all non-elected employees of government work in bureaucracies, although public organizations vary greatly in the extent to which they reflect the various characteristics of bureaucracy. Thus, we tend to think of teachers and planners as being in less bureaucratic organizations than police or the military. Ask a teacher whether she answers to someone in a hierarchy or is bound by rules and you will find that bureaucracy is a reality of her world.

The Promise of Bureaucracy

The bureaucratic ideal is the antithesis of the swamp. The swamp is murky, disorderly, and unpredictable. Bureaucracy thrives on clarity, order, and predictability. By creating legal, rational order and formal procedures for the accomplishment of organizational goals, bureaucracy attempts to ferret out the alligators, shed light on the darkness, and plan for dealing with the rising water. The promise of bureaucracy is rationality, objectivity, and thoroughness, thereby implying predictability, clarity, and consistency in the application of authority (Weber, 1968). Bureaucracies, however, often do not live up to this promise. And, in the case of public organizations, this leaves bureaucracies open to a great deal of political and intellectual criticism.

Bureaucracy, in the ideal form as portrayed by Max Weber, is based on a hierarchical system of authority where roles, rules, and regulations serve as the basis for action. Decisions regarding personnel are based on merit suggesting that expertise, knowledge, and performance are the major criteria for the evaluation of employees. Additionally, employees work full-time for regular pay rather than having a property right to their positions, and professional neutrality is a hallmark of the system. Specialization of knowledge and task are important components; they allow the greatest efficiency in accomplishment of individual tasks. The hierarchy of authority is the coordinating mechanism that brings all of the specialized activities together in pursuit of common organizational goals.

The Weberian model, as idealistic as it seems, was consistent with developments in business and government in the United States in the late 19th century. The development of large industrial firms led to many bureaucratic organizations in business. Historically, bureaucracies have been so successful in the private sector that to this day, they are the dominant forms of large-scale private firms.

In the public sector, the civil-service reform movement, which had its beginning in the early part of the 19th century, came to fruition with the passage of the Pendleton Civil Service Act of 1883. The act incorporated many of the concepts found in Weber's ideal construct of bureaucracy, especially neutrality and emphasis on merit in personnel processes. These approaches were affirmed by Woodrow Wilson's famous essay, "The Study of Administration" (1887).

During the Golden Era of Public Administration—the 1930s to the 1950s (Newland, 1984b)—the intellectual traditions of the field were firmly established. The traditions took their clues from the likes of Woodrow Wilson, Luther Gulick, and Lyndall Urwick (1937); Leonard White (1926), and Max Weber. The field of public administration grew with a focus on the structure of organizations utilized to administer policies. The separation of politics and administration, or policy and administration, was accepted as a given and appeared in the titles of major books in the early development of the field. Public bureaucracy developed with an emphasis on the separation of the administrative process from the policy-making process and from partisan political activities. This development was especially important at the national level. It was not until the 1920s and thereafter that state and local governments witnessed widespread reform efforts aimed at making administration neutral. Although there still are unreformed governments, the principles associated with Weberian bureaucracy are almost universal in government in the United States. Through mandates from the national government and initiatives of their own, state and local units share some of the features of the bureaucratic form of organization. Even in the face of bureaucrat bashing and considerable repoliticalization of administration since the 1980s, the vast majority of public administrators today work in settings the earlier reformers would recognize.

Many people view bureaucracy as a superior form of organization for handling complex problems and issues. Even in the face of more wicked problems, public authority most often finds expression through some variation of bureaucracy. Despite the revitalization of conservatism and market-imitating reforms since the 1970s (Johnston, 2000), people continue to demand ever-expanding services from government. Trying to run governments like private firms coupled with constraints on taxes has altered the mode and scale of public services delivery in many governments. Nonetheless, even with increasing reliance on private vendors and nonprofits in service provision, we see continued growth of government and bureaucracy which implies greater state control over the activities of individuals.

Leaders and citizens share common concerns about the possible loss of liberty and often articulate a need for reduction in governmental activity. There is, however, often little agreement about how the size and scope of government can be reduced because individuals and interest groups usually do not support a reduction in those activities that benefit them. They aim the reductive arrows at others. For example, older Americans, as nominal fiscal conservatives, often push for lower taxes and reduced federal spending for public education, but fiercely reject any proposed reductions in social security benefits or Medicare. Likewise, younger persons question the entire social security system as being insolvent and unjust, but insist on continued public subsidies for highways and small businesses. Because so many persons and pressure groups have a personal stake in maintaining each governmental activity at every level, reduction or elimination of a given program or public outlay is difficult to accomplish. The net result is that bureaucracy has grown to the point where it is seen by some as the dominant force in our political system. This raises the issue of what happens when bureaucrats behave badly.

Bureaucratic Pathology

Although the characteristics of bureaucracy described by Weber are supposed to lead to efficiency, predictability, objectivity, thoroughness, consistency, and rationality (Argyriades, 1982), those characteristics also affect the way members of the organization behave. Their behavior can be functional or dysfunctional. Their behavior may serve the interests of one part of the organization at the expense of another part or to the detriment of the organization as a whole. The behavior in which survival of the bureaucracy and protection of its members displace the nominal goals for which the organization was established has been referred to as *bureaupathetic behavior* (Merton, 1940; Thompson, 1961).

Bureacracies rely on a well-defined hierarchy and formal authority to control the activities of members in the organization. The purpose of this control is to ensure that the efforts of all members are coordinated toward reaching the substantive goals of the organization. Although some control is necessary, many bureaucratic organizations demand complete conformity. The tendency toward conformity is powerful and is reinforced by the rewards management has to dispense. Rosabeth Moss Kanter (1977), for example, found that success in the organization is highly dependent on effective team membership displayed largely through conformity to the team's norms.

Other key forces that support conformity are the socialization processes of the organization, desire to belong, self-interest, peer pressure, and lack of self-confidence. Fear of punishment such as the loss of job and security also are important to many members and help ensure conformity. Each of these factors affects individuals differently, but there is little disagreement that the pressures to conform are strong and present forces in most organizations, especially large bureaucratic organizations.

Although conformity contributes to the coordination of efforts within the organization, it produces grave negative effects when carried too far. The organizational culture that develops in bureaucracies can lead to situations in which members operate only within the sphere of formal authority they perceive themselves to have. Thus, they look for specific authorization to do anything. Such a preoccupation with formal authority often means that the bureaucrat is internally responsible but is able to avoid external accountability for actions. The bureaucrat can decline to act because of the lack of formal authority or can hide behind the performing of a narrow action that is insufficient to deal effectively with the problem at hand but that satisfies the need to operate within the scope of legitimate authority. To the frustrated citizen who has been shuffled from one desk or office to another, the issue of getting action is more important than who has formal authority to accomplish the task.

Conformity can also be dysfunctional to the organization as a whole because it is strongest in the most homogeneous subunits of the organization. Thus, the further down the hierarchy one goes, the greater is the sense of group norms and conformity to them. The conformity in a small subunit may be so strong that members of the subunit resist the authority that is supposed to be the coordinating force in the organization. The subunit may become so cohesive that it becomes insulated from the organization as a whole. The high *esprit de corps* and conformity to special group norms in police SWAT units, for example, may cause open conflict with other units and the commanders of other units in field operations. In universities, athletic teams and programs, likewise, are notorious for their sense of separateness and elite status, which often effectively insulate the team members, coaches, and activities from the nominal authority of the university president.

Along with the hierarchical structure of bureaucracy, the specialization of activities can be detrimental. Specialization fosters the application of the greatest expertise to any given part of the organization's work. By concentrating on their particular activity, bureaucrats can develop great proficiency in what they do and enhance organizational efficiency. On the negative side, however, they can use their narrow expertise as a way of resisting control by those in high-level positions. The expertise gives special status, and this can be used as leverage in dealing with other parts of the organization. Because others are unlikely to have full knowledge of the area of activity of the specialized unit, it is difficult for others to make judgements about recommendations, requests, or actions of those subunits. Elementary and secondary school special education programs, for example, often resist coordination and cooperation with other educational programs and units in schools and frequently receive special, earmarked appropriations and special facilities. This sets them apart and often permits them to operate independently of direct control by district administrators. At the national level, members of the intelligence and defense communities, such as the CIA, the Department of Defense, and the FBI, play the specialized knowledge and status game to the hilt and often successfully resist efforts by the president and Congress to manage them. Sharing of information and coordination among these agencies even in the face of national danger is difficult to secure.

The terrorist attacks of September 11, 2001 focused attention on the lack of communication across agencies and provided George W. Bush the opportunity for a massive reorganization of national security agencies. The new Department of Homeland Security combined twenty-two existing agencies employing 170,000 workers. One of the arguments in favor of the reorganization was that combining the various agencies into one department would help coordinate information and action by the various units that affect national security both internally and externally. Critics point out that the Department has had difficulty achieving the goal, citing lax airport security, the ability of investigators to get into sensitive federal agency buildings carrying contraband items, and the disastrous response to Hurricane Katrina as examples of an agency that did not come together very well.

As specialized functions develop, professional standards and norms also develop around those activities. The professional standards and norms cloak the specialists with a sense of neutral competence that contributes to greater credibility with the rest of the organization and the external environment. This credibility, in turn, may be used in resisting legitimate attempts to collaborate by those outside the particular unit. Some good examples in local government include librarians, fire chiefs, police chiefs, judges in municipal courts, prosecuting attorneys, and heads of computing services. These managers, often excellent in their fields of specialization, frequently find it difficult to coordinate with other departments and to operate in an inclusive manner.

Efficiency of operation in a particular activity may be enhanced by specialization, but highly specialized units may lose sight of the overall policy goals and objectives of the organization. The city manager of a large western city, for example, in pushing the city toward a more strategic approach to budgeting and other resource allocation under conditions of financial constraint, found that only he, the city auditor, and the budget director had an overall, system-view of the city administration. The other top managers—assistant city managers, department heads, and program directors—although nominally members of a *top management team,* took much more specialized and localized views based on individual departmental needs, functions, and resources. The city manager's experience was not atypical.

By focusing on their departments' and programs' specialized objectives and activities, bureaucrats exaggerate the importance of their activities and lose sight of how they relate to the rest of the bureaucracy and policy processes. They focus on their activities and the capacity of their department to function under stress, thereby inhibiting the capacity of the organization as a whole to cope and function properly. This kind of decentralization of focus and effort is common. Success in the specialized activity often becomes the real day-to-day objective of the bureaucrat to the detriment of the broader mission of the organization.

The concentration on specialized activity may also lead to loss in communication across subunits of the organization. For example, typically, cities of 150,000 have more than thirty individual departments and free-standing programs. Even if management of each of the departments is effective, the fragmentation and decentralization do little to promote interdepartmental communication. Although city managers may promote cross-department activities and use crosscutting teams for special projects, interdepartmental competition tends to be high, and interdepartmental coordination and cooperation low, resulting in minimal exchange and cross-fertilization of ideas.

The loss of new perspectives leads to stagnation in the organization and reduces its effectiveness. Too little openness and understanding of what is going on in other subunits or too little interaction with others reduces the variety of ideas and inputs to organizational activities. Further, it reduces the possibility of using horizontal communication networks to coordinate activities among different units or agencies, all of which have some part of the action in implementation of a given policy.

Specialization can result in isolation from outside ideas. This, in turn, often leads to a phenomenon known as *groupthink,* in which group norms are so strong that realistic appraisal of a situation is difficult or impossible. Irving Janis (1972) studied decisions regarding such situations as the attack on Pearl Harbor, invasion of North Korea, Bay of Pigs, and expansion of the war in Vietnam. He found that United States decision makers were severely hampered by groupthink. More recently, American defense and intelligence planners and decision makers appear to have suffered from groupthink in our unsuccessful military efforts in the civil war in Somalia, the war in Iraq, and our support for the Islamic insurgents in Afghanistan in their war of liberation against the Soviets. In each case, one-dimensional thinking caused our government to pursue policies that proved disastrous. In the case of Afghanistan, narrowly-defined American anti-Soviet efforts helped lead to rule by the Taliban, who later became the focus of American military effort. It took the events of September 11, 2001 to alert American leaders to some of the more complex issues of the international situation in south Asia and their potential impacts for the rest of the world.

As Janis found in his studies, groups dealing with these situations become so close-knit that they develop norms that cause them to avoid negative feedback and develop mechanisms to keep such feedback from their leader. Additionally, warning signals are ignored, and information that contradicts their norms is reasoned away. Members of the groups tend to screen their own input, and critics are dismissed as not understanding the situation. Members lose the ability to identify with the concerns of those outside the group. Acceptance of the group viewpoint becomes paramount.

Clearly, such a situation does not contribute to the most rational decision-making process for government. The experience in these situations is repeated every day in organizations. The Watergate scandal of the Nixon administration, the infamy of the Iranian arms deals in the Reagan administration, the failure to secure a national health care insurance system in the Clinton administration and the decision to invade Iraq by the Bush administration represent the "us-against-them" mentality symbolized by groupthink. On a much smaller scale, decision making in subunits of bureaucracy reflects similar characteristics. An example of both the garrison mentality and arrogance of groupthink is the Ramparts Division of the Los Angeles Police Department in the late 1990s. Members of an antigang unit fabricated evidence, used intimidation and torture to force confessions, filed false reports, lied to superiors, and gave false and misleading testimony in court. Additionally, some group leaders used intimidation to coerce other members of the unit to toe the line and support group norms. Over seventy officers were implicated in the scandal.

Rules, regulations, and procedures have a tendency to become more important than substantive goals in many organizations. This phenomenon is referred to as *goal displacement* where abiding by the rules and regulations becomes the real goal or takes precedence over doing what the rules were created to accomplish. Rules may ease the work of the bureaucrat and provide predictability to organizational activities. For the client wishing to be well served, however, rules may get in the way of effective service. The question arises as to whether the organization exists for the provision of service or for the protection of the bureaucrats. Obviously, there is much room between these extremes. It is also certain that some people become so frustrated by the rules that they give up and never receive the service. In some instances, however, the client has little choice. If individuals want to receive a Social Security check or drive an automobile, then they must put up with the rules and regulations of the regional office of the Social Security Administration or state auto-licensing bureau. Stories and complaints about poor service at Social Security offices and Departments of Motor Vehicles service centers are legend.

Bureaucracies are expected to be impartial and neutral to promote fairness and equitability in dealing with the public. Once again, a noble objective of the bureaucratic form often results in a less than desirable effect. Neutrality and impartiality can be carried to the extreme so that bureaucracy becomes impersonal. Equality of treatment may lead to an inappropriate outcome or remedy for a specific situation, and the bureaucrat becomes viewed as unresponsive. Although bureaucrats may hide behind the rules as a way of avoiding doing something creative, they frequently have little power to mitigate the negative effects of rules.

Zero tolerance as practiced in most school districts is an instructive example. In response to the 1999 Columbine school tragedy, school districts adopted zero tolerance policies, rules, and regulations regarding controlled substances and weapons on campus. In many instances, literal application of zero tolerance rules resulted in suspension and expulsion of students for petty offenses. Thus, students have been suspended from school for actions such as offering pain pills to a student suffering from menstrual cramps and giving chewing gum to another student. A ten-year-old student was suspended for unknowingly bringing a knife to school packed in her lunch bag by her mother for the purpose of cutting an apple. Zero tolerance policies have their place, but unthinking, inflexible enforcement—often without any discretion permitted by the rules to the teacher, principal, or district administration—shows the absurdity of rigid enforcement of rules and regulations as a norm of equal treatment.

Bureaucracies develop personalities of their own. Often bureaucratic behavioral norms are self-protective and border on the pathological (Merton, 1940; Thompson, 1961). Such norms and behaviors help bureaucrats defend themselves from others such as superiors, political leaders, clientele groups, and the general public. Some of the activities explained in our discussions above constitute protective behavior.

Agencies and their bureaucrats often develop a language of their own called *bureaucratese*. Bureaucratese allows members of the organization to communicate precisely with each other, but it also allows bureaucrats to better control the situation when dealing with outsiders, including their political superiors and clients. Ralph Hummel (2008) claims that bureaucratese's primary function "is to make outsiders powerless." Whether or not this is its main function, this jargon intimidates those who have to deal with the agency because they do not know the language. Academic disciplines including public administration have developed their own jargon specific to their fields. The ethereal jargon of academic written and oral communication differs significantly from ordinary English, and the jargon of practice and is a difficult nut to crack. Remember the first time you experienced scholarly terminology in academic public administration. A special language builds group and organizational cohesion, but it may impede effective service delivery if the clients cannot understand what is expected and required of them or what is available to them.

Many students of bureaucracy have identified several common tendencies in bureaucratic behavior (Downs, 1967; Merton, 1940; Schon, 1971; Terry, 2003; Thompson, 1961). Generally they conclude that bureaucracies and bureaucrats have conserving tendencies. They attempt to hold on to what is comfortable and known, and resist efforts to change them. In protecting their turf, they develop habits, routines, and procedures that serve their interests and limit the ability of outsiders to influence their activities. They effectively resist control by others and have perfected survival strategies (Greenberg, 1974; Kaufman, 1976).

Although bureaucracies are effective in socializing members to their norms, there are always some people who cannot or will not conform because of the incompatibility of their own values with those of the organization. These individuals may withdraw from the life of the organization, try to change the organization, or rationalize their activity within the organization on the grounds that it permits them to earn money to do what they really value outside of the organization. In extreme cases, some individuals choose to be guerrillas and attempt to sabotage the organization (Needleman & Needleman, 1974; O'Leary, 2005)

As noted by Mary Parker Follett (1924), Chester Barnard (1938), and Robert Merton (1940), informal organizations develop within formal organizations. Informal organizations inside the shell of the formal institution offer one major way for members, including dissidents, to cope with the demands made on them by the formal rules and structure. Classical organization theorists and early pioneers in public administration believed that informal organizations constitute a negative force. They felt that informal organization should be discouraged and that effective management would prevent its development (Gulick & Urwick, 1937; Blau, 1963). The Hawthorne Studies of worker motivation and productivity begun in 1927 led to reassessment of this position. Management literature began to consider the functional effects of informal organization (Barnard, 1938; Mayo, 1933). These issues will be addressed more fully in the next chapter. For now, it is important to note the natural tendency for informal organizations to develop inside of formal organizations.

Popular Criticisms of Bureaucracy

Although bureaucracy is a positive instrument for the implementation of governmental policies and programs at all levels in the United States, popular sentiment about bureaucracy is largely negative. As Allen Barton notes, popular complaints about public bureaucracy focus on three major issues: (1) personal traits of bureaucrats, (2) the structure of bureaucracy, and (3) the relationship of the bureaucracy to the larger political system (Barton, 1980).

Personal Traits

Bureaucrats are often characterized as being uncaring and interested only in following rules and regulations because when an individual case does not fit into the rules or regulations, bureaucrats often see no way of handling it. To the individual seeking service, the bureaucrat seems insensitive and rigid. Red tape—the slavish following of complex rules and procedures—is usually blamed for such lack of responsiveness and delays to individual cases. Public bureaucrats are often viewed as people who cannot make it in the private sector and are thus less competent than their private sector counterparts. Similarly, they frequently are considered less motivated and overly rigid. Citizens often complain that bureaucrats are more interested in serving their own interests and controlling the public than in serving it. Though these views are largely inaccurate, they are commonly held among the general populace. One bad personal experience with an inept bureaucrat or agency is often over-generalized into an indictment of the bureaucracy and government in general. The hard, effective work of the vast majority of the millions of people who serve the public well is not visible or acknowledged.

Structural Aspects

Some structural constraints placed on bureaucracy limit its effectiveness and lead to popular criticism of it. Constitutional law and public policy often impose specific restrictions on bureaucrats to prevent them from abusing their power. For example, public bureaucrats in the United States are permitted to operate only on the basis of a specific grant of authority. They cannot create authority to act on their own. Thus, dealing with a specific situation that may fall outside the specific grant of authority is difficult if not impossible. There also are restrictions on the political activity of public administrators. Personnel rules are protective of the individual employee. Thus, agency managers often feel frustrated when attempting to make employees more responsive because they generally have only limited authority to discipline employees and dismissal of public employees is difficult. Procedural protections in the form of formal hearings and due process rules, as required by the constitution for public employees, are much less common in the private sector.

The practice of *employment-at-will* that allows an employer to dismiss an employee at any time for any reason is common in the private and nonprofit sectors, but is not operative in the public sector to any great extent. In the public sector, employees normally may be terminated only for cause, usually a grievous cause such as willful violation of the law in performance of duties, theft, or insubordination. Over time, laws and court decisions have limited the employment-at-will doctrine in the private and nonprofit sectors. Some states, notably Georgia and Florida, reformed their systems to move toward at-will employment. Nonetheless, there still is a major difference in the public sector, where even dismissal for cause is difficult.

A common view of some accuracy is that public budgeting systems work against accountability and economy by rewarding those agencies and programs that spend their monies regardless of what they accomplish through the use of their resources. Saving money while performing the expected job often is rewarded by budget cuts, whereas those who spend all that they are appropriated and ask for more often have a justification for greater resources. In this system, there are few incentives for efficiency and many rationales for increased funds and expansion of activities. Through expansion, bureaucratic managers gain larger domains to control and thus greater power, usually accompanied by a larger salary to reflect the greater responsibility. For example, many city managers try to keep cost per unit of service low but seldom try to retard the expansion of the city population and territory. Under severe fiscal constraint, city managers may actually cut service levels, reduce the size of the city work force, and trim fat from the expenditure budget. Nonetheless, in the long run, the city grows, the budget increases, and the city manager is commensurately rewarded.

Performance management using program evaluation based on outcome and impact measures and *sunset reviews* (in which agencies are automatically reviewed at the end of a specific time period to determine the need for their services and continued existence) is an example of efforts to control these activities. We will discuss these issues more in Chapters 5 and 6. For now, it is important to note that program and sunset reviews do not function well at any level in part because of political and clientele support for specific agencies and programs. For example, public safety services—fire and police protection—often are the most costly services provided by local governments. Yet support by the public, by pressure groups such as employee associations and by unions, and elected officials is so strong that police and fire departments are nearly immune to budget reduction except in the most extreme fiscal situations.

The expertise of bureaucrats and agencies and their control over information lead to a concentration of bureaucratic power in this age of information and electronic communication. Through its store and use of information, bureaucracy has the upper hand in many policy-making functions. They impact many decisions even at the expense of the legislative body, which is supposed to be the policy-making apparatus. Similarly, the chief executive frequently is powerless to do much to influence the course of events in particular agencies. For example, only a few members of Congress ever have anything approaching full and accurate information about military spending. Even the president often has trouble becoming fully informed about military expenditures. Given the complexity of the appropriations for the military, it may be that not even many of the top officers in the Pentagon have full information about how funds are spent. Ironically, they may not want to know.

As areas of expertise develop, professionalization of the bureaucracy also grows. Professionalization implies the application of knowledge and expertise in ways consistent with standards and codes developed by fellow professionals. These standards and codes benefit the public to the extent that they insure proper and ethical behavior. Professional groups, however, may also help insulate the member bureaucrat from external controls. The professional association may attempt to dominate the decision-making process or may claim the allegiance of the bureaucrat. Loyalty to the agency or to the public may be weakened, thus further limiting accountability. An interesting example is the effort by teachers' unions and associations to protect the seniority and status of long-time faculty in schools and universities against posttenure review programs. Academic freedom and tenure in position are so strongly held as professional norms that attempts to systematically review the effectiveness of tenured faculty meets fierce resistance from such organizations as the American Federation of Teachers and the American Association of University Professors. Although many states now have annual review of teachers and a weak form of posttenure review, the faculty associations continue to battle to protect tenured faculty.

The bureaucrat combines expertise with professionalism and the authority of the state to form a "formidable source of power" (Lewis, 1977). Cloaked in this power, bureaucrats can be intimidating to citizens and clients. Professionalism also gives an aura of neutrality and competence, important ingredients in dealing with persons, groups, and organizations outside the agency. Professionals often use this image of professionalism and neutrality to attempt to influence decisions outside their areas of competence, especially in decisions about the distribution of resources (Lewis, 1977). It is not uncommon, for example, to find managers of recreational facilities that deal with children raising questions about the effectiveness of schools and police. Their shared concern for the welfare of children and families leads them to challenge the effectiveness of other programs for children.

Political Relationships

Mark Moore (1995) argues that politics with outside authorities, along with deliverance of services to clients and management of internal affairs of the agency, constitute an equilateral triad of activities that all effective managers must master. He maintains that the creation of public value by bureaucrats requires them to be proficient in political communication, negotiation, and exchange. This relationship of bureaucrats and bureaucracy to the larger political system, however, provides another area of popular criticism. The bureaucracy, as the one permanent institution in the executive branch at all levels, enjoys a certain degree of autonomy. Elected executives and their *exempt appointees* —politically-appointed high-level administrators not protected by civil service status—usually serve fixed terms, and so they come and go. Even mayors and city managers of long tenure find they must relinquish their posts from time to time. In contrast, the bureaucrats in the protected civil service may stay on indefinitely. As a result, they have personal contacts and support systems that insulate them from newly elected officials (Pfiffner, 1987). The bureaucrat has many tools to make it difficult for the elected official or the exempt appointee, including capacity to interpret policy and to slow down action. As noted earlier in Chapter 2, newly elected presidents often find that the career service employees in such agencies as the Department of State, Forest Service, Environmental Protection Agency, Army Corps of Engineers, and Drug Enforcement Administration can successfully resist attempts to force them to speedily carry out changes in agency procedures and rules.

External groups align with bureaucracy to provide continuity and predictability for both of them in the political swamp. External clientele groups provide nearly permanent, predictable support systems for agencies. Often these clientele groups are the main source of political support in legislative hearings and budget considerations. Critics of American politics view the long-lasting alliances between bureaucracies and interest groups as a major problem because the agency responds to the special, private interests of the pressure group rather than to the general public interest (McConnell, 1966). Despite the fact that it is hard to operationally define the public interest (Lewis, 2006), the administrative system does favor those interests that are well mobilized, have resources to participate in political exchange, and are willing to support bureaucratic ends. As a result, many legitimate demands and concerns may be ignored because the champions of such concerns have little opportunity to voice them (Box, 2006).

The Iron Triangle of interest groups, bureaucracy, and legislative committees reinforces the tendency to react to special interests. Legislative committees depend on bureaucratic agencies for much of their information and assistance in the policy-making process. Long-lasting alliances often form between particular committees and agencies. Affected interest groups, through their lobbyists, usually maintain close ties with agencies and legislative committees, and the three elements work together in mutual support and harmony. For example, agricultural committees of Congress, the Department of Agriculture, and large agriculture businesses usually work together and understand each other's needs. They realize that if they work together, they can accommodate part of each participant's needs and desires. Whether or not the result is conducive to the general public interest is not a high priority of the alliance. In Fritschler and Rudder's (2007) terms, these alliances are subgovernments in which the bureaucracy, interest groups, and congressional committees come together to fend off forces detrimental to their common interest.

The electoral system also encourages these coalitions of interested parties. Although it is theoretically possible for voters to exert control through elections at all levels in American politics, even with term limits in many states, incumbents have advantages over their challengers. As incumbents, even second-term (which sometimes is their last term) legislators have public visibility rarely available to challengers. Furthermore, incumbents often can call on interest groups for funds and other support in re-election efforts. Similarly, agencies can be helpful by providing important information or in the timing of announcement of programs. The result is that the bureaucracy responds as much or more to the needs and values of the incumbent than to the interests of the citizenry at large.

Bureaucrats also have an advantage over other political participants because many of the activities in which they engage never become major issues debated in the public arena (Lewis, 1977; Kingdon, 2003). Thus, they are able to work on particular issues or agendas over concerted periods without much time in the public spotlight. Media are fickle, and public attention is short. The spotlight shines on an issue for short periods and then shifts as people get tired of an issue or a new issue gains media attention. The bureaucrat can focus on a given issue such as disposal of nuclear wastes long after the general public, the media, and the elected official may have forgotten about it. Bureaucrats thus dominate the policy process on many issues. Bureaucratic tenure and lack of public exposure also have positive effects. Bureaucrats ensure stability of governance in an unstable world and promote continuity of policy and service through these times of continuous political change.

While criticisms of bureaucracy are common and imply dysfunctional effects, the positive aspects of bureaucracy are undeniable. As Gerald Caiden (1981) indicates, there is a culture of public organizations that involves adherence to laws, rules, and regulations. The public service is based on the belief that bureaucracy serves the people and is expected to uphold the highest levels of integrity while operating on the basis of merit and performance. These values, and others, form what Caiden calls the "ideology of public service." Implied in the criticisms people have of the bureaucracy is the expectation that public servants should behave in concert with the values Caiden has outlined. The criticisms about lack of integrity and higher norms often stem from the perception that bureaucrats have not lived up to the standards the public has for them.

Despite the bleak picture painted by the critics, there are those who believe that the critics misrepresent bureaucracy (Kassel, 2008; Wagenaar, 2004). While the supporters of the bureaucracy accept the fact that some individuals abuse their positions, they present a picture of a hard-working and ethical public service. Their concern is with the way the work of the bureaucracy can be facilitated, along with protections from abuse by the few who do not live up to the promise of bureaucracy (Goodsell, 2004; Mainzer, 1973; Newland, 1984a, 1987; Rosen, 1978).

Reform

Reorganization and bureaucratic reform are major preoccupations of many people interested in public administration and policy. Harold Seidman opens his influential book (1997) with the statement, "Reorganization has become almost a religion in Washington." Reorganization and reform abound at the state and local level as well. As soon as any problem is identified with any governmental program, policy, or agency, there are advocates of ways to fix the problem through reform. Of course, reform movements characterized much of the early development of American public administration. The personnel reform efforts of the late 19th century and the local government (good government) reforms of the early 20th century are good examples of that era. The main objective of reform during this era was to ensure neutral competence of public officials.

Reform efforts through the 1920s, 1930s, and 1940s focused on centralizing executive leadership, authority, and responsibility in agencies and in levels of government. The 1921 Act creating the Bureau of the Budget is one of the significant examples of this focus. By the 1950s, the centralizing trend had succeeded in focusing responsibility in department headquarters in national agencies as well as many state and local levels. In addition, the national government began the process of centralizing political authority on the national level through public policies that required state and local units to comply with national rules if they were to receive funding from the national government. Among the most celebrated events accomplishing such an effect was the passage of the Social Security Act of 1935 and its programs. During the 1950s, however, there was an attempt to reverse some of the centralizing tendencies and to disperse authority (Rourke, 1984). The pendulum continues to swing back and forth depending on the political philosophy of those in office. During the 1960s there was a resurgence of the centralizing tendency followed by the decentralizing emphasis in the 1970s until the beginning of the 21st century. Although President George W. Bush advocated the devolvement of programs from the national government to the states, his administration pushed many policies, such as No Child Left Behind in education and "smart" drivers' licenses, that actually centralized power. The Obama administration began its term in 2009 with national policies that also centralized power to address serious financial and economic instability.

Reform Objectives

Most calls for reform suggest that there is a need to make bureaucracy more responsive to the elected political leaders and the general public (Garnett, 1987). In every election there are advocates of making government responsive and accountable, usually meaning that the bureaucracy has to be brought under control. The assumptions supporting such efforts are that gov-

ernment bureaucrats are serving their own interests or are overly responsive to special interests, both of which are detrimental
to the public good (Greenberg, 1974; Weiss, 1980). Reform proposals often focus on reducing the size and cost of government
programs and agencies.

Reform has been pursued with a moral fervor in the United
States. The personnel reforms of the 19th century were couched
in terms of getting rid of the evil of spoils and replacing it with
the virtue of merit. The good government movements of the 1920s
and afterward had the same good versus evil character to them.
Machine politics was viewed as corrupt and in need of disman-
tling. Administrative reform built on principles of management
and separation of partisan politics from administration assumed
a major status in public affairs. Many of the principles are em-
bedded in the early classics of American public administration
(Gulick & Urwick, 1927). Perhaps the most influential public
document in public administration history, the Hoover Commission report (The Commission on Organization of the Executive
Branch of Government 1949), emphasized these principles and
values.

Consequently, bureaucratic machines replaced the political
party machines. While merit systems and reformed cities abound,
bureaucracies dominate the political decision-making process.
The interests of the bureaucracy—especially the interests of
the middle class who work in it and whose values dominate it—
supplanted the interests of the political parties and their followers (Lowi, 1967). The New Public Administration and equal em-
ployment/affirmative action policies so important to the 1970s
and the post-modern criticisms of American public administration in the 1990s were, in part, reactions to the bureaucratic machine. Reforming the bureaucracy is viewed as a way of return-
ing power to the citizenry (Cox & Mair, 1991; King & Stivers,
1998).

Reform and organization efforts are justified on many other grounds. Especially popular are promises that the reform or
reorganization will lead to greater economy, efficiency, and improvement in ability of government to deliver services. As Aaron
Wildavsky (1961) noted, these kinds of justification for reform
often mask political agendas. Reform and reorganization usually
have profound effects on the distribution of political power and
on who gets what in the political system. Thus, those who hope

to benefit directly from certain changes support reform efforts that further their interests.

Bureaucratic reform also is supported because it is expected to solve substantive problems of all kinds (Seidman, 1997). These justifications usually are linked to improving the ability of the organization to operate more efficiently, thus improving its chances of doing its job. Thus, the military establishment is reorganized every once in a while in order to reduce waste, and also because it is assumed that reorganization will improve defense capability.

The promises made by reformers and proponents of reorganization are often unrealistic. When the expected results do not come, people become frustrated, and the bureaucracy's image becomes even more negative. The lack of coherence between problem definition, reorganization gambits, and lack of actual positive consequences produces a self-serving cyclical culture of change in bureaucratic structures.

Approaches to Reform

Bureaucratic reform occurs in many ways, but there are two fundamental approaches. Reform attempts either to restructure the bureaucratic organization or to change the procedures through which the bureaucracy operates. Most efforts combine elements of both approaches, but usually a reform proposal will fit primarily into one or the other category.

Structural reform is prevalent throughout the history of our political system. The development of our governmental system relied on structural features that were expected to limit the ability of government to infringe on the liberty of its citizens. The constitution spells out structures that many now consider inefficient and outmoded. Thus, there are always suggestions for changes that would allow one branch of government or the other to operate with fewer hindrances. Of course, presidents usually want the executive branch unshackled. Leaders in Congress usually want greater freedom for its two houses. Even members of the Supreme Court call for changes that would speed up the judicial process. These structural elements were placed in the Constitution so that no one branch would be able to operate entirely on its own. Separation of powers and the attendant checks and balances were intended to slow things down and permit careful consideration of any anticipated action.

Public administration in the United States was built largely on reform of government structure as a way of increasing the efficiency and responsiveness of the executive branch. The personnel reforms of the 19th century were based on separating administrative systems from the partisan political environment. Separation of politics and administration or policy and administration was the major theme of much of the reform movement. Although many of the advocates of good government and more efficient government administration during the 1920s, 1930s, and 1940s placed much emphasis on management practices, they also held separation of politics and administration as a sacred tenet.

One of the major features of structural reform is reflected in personnel systems. They are constantly targets of reform. At the national level, in 1883, the personnel system was made semiautonomous through the creation of the civil service system. Though it took many years to develop fully, this civil service system was set up so that it could not be controlled entirely by the chief executive. The same type of development took place at the state and local levels with some actually preceding the national government in development of independent civil service and/or merit systems. Reformers theorized that government would become more efficient and less responsive to particular interests (political machines) with independent personnel systems. As pointed out earlier, the bureaucracies that have developed have their own agendas and respond to particular interests so they may be characterized as machines. Those with access to the bureaucracy reap the spoils. Clearly, personnel reform also involves procedural changes that will be addressed below.

By the 1970s, many leaders were calling for structural change in personnel management again. With the leadership of President Carter, the Civil Service Reform Act of 1978 was passed, restructuring the personnel function in national government. The act made many specific structural changes. Chief among them was the division of the U.S. Civil Service Commission into three major units: the Office of Personnel Management, the Merit Systems Protection Board, and the Federal Labor Relations Authority. The effect of the changes was to bring the personnel function more closely under the president again, with the Office of Personnel Management being integrated into the executive management function. These same experiences, in varying degrees, are found at the state and local levels. Many state and local units followed suit after the national government reforms. Ironically, now there are calls for change again at the national level as there is evidence of continued politicization of the personnel function under Presidents Reagan, George H.W. Bush, Clinton, and George W. Bush.

Virtually every agency of government at all levels develops reorganization plans on a recurring basis. Some are implemented; many remain just plans. It is nearly axiomatic that a newly elected president, governor, or mayor comes to office with major plans to improve efficiency and effectiveness, reduce waste, save tax money, and improve responsiveness in government through reorganization. The high hopes of this ritual are often dashed by the reality of having to work with the bureaucracy that has power of its own (Brown, 1977; Stanton, 2008).

A highly visible area of structural change is the way presidents try to improve performance through the organization of their own offices and staffs. In 1921, the Bureau of the Budget was created with the responsibility of coordinating the executive budget process. In 1939, it was moved to the Executive Office of the president, reflecting increasing consolidation of presidential control of the budgeting function. In 1970, the Bureau of the Budget was renamed the Office of Management and Budget (OMB) to reflect changes in its responsibilities over time. Since that time, this office has undergone several changes in mission and responsibilities. Two interesting responsibilities added in the 1990s reinforced OMB's central role in national efforts in program performance assessment and the utilization of electronic data in governance. OMB is the lead agency in the implementation of the Government Performance and Results Act of 1993 (GPRA). This GPRA required the national government to institute strategic planning and performance measures for its programs and agencies. Setting aside issues of the effectiveness of strategic planning at the national level, OMB assists agencies in the development and use of measures of program effectiveness. OMB maintains a Performance Improvement Council to aid it in these efforts. It also uses a Program Assessment Rating Tool (PART) as part of its system for assessing programs and making decisions on budget plans.

The Office of Information and Regulatory Affairs (OIRA), which is part of OMB, oversees federal regulations and information requirements. It also develops policies to improve government statistics and information management. In the age of the Internet, the OIRA promises to be useful in administration efforts to engage in data-driven program evaluations.

In the end, however, exactly what the OMB does and how influential it is depends on how much the President seeks and uses its advice, counsel, and information. In each administration, there are differences about which members of the cabinet, Executive Office of the White House, and personal staff have access to the president and, thus, influence with him. For example, there is always speculation over whether the National Security Advisor, the Secretary of State, or the Secretary of Defense is more important in foreign policy. All three seemed to have important roles in the administration of George W. Bush, but the issue of who had the most continuous counsel and influence is an open question. There is evidence that Vice President Dick Cheney may have been the most influential, at least until the last year. The Obama administration faces the same questions with strong personalities in National Security, State, and Defense departments, as well as a vice president very well versed in foreign affairs. In every administration, the mix and status is different in part because of the way the president's office and internal communication system are structured.

Another structural issue, in some ways most important at the local level, is the degree to which government should contract with the private sector in performing many functions, thus eliminating some governmental agencies and changing the structure of service delivery (Cooper, 2003; U.S. General Accounting Office, 1997). Contracting for weapons development is a prime example at the national level. On the state and local level, Western states contract with the private sector for many kinds of services, including fire, sanitation, library, and water services. Contracting with the private sector for highway building and construction of other major facilities is common. Since 1970, some states and local governments have contracted with private firms for jails, prisons, and other corrections' services (Palumbo, 1986). The general trend toward privatization has grown since the 1970s but appears to be less of a focus in the Obama administration. This reform usually is justified as facilitating more efficient delivery of services, although there is disagreement about how much, if anything, is actually saved through contracting and other forms of privatization (Gerber, Hall, & Hines, 2004; Lamothe, Lamothe, & Feiock, 2008; Seidenstat, 1996).

Procedural reform is also common. Proponents usually argue that if procedures could be improved and streamlined, government services could be delivered more efficiently and effectively, and at great cost savings. The budget process is a popular area of procedural reform efforts (Caiden, 1987; Wildavsky & Caiden, 2005). During the 1960s, 1970s and 1980s, each new national administration seemed to have a new budgeting system that was going to revolutionize the federal budgeting and management process. We went through program budgeting, planning programming budgeting system (PPBS), strategic budgeting, zero-based budgeting (ZBB) and other variations. Each strategy had features attractive to those who wanted to improve governmental services, but each system has been short lived because of the strong routines inherent in the bureaucracy and the Congress. Although each of the systems may have been used by an administration in its own decision-making processes, they usually have had little impact on how the bureaucracy and Congress proceed. Most of the tradition of line item budgeting lives on (see Chapter 5 for more discussion of line item and other forms of budgeting).

Management and decision making are areas in which reform is constant. Elements of a variety of decision-making approaches are evident in governmental agencies. Among others, there has been management by objectives (MBO), strategic planning, flow charting, quality services, management for results, performance management, program evaluation and review techniques (PERT), cost-benefit analysis, cost-risk analysis, and many others. Most approaches and techniques are advocated in the hope of making better-informed decisions in a more timely fashion, thereby improving the management of agencies for the public interest. Disagreements, however, arise over who is actually being served best by a particular approach. Some critiques see these approaches as a kind of management flavor of the year that basically serve the reputation and interest of a given chief administrator.

Evaluation of government agencies and programs has also been a popular cause with reformers. For example, the zero based budgeting system implemented by President Carter built in an evaluation process that was supposed to force units to examine themselves thoroughly in the budget development process. Although this process did not survive the Carter administration at the national level, many cities and some states use a form of formal annual performance evaluation in their administrative planning and budget-making processes. The George W. Bush administration instituted a form of balanced scorecard in which each agency was required to evaluate itself annually on improvement on five dimensions:

1) strategic management of human capital
2) competitive sourcing
3) improved financial performance
4) expanded electronic government
5) budget and performance integration

The Obama administration chose to build on the Bush administration approach, but changed from a focus on grading specific programs to assessing progress in achieving stated goals and explaining trends in performance. To do so, the administration outlined six themes:

1) putting performance first using a new performance improvement and analysis framework
2) ensuring responsible spending of Recovery Act funds
3) transforming the federal workforce
4) managing across sectors
5) reforming federal contracting and acquisition
6) embracing transparency, technology, and participatory democracy

(Office of Management and Budget 2009).

Originally a part of ZBB, sunset review has been particularly popular at the state level. Sunset legislation tries to assure that governmental agencies and programs do not continue on in perpetuity once their original goals have been accomplished. In sunset review systems, all agencies and programs have a specific life span or are reviewed on a recurring cycle such as every five years. If the reviewing authority—sometimes a legislative committee and sometimes a special administrative agency or commission—finds that continuation of a given agency or program is not justified, it recommends abolition to the legislature. So far, few programs and agencies have gone out of business as the result of sunset review because every program or agency has constituents or stakeholders who lobby for their retention.

Evaluation systems using outcome and impact data are off-shoots of sunset review systems. One outcome system, benchmarking, became popular in the 1990s (Ammons, 2001). As practiced in states such as Oregon, Minnesota, and Arizona, *benchmarking* is a system of assessing program effects through time using measures based on past performance and carefully established future performance levels. A series of outcome-based benchmarks are established for every program and subprogram. Programs are then assessed in terms of whether they achieve the benchmarks. One key feature of this system is that the agency, the legislature, and a special component of the executive branch jointly develop benchmarks and outcome measures. Another feature is that the benchmarks require progressive improvements in both the quantity and quality of the program outcomes. For those states that use it, benchmarking has improved state capacity to assess outcomes of their programs.

Many municipalities adopted and modified benchmarking and outcome assessment systems using some form of outcome and impact measures in their annual budgeting processes (Ammons, 1995; 2001). For example, Portland, Oregon; San Diego, California; Reno, Nevada; and Ontario, Canada have developed refined impact measures for every program and department. The quarterly and annual reports as well as the budget proposals from each department are based on outcome and impact measures. Although these systems can be overly slavish in application, benchmarking and outcome measurement systems have changed the way local governments are managed (Ammons, 2001).

During the early 20th century, much of the effort in procedural reform focused on attempts to ensure that individuals were assured their procedural rights in dealing with bureaucracy. For several decades, regulatory agency activities and court cases regarding procedures of regulatory agencies produced many procedural guarantees (Davis, 1975; Kerwin, 2003). Other rules may be found in legislation authorizing programs and agencies. In 1946, as part of an effort to develop uniform practices, the national government passed the Administrative Proce-

dures Act which codified procedural rules required of administrative agencies. State and local governments followed the lead
of the national government, and now there is a strong body of
procedural protections for anyone dealing with a governmental
agency at any level. The activism of the courts in the 1960s and
early 1970s added to and strengthened procedural protections
(Rosenbloom, 1987). In the 1990s, the courts adopted what they
call a *balancing principle*. This principle involves balancing the
procedural rights of the parties involved with the interests of the
government in carrying out its activities. The Roberts court has
demonstrated a tendency to side more with government but still
uses the principle.

Allied with and arising from the procedural protections are
open government and sunshine laws. All levels of government
have policies that require open meetings, open records, and access to governmental information. The Freedom of Information
Act of 1966 at the national level is a primary vehicle for opening
the federal government to the average citizen. The assumption
behind the act is that taxpayers support the development of the
information and thus have a legal right to it. The act also builds
on the belief that control over the bureaucracy and government,
which is essential in a democracy, is impossible without information about what the government is doing and why it is doing it.

Issues of domestic and international security invite government secrecy. Using the act, for example, a reporter found that
former FBI director J. Edgar Hoover, now deceased, developed a
considerable secret file on the supposed un-American and pro-
Soviet activities of Albert Einstein (Jerome, 2002). Einstein, a
noted pacifist, did oppose America's entry into World War II, but
it is well known that he put aside his pacifist stance and supported American efforts to develop nuclear weapons. There is
actually no evidence that Einstein was anything but a loyal citizen. This did not, however, prevent Hoover from building the file.
In passing, it is worth noting that Hoover also kept secret files
on a wide array of persons including Martin Luther King, John
F. Kennedy, John Lennon, and Bob Dylan, among many others
(Gentry, 2001).

More recently, the George W. Bush administration, like others before it, attempted through executive privilege and control
to make access to government information more difficult. This
effort was partially successful because of the threat of terror-

ism, but individuals have been able to use the courts to force the release of information (Roberts, 2008). As rumors persist about what an administration or agency may or may not be doing, there is pressure to find out more. Partisan politics play a role in this. The citizen's right to know plays a more important role, and public information about what happens under the cover of national interest is a major tool for keeping bureaucracy and government responsible to the people.

The states generally follow the lead of the national government on freedom of information. State laws affect both state-level practices and those of local government. It is difficult for state and local officials to curtail public access to records and information. As in the case of the national experience, the courts have defended and extended the right of citizens to know.

Along with freedom of information policies, open meeting laws give public access to governmental decision-making processes at all levels. Open meeting laws generally dictate that a governing body can discuss or make policy only in meetings open to the public. Exceptions are made for some personnel decisions, lawsuits, and purchase of land. Otherwise, an agenda for the meeting must be publicly posted some prescribed time in advance. The subsequent meeting is bound by the publicly announced and printed agenda. The idea is to allow the public to be part of the decision-making process and to make sure that the decision-makers are not making decisions without consideration of public input. Open meeting policies also allow the public to be informed about what is happening and who is advocating or opposing what.

Obstacles to Bureaucratic Reform

Reform of bureaucracy is viewed from different perspectives. Advocates of bureaucratic reform view it as the solution to particular problems. Bureaucrats, who are likely to be affected by reforms most directly, usually are less enthusiastic about the need for and the impacts of reform. As Siedentopf (1982) states, "structural innovation underestimates administrative conservatism, bureaucratic inertia, and human resistance to change."

Ownership is a powerful force for social change. Bureaucrats and their agencies often feel threatened by the changes others wish to make. When bureaucrats are involved in the change process, they are more likely to support it. When outside reform movements that are critical of bureaucracy suggest changes, however, bureaucrats are likely to be less supportive of the change and, resist it.

Bureaucratic Resistance to Change. Stability produces many benefits, including making the swamp more predictable and navigable. Social systems may be viewed as naturally conserving and striving toward equilibrium (Kaufman, 1995; Schon, 1971). Bureaucratic routines, standard operating procedures, and rule-bound behavior are strong impediments to change (Rainey, 1997; Thompson, 1969). The comfort of routine preserves internal order and predictability. People in bureaucracy feel comfortable with the way things are done, thus making it difficult for them to accept the discomfort of change. They cannot easily see how change will improve operations and make their lives better. This reaction is simply human nature and common in all types of situations.

Bureaucrats become narrow in the perceptions of what is important because of specialization in function and knowledge. They tend to view the activity in their own units as most important and to be unconcerned about effects of their actions on the organization as a whole. Their sense that their unit is doing well prevents them from acknowledging the need for change because they do not have a good understanding of the rest of the system and how well it is doing overall. They are likely to have close ties with clientele and others outside the organization who support them in resisting change because of the fear of possible negative effects for them. Changes may disrupt these comfortable, predictable, and productive ties to legislative committees, lobbyists, journalists, or other supportive elements. The sense of potential disruption and uncertainty is not easily overcome.

Potential changes abound with costs that reduce the willingness and capacity of bureaucrats to accept them. There are sunk costs that arise from previous investment of money, time, and effort in established routines. Once resources are committed, no one likes to see them wasted. Agencies make serious efforts to produce results from the sunk costs once invested. Any change that might interfere with perceived payoffs may be resisted. When an organization puts resources into a particular set of operations such as building freeways, it is not likely to abandon the current system just because someone else likes high-speed trains better.

Psychological costs also are important in human undertakings. Commitment of individuals to an approach, a program, or a system is not easy to change. Sense of mission and method help organizations do their work well, but impede receptivity to change.

Power is a commodity in political life and change incurs political costs. The political stakes of managers, employers, clientele, and others affected by the organization and its activities are important considerations when contemplating change. Political actors always protect their interests and preserve their turf. Actors who have influence in and around the organization are likely to influence its structure and processes in such a way as to preserve and protect their interests. For example, neighborhood and homeowners associations sometimes are well connected with city council members, staff of municipal planning departments and members of planning commissions. Though not as well connected as the housing and development interests, they do have political clout. It would be illogical to believe that they would give up their influence and the capacity to protect their turf in the face of a proposed change in the role of local associations in the land-use planning processes. NIMBY (not in my back yard) is such a strong force in land-use decisions that neighborhood interests jealously guard any political access and influence they may have.

In spite of organizational, psychological, and political constraints, many proposed changes are popular and acceptable. Alas, the agency may lack financial, personnel, and time resources needed to effect the change. Of course, a proposed change may itself affect the agency resource base. Thus, it might still encounter a double negative response: "We don't have sufficient resources to do this, and even if we did, it is a bad idea because it would use valuable resources and prevent us from doing a good job on other things." Generally, agencies do everything they can to protect their base resources and add to them.

Overcoming Resistance to Change. Resistance to change is strong, but there are ways to reduce the resistance. Perhaps the most important strategy is to involve those affected by the change in the process of developing the reform. They are more likely to endorse and implement a change if involved in the decision-making process. Conversely, if the change originates outside the agency, members often rally around the defense of the status quo in their organization. If the same change is internally developed and proposed, however, the members have the opportunity to structure and influence the scope of the proposed change. This experience may even lead them to be supportive of greater change over time.

Acceptance of change depends on clear understanding of the proposed change and its implications for improving the life of the agency, bureaucrat, and client. If the bureaucrat understands the change and is convinced that its implementation would be in his or her self-interest, acceptance is enhanced. Similarly, if the bureaucrat's perception of organizational goals is consistent with the proposed change, acceptance is more likely. Finally, understanding the consequences of not accepting or supporting the change may have an impact. Heavy-handed explanations and threats of negative consequences for nonacceptance, however, can also backfire. Tickling and mobilizing the bureaucrat's self-interest is a delicate, unpredictable undertaking.

Prospects for Bureaucracy

Bureaucracies are dynamic. They permeate our governmental system. They have features that facilitate their ability to accomplish public purposes, and they also have features that inhibit their effectiveness and their responsiveness to leaders and to the public. As a result, continual emphasis on reforming bureaucracy permeates political discussion. As those in power and ideology shift, they bring pressure for change in government and bureaucracy. As long as the political pendulum continues to swing, so will the desire for reform and change.

Carol Weiss (1980) suggested some time ago that several trends will keep bureaucratic reform on the public policy agenda. Her keen analysis is still apt. First, declining public confidence in government is an important factor. Public institutions have suffered greatly in reputation and image since the 1970s. Scandals in government, especially the presidential office, leave people wondering if any public institution can be trusted. Common reactions are reduction in government efforts and (governmental) reform to protect the public against such abuses.

Second, economic downturn, public economic stringency, and taxpayer resistance are interrelated phenomena that also promote desire for change. As the economy struggles, especially after a long period of flush growth, there is support for reform to lighten the burden of government and public spending. The "war" on terror led to increases in spending for defense, foreign aid, and homeland security. More recently, the stimulus package to address economic distress led to more spending causing citizens and political leaders to sound the alarm. They now look for policies to rein in spending over the long term.

However, no clear pattern of planned reductions, increases, and plateaus has arisen from leadership in either the executive or legislature at the national level. The same leaders that voice support for reducing the national debt, stabilizing social security and Medicare, and supporting local education also support and pass bills creating massive subsidies and protections for selected productive sectors such as energy, agriculture, and the auto industry. The outcomes are a mixed bag. Still we have nominal intention to reduce the heavy hand of government regulation, the size of bureaucracy, and the tax burden. Various proposed reforms abound, but not much normally changes.

The first decade of the 21st century was not a happy time for state and local government. Most of the states and many localities face desperate financial problems. Local and regional private economies are doing terribly. State and local tax revenues are down. In meeting their constitutional mandate for a balanced budget, state governments, at least on paper, must balance revenues and expenditures. However, this has not prevented most states from engaging in deficit spending. Even with drastic short-run budget reductions, nearly all of the states face potential public economic ruin.

Many if not most localities lack fiscal resources to provide basic services and face continued reductions of shared revenues from federal and state sources. Even before the current hard times, taxpayers have been disinclined to raise government revenues. Instead, they call for cutbacks in governmental activities. Reforms, including privatization and more reliance on the nonprofit sector, are supported as ways of reducing state and local government effort and costs.

Third, scale and complexity are important. The size, complexity, interdependence, and uncertainty of government programs and agencies lead to questions about governmental effort and effectiveness. Wicked problems have no reasonable solution. In many cases, only the most extreme marginal effects can be mediated, and the root problem persists. For example, there is no easy solution to poverty in the United States. Many public and nonprofit bureaucracies have the nominal purpose of assisting the poor. Few programs work well. In spite of recent welfare reforms, including workfare and back-to-work programs, poverty has increased. This frustrates a society based on materialistic values and a sense that all problems can be fully solved.

Likewise, the American people cannot accept the fact that drug dependence is not actually solvable. Since the 1970s, governments at all levels have tried, in Harmon's (1994) terms, to put a public organizational boundary around the drug problem. The hope was that giving public responsibility for curbing the drug trade to a series of law enforcement agencies would be a means of rationally dealing with a truly wicked problem. As a series of national drug czars, the DEA, the local DARE programs, and zero-tolerance schools continue to fail to reduce drug abuse and addiction, the public becomes impatient and demands additional reforms in the form of stricter policies, stronger law enforcement, and harsher penalties. It is easy to blame inept officials, overlapping jurisdictions, duplication of effort, lack of resources, and weak resolve. It is difficult to understand and accept the limits of social intervention in dealing with wicked problems.

Fourth, fragmentation of political parties and proliferation of pressure groups are two additional interrelated factors that Weiss believes foster efforts toward bureaucratic reform. Parties at all levels are weak and cannot really bring people together under specific integrating values. All political parties in the United States, including the fringe parties, have difficulty in generating support for a given approach to dealing with policy issues. Their members can influence the outcome of elections, but the party organization and leaders cannot govern effectively once the election is won.

Single-interest pressure groups fill the gap left by the absence of party-based governance. They are more able to focus on special issues and to rally public as well as inside support for their particular interest or program. Pressure group efforts often include reforms designed to mold programs and agencies to better serve their interests and special needs. The deregulation of the energy market in California in the late 1990s and elsewhere is a good example. In retrospect, it becomes clear that large energy companies pushed deregulation at the state level to promote their capacity to manage the supply and price of energy. The reforms—doing away with state regulation of prices paid for wholesale and retail energy—were sold to the public on the promise of lower energy costs to the final user. In most cases, the opposite occurred.

Reform of bureaucracy seems to be part of the American ethos. There is no doubt that reform efforts will continue to be part of the public debate about government and bureaucracy. What the result of these efforts may be is much more open to question. Chapter 4 continues our discussion of public life with bureaucracy. The emphasis shifts to the individuals working in, and the changing forms of, government bureaucracies.

Review and Study Questions

1. How does bureaucracy help tame the swamp?

2. What are some of the important positive and negative consequences of the use of hierarchy and formal authority as a means of controlling members of an organization? Do the positive outcomes outweigh the negative ones?

3. Is "bureaupathic" behavior inevitable? Why or why not?

4. Which of the many popular criticisms of public bureaucracy seems most apt? Least apt? Why?

5. Why is there so much emphasis on reform of public bureaucracy?

6. Have procedural reforms actually resulted in a more effective, responsive, fairer, and kinder bureaucracy? Why or why not?

7. Given the many obstacles to effective reform, what may be done to overcome key obstacles? Do you think these strategies will work? Why or why not?

8. What is your favorite bureaucratic reform? Why?

Exercises

1. Set up an interview with a local police chief. In your interview, ask her or him to tell you why she or he became a police officer. Also ask why she or he became a police chief. Try to find out if the chief's point of view about what constitutes effective policing changed as she or he moved up the ladder of command. What does the experience of this person tell you about the role of formal authority and hierarchy?

2. Attend a planning commission, school board, police commission, city council, or a tribal council meeting. Pay special attention to council/commission member and staff responses to questions raised by presenters or members of the audience. Can you detect examples of "groupthink?" What does this suggest to you about the usefulness of public discussions in open meetings?

3. Municipal leaders and city staff often go on retreats. The nominal purpose of such retreats is to open up the channels of communication and to establish the foundation for continuing dialogue. Cynics say the real purpose is to play golf and sit around the bar feeling good. Talk with the mayor or city manager and try to get an understanding of what good things she or he thinks resulted from their most recent staff or council–staff retreat. Do you think long-term benefits will flow from these results? Why or why not?

4. Visit the local office of a motor vehicle/drivers license office. Sit around for a while and observe how clients are treated. What is your impression of how receptive and caring the staff are? Whatever the current level of responsiveness, what could be done to make the process better?

5. Think about the last time you were engaged by a traffic officer (You may have been walking, riding your bike, or driving your automobile). Were you treated with respect? Was the officer's comportment professional? Was his or her behavior ethical? Was your behavior ethical? Was the outcome fair? What lessons about bureaucratic behavior and evaluation of bureaucrats does this experience offer?

References

Ammons, D. N. (1995). *Accountability for performance: Measurement and monitoring in local government* (Practical Management Series). Washington, DC: International City/County Management Association.

Ammons, D. N. (2001). *Municipal benchmarks: Assessing performance and establishing community services standards* (2nd ed.). Thousand Oaks, CA: Sage.

Argyriades, D. (1982). Reconsidering bureaucracy as ideology. In G. E. Caiden and H. Siedentopf (Eds.), *Strategies for administrative reform* (pp. 39-57). Lexington, MA: Lexington Books.

Barnard, C. I. (1938). *The functions of the executive.* Cambridge, MA: Harvard University Press.

Barton, A. H. (1980). A diagnosis of bureaucratic maladies. In C. Weiss &. H. Barton, (Eds.), *Making bureaucracy work* (pp. 27-36). Beverly Hills, CA: Sage.

Blau, P. (1963). *The dynamics of bureaucracy: A study of interpersonal relationships in two agencies* (2nd ed.). Chicago: University of Chicago Press.

Box, R. D. (2006). *Democracy and public administration.* Armonk, NY: M.E. Sharpe.

Brown, D. S. (1977). "Reforming" the bureaucracy: Some suggestions for the new president. *Public Administration Review, 37,* 163-169.

Caiden, G. E. (1981). Ethics in the public service. *Public Personnel Management, 10,* 146-152.

Caiden, N. (1987). Paradox, ambiguity, and enigma: The strange case of the executive budget and the United States constitution. *Public Administration Review, 47,* 84-92.

The Commission on Organization of the Executive Branch of the Government. (1949). *General management of the executive branch, a report to the Congress.* Washington, DC: Government Printing Office.

Cooper, P. J. (2003). *Governing by contract: Challenges and opportunities for public managers.* Washington, DC: CQ Press.

Cox, K., & Mair, A. (1991). From local social structures to localities as agents. *Environmental Planning, 23,* 194-213.

Davis, K. C. (1975). *Administrative law and government.* St. Paul, MN: West.

Downs, A. (1967). *Inside bureaucracy.* Boston: Little, Brown.

Follett, M. P. (1924). *Creative experience.* New York: Longmans, Green.

Fritschler, A. L., & Rudder, C. E. (2007). *Smoking and politics* (6th ed.). Englewood Cliffs, NJ: Prentice-Hall.

Garnett, J. L. (1987). Operationalizing the constitution via administrative reorganization: Oilcans, trends, and proverbs. *Public Administration Review, 47,* 35-44.

Gentry, C. (2001). *J. Edgar Hoover: The man and the secrets.* New York: Norton.

Gerber, E. R., Hall, C. K., & Hines, J. R. Jr., (2004). *Policy report: Issues in local and state service provision.* Ann Arbor: University of Michigan Center for Urban Policy. Retrieved from http://www.closup.umich.edu/research/reports/pr-1-privatization.pdf.

Goodsell, C. (2004). *The case for bureaucracy: A public administration polemic* (4th ed.). Washington, DC: CQ Press.

Greenberg, E. S. (1974). *Serving the few: Corporate capitalism and the bias of government policy.* New York: Wiley.

Gulick, L., & Urwick, L. (Eds.). (1937). *Papers on the science of administration.* New York: Institute of Public Administration.

Harmon, M. M. (1994). *Organization theory for public administration.* Burke, VA: Chatelaine Press.

Hummel, R. P. (2008). *The bureaucratic experience* (5th ed.). Armonk, NY: M.E. Sharpe.

Janis, I. (1972). *Victims of groupthink.* New York: Houghton Mifflin.

Jerome, F. (2002). *The Einstein file: J. Edgar Hoover's secret war against the world's most famous scientist.* New York: St. Martin's Press.

Johnston, R. V. (Ed.). (2000). *Entrepreneurial management and public policy.* Huntington, NY: Nova.

Kanter, R. M. (1977). *Men and women of the corporation.* New York: Basic Books.

Kassel, D. S. (2008). Performance, accountability, and the debate over rules. *Public Administration Review, 68,* 241-252.

Kaufman, H. (1995). *The limits of organizational change* (rev. ed.). New Brunswick, NJ: Transaction.

Kaufman, H. (1976). *Are government organizations immortal?.* Washington, DC: The Brookings Institution.

Kerwin, C. (2003). *Rulemaking: How government agencies write law and make policy* (3rd ed.). Washington, DC: CQ Press.

King, C. S., & Stivers, C. (Eds.). (1998). *Government is us.* Thousand Oaks, CA: Sage.

Kingdon, J. (2003). *Agendas, alternatives and public policy.* New York: Longman.

Lamothe, S., Lamothe, M. & Feiock, R. C. (2008). Examining local government service delivery arrangements over time. *Urban Affairs Review, 44,* 27-56.

Lewis, E. (1977). *American politics in a bureaucratic age.* Cambridge, MA: Winthrop.

Lewis, C. W. (2006). In pursuit of the public interest. *Public Administration Review, 66,* 694-701.

Lowi, T. J. (1967). Machine politics—old and new. *The Public Interest, 9,* 83-92.

Mainzer, L. C. (1973). *Political bureaucracy.* Glenview, IL: Scott, Foresman.

Mayo, E. (1933). *The human problem of an industrial civilization.* New York: Macmillan.

McConnell, G. (1966). *Private power and American democracy.* New York: Knopf.

Moore, M. (1995). *Creating public value.* Cambridge, MA: Harvard University Press.

Merton, R. K. (1940). Bureaucratic structure and personality. *Social Forces, 18,* 560-568.

Needleman, M. L., & Needleman, C. E. (1974). *Guerrillas in the bureaucracy.* New York: Wiley.

Newland, C. A. (1984a). Crucial issues for public personnel professionals, *Public Personnel Management, 13,* 15-46.

Newland, C. A. (1984b). *Public administration and community: Realism in the practice of ideals.* McLean, VA: Public Administration Service.

Newland, C. A. (1987). Public executives: Imperium, sacerdotium, collegium? Bicentennial leadership challenges. *Public Administration Review, 47,* 45-56.

Office of Management and Budget. (2009). *Analytical perspectives, budget of the U.S. government, fiscal year 2010.* Retrieved from http://www.whitehouse.gov/omb/budget/fy2010/assets/spec.pdf

O'Leary, R. (2005). *The ethics of dissent: Managing guerilla government.* Washington, DC: CQ Press.

Palumbo, D. J. (1986). Privatization and corrections policy. *Policy Studies Review, 5,* 598-605.

Pfiffner, J. P. (1987). Political appointees and career executives: The democracy-bureaucracy nexus in the third century. *Public Administration Review, 47,* 57-65.

Rainey, H. G. (2003). *Understanding and managing public organizations* (3rd ed.). San Francisco: Jossey-Bass.

Roberts, A. (2008). *The collapse of fortress Bush: The crisis of authority in American government.* New York: New York University Press.

Rosen, B. (1978). Merit and the President's plan for changing the civil service system. *Public Administration Review, 38,* 301-304.

Rosenbloom, D. H. (1987). Public administrators and the judiciary: The new partnership. *Public Administration Review, 47,* 75-83.

Rourke, F. E. (1984). *Bureaucracy, politics and public policy* (3rd ed.). Boston: Little, Brown.

Schon, D. (1971). *Beyond the stable state.* New York: W.W. Norton.

Seidenstat, P. (1996). Privatization: Trends, interplay of forces and lessons learned. *Policy Studies Journal, 24,* 464-477.

Seidman, H. (1997). *Politics, position, & power: The dynamics of federal organizations* (5th ed.). New York: Oxford University Press.

Siedentopf, H. (1982). Introduction: Governmental performance and administrative reform. In G. E. Caiden & H. Siedentopf (Eds.). *Strategies for administrative reform,* (pp. ix-xv). Lexington, MA: Lexington Books.

Stanton, T. H. (2008). Improving the managerial capacity of the federal government: A public administration agenda for the next president. *Public Administration Review, 68,* 1027-1036.

Terry, L. D. (2003). *Leadership of public bureaucracies: The administrator as conservator.* Armonk, NY: M.E. Sharpe.

Thompson, V. (1969). *Bureaucracy and innovation.* Tuscaloosa, AL: University of Alabama Press.

Thompson, V. (1977). *Modern organization* (2nd ed.). New York: Knopf.

United States General Accounting Office. (1997). *Privatization lessons learned by state and local governments.* (GAO/GGD-97-48). Washington, DC: Governmental Printing Office.

Wagenaar, H. (2004). 'Knowing' the rules: Administrative rules as practice. *Public Administration Review, 64,* 643-655.

Weber, M. (1968). Economy and society: an outline of interpretive sociology. G. Roth & C. Wittich (Eds.). Ephraim Fischoff et al., (Trans.). Vol. I, Ch 3. New York: Bedminster Press.

Weiss, C. H. (1980). Efforts at bureaucratic reform: What have we learned? In C. Weiss & A. H. Barton (Eds.) *Making bureaucracy work* (pp. 7-26). Beverly Hills, CA: Sage.

White, L. D. (1926). *Introduction to the study of public administration.* New York: Macmillan.

Wildavsky, A. (1961). Political implications of budgetary reform. *Public Administration Review, 21,* 183-90.

Wildavsky, A., & Caiden, N. (2004). *The new politics of the budgetary process.* New York: Pearson.

Wilson, W. (1887). The study of administration. *Political Science Quarterly, 2,* 197-222.

Web Sites

Executive Office of the President (EOP). (The EOP coordinates the major management agencies of the US President.) http://whitehouse.gov/administration/eop

Federal Executive Institute (FEI). (The FEI is the federal government's Management development and training center for senior executives.) http://www.leadership.opm/fei

Office of Management and Budget (OMB). (OMB assists the President in budget, policy, legislative, regulatory, and other affairs. It also evaluates implementation of policies and programs.) http://www.whitehouse.gov/omb

Government Accountability Office (GAO). (GAO is the investigative arm of Congress. It helps to insure that the bureaucracy implements the policies as Congress intended them.) Office of Information and Regulatory Affairs (OIRA). (OIRA is part of OMB. It oversees information and regulatory affairs for the president. Its suboffices often lead reform efforts in the executive branch.) http://www.whitehouse.gov/omb/inforeg

Office of Personnel Management (OPM). (The main human resources management agency for the federal government. Keeper of the federal civil service system.) http://www.opm.gov/

The Public Manager. (A quarterly publication for public practitioners.) http://www.thepublicmanager.org

4

Administrative Life: People in Organizations

Organizations are social units created to attain one or more particular goals. To accomplish their goals, organizations require individuals to work in groups. They must establish tasks and procedures governing the interactions of members and must assign responsibilities and duties to each member of the organization.

The method by which procedures are established and activities assigned varies greatly by organization. In the case of public sector organizations, some external body such as a legislature or executive office establishes the basic purpose and rules for the operation of the organization. However, each agency usually is given some discretion in how it operates. Internal methods for determining procedures and assigning responsibilities differ greatly among organizations and will be discussed later in this chapter. What is important now is that the organization has the responsibility of establishing the framework for how the work is done.

As social units created to attain one or more particular goals, organizations limit individual behavior that may hinder collaboration. The organization attempts to reduce uncertainty in human relationships and enhance the predictability of individual behavior. By circumscribing individualistic actions, the organization attempts to minimize conflict and coordinate the efforts of all members of the organization toward the common goal.

As attempts are made to bring together the values of the organization, individuals, and society, tensions among them breed indeterminacy. The competing values create tension and erode certainty, thus producing instability within. Internal instability coupled with the cross-pressures from the environment lead to even greater swampy conditions. Faced with such uncertainty and pressure, individuals in the organization often return to what they know best. They become pathogenic in protecting their own interests as suggested in the previous chapter and become rigid and inflexible in attempting to find more stable footing and negotiable paths (Thompson, 1961).

At the same time that organizations attempt to mold the behavior of individuals, the members of the organization seek fulfillment through it. Individuals join organizations for many reasons. Most join work organizations initially out of economic and physical necessity. Once their physical and economic needs are met, they may fulfill other needs through the organization. Through organizational life, they may achieve a sense of self-worth, accomplishment, or a feeling of being needed. The administrative process must accommodate both organizational and individual concerns.

Individuals come to organizations with their own values and behavior patterns. As noted above, the organization attempts to constrain the behavior pattern in the interest of coordinating collective effort. As a result, an organization assumes an identity and consciousness of its own that differs from the summation of the behavior of its individual members. As Herbert Simon notes, individuals in a group are affected by a new force, the concern or consideration of the actions of others (Simon, 1997). Sigmund Freud studied the relationship of individual behavior to group interaction and found that groups have unexpected impact upon the behavior of individual adults (Freud, 1955; Denhardt, 2007).

Theories of Organization

Although theories of organization have emphasized different elements of the organization, they continue to struggle with the same basic issues. The dominant issues are views of the roots of individual behavior and authority, and getting the individual to do what the organization wants done. Theoretical efforts continually redefine what is meant by organizational life, but they are cumulative in building upon one another. Management and organizations are characterized by complex relationships and behaviors. Relationships exist among individuals, organizations, subunits of organizations, superiors, and subordinates, groups, and between organizations and their environments. This variety of relationships affects the behavior of organizations and their members.

Michael Vasu, Debra Stewart, and G. David Garson (1998) suggest six approaches to the study of organizations. A modification of their typology will be used here to illustrate the various ways individuals have been viewed relative to organizations. The six approaches to organizational theory are: Classical, Human Relations, Decision Making, Neo-Human Relations, Systems, and Bureaucratic Politics approaches. Each rests upon a different set of assumptions and expectations about human beings and their behavior. Different models and metaphors of organizations allow us to analyze organizations by developing an overview that makes sense of the organizations (Morgan, 1986).

Classical

The Classical approach to organization theory and behavior has its roots in the traditional view of public administration discussed in Chapter 1. Weber's ideal construct of bureaucracy is consistent with the traditional view and became a major theoretical justification for it. Basically, proponents of this approach assume a formal-legal framework for the organization. Authority is based on law or formal rules, and work is structured according to a hierarchy of authority. Organization charts, rules and regulations, and job descriptions are relied upon for organizing the work. A major expression of the Classical approach is the Scientific Management School, which was intent upon increasing productivity and efficiency through systematic management. The leading proponent of Scientific Management was Frederick W. Taylor (1913), an engineer who turned his attention to the design of work. The Classical approach assumed that human beings are rational, motivated by economic needs, and that payment for work is the best incentive.

Based on these assumptions about human nature, the Scientific Management School conducted empirical studies of the work situation to determine the one best way to perform any task. Proponents of the approach believed that they could discover universal laws for all activity; thus, management could determine what are the best processes for workers and train and direct workers in performing those processes. Workers have little discretion in such a situation; instead, they must learn standard operating procedures and apply them to work tasks.

To accomplish their objectives, the Scientific Management School conducted time and motion studies and job analyses. Worker tasks were studied in minute detail, and those movements and actions that contributed to the organization's goals would be incorporated into the job whereas those that were counter-productive would be eliminated. To encourage individuals to work at their highest levels of productivity, piece-rate incentives were incorporated into the pay scale.

Employees had an unanticipated reaction to these "scientific" approaches; they became dissatisfied. The very antagonism between labor and management that Taylor attempted to obviate through his scientific approach emerged in reaction to it. Eventually, under union pressure, Congress prohibited the use of federal monies in any time and motion studies that came to symbolize the Classical approach.

For the Classical theorists, organizations are defined by roles and positions that describe the tasks to be performed and by lines of authority and responsibility (hierarchy). Furthermore, the organization is formal and can be described by organization charts and rules and regulations directing individual behavior. The way to make individual behavior compatible with organizational needs is to direct or order people to perform in specific ways. For the Classical theorists, human beings are valued for their physical abilities that fit the needs of the organization; the organization has no interest in the individual outside organizational activities. Management is supervisory and does not make policy; thus administration is separate from politics, and authority is only formal and legal. Administrative efficiency is increased as specialization of the work process takes place (Gulick & Urwick, 1937).

The Classical theorists looked at the organization as a rational instrument and assumed congruence between personal and institutional rationality. The shortcoming of Classical theory is that it looks at only a small part of rationality (the means to a specific end) and a small part of individual behavior. It does not look at the whole range of human behavior and thus does not attempt to fashion the organization around that reality. Instead, it attempts to mold individual behavior to the needs of the organization. Individuals are viewed as cogs in the organizational machine. Despite its shortcomings, Classical organization theory is evident in most large organizations in abundance. Position classification, for example, is still a key element of most large organizations, as are formal rules and regulations, hierarchies of authority, and specialization of tasks.

Human Relations

Application of the principles of the Scientific Management School led to outright hostility from workers. As a result, industrial psychologists became part of the efficiency teams of management. The role of the industrial psychologist was to aid in the selection of the best employees, examine the effects of the work situation, and help to design optimum working conditions. The concerns of the industrial psychologist were the same as those of the Scientific Management School, namely the efficiency and productivity of the employee. However, they developed new ways of looking at efficiency and productivity. The findings of industrial psychologists led to the development of the Human Relations School.

The beginnings of the Human Relations School are found in the Hawthorne Plant Studies of Western Electric in Chicago from 1927 to 1932 (Brown, 1987; Homans, 1951; Mayo, 2003), although Mary Parker Follett had suggested similar ideas before this time (Follett, 1924; Metcalf & Urwick, 1940). The primary aim of the studies was to examine the work situation through scientific methods for purposes of developing greater productivity. Physical working conditions were considered to be the determinant of worker productivity; thus, experiments were conducted with lighting and other physical aspects of the environment. The results were confusing in that changes in lighting in both directions (increased or decreased) seemed to lead to a slight rise in productivity. Similarly, other changes in the physical environment had conflicting results.

Consequently, the researchers decided that there must be something about the individuals' group interaction that is also of importance. They then began conducting interviews focusing on satisfaction of employees. They concluded that psychological and social factors are important to behavior and thus to productivity. In the interviewing it became apparent that individuals do not react as isolated beings but as social beings. This finding led industrial psychologists to analyze group dynamics. The informal organization by which people interacted with others within the formal organization became the object of much study (Blau, 1963; Blau & Meyer, 1987). The informal organization was viewed by the Human Relations approach as the most important element in promoting efficiency. The researchers also concluded that just paying attention to the employees caused them to act differently. This phenomenon is now referred to as the *Hawthorne Effect.*

Five principal conclusions emerge from the Hawthorne Studies and form the basic foundation of the Human Relations School:

(1) *Group (social) norms* (shared values, beliefs, and assumptions), not physical factors, are the most significant determinants of levels of production.

(2) Behavior of workers is affected significantly by noneconomic sanctions and rewards.

(3) Workers tend to react as members of groups rather than as individuals. The group norms influence the decisions and actions of individuals.

(4) There is a need for leadership in creating and enforcing group norms different from the formal organizational leadership.

(5) There is a need for democratic leadership and communication between levels of the organization and a need for participation by employees in decision making.

Many managers accepted the Human Relations approach, but it was really an extension of the Scientific Management School. Human Relations resulted from the Scientific Management School's own studies and pursued the same goals, especially increasing the efficiency and productivity of the employee. Now the search for universal laws of productivity focused on laws of human behavior rather than physical movements. Productivity was now seen as depending upon the psychological and social aspects of workers in organizations. During the 1950s, in particular, employers attempted to make the workplace a pleasant place and tried to create a family-type setting. Thus, office picnics and other activities to get employees and their families involved became common. To facilitate a sense of participation, suggestion boxes and other such efforts were developed. The problem with most such programs was that they gave the appearance of an interest in employees but often did not go beyond appearances. Once employees realized that the organization did not take suggestions seriously or did not want real participation, they became alienated.

The major change in work organizations fostered by the Human Relations approach was that it focused attention on the individual as a human being rather than as a cog in the organization. Organizations began to recognize that employees responded to incentives other than monetary rewards and thus began the process of humanizing organizations. The implications were many. Authority was no longer defined only in terms of formal, rational factors. Instead, informal, nonrational factors also were viewed as affecting authority relationships. Although Scientific Management's goal of efficiency was still paramount, the issue now became how the individual worker could be induced to act the way the organization wanted through psychological and social means. Legitimate authority was now viewed in diverse ways.

In recognizing informal organizations within the formal structure, the Human Relations approach tended to downplay much of the formal authority relationship. A greater understanding of group dynamics resulted, and organization theory began to focus on social codes, group norms, perpetuation of informal groups, and resistance to change as important elements in understanding the behavior of individuals in organizations. In dealing with the individual, it also became apparent that security could be defined not only in terms of economics but also in terms of such things as status, prestige, and acceptance.

The Human Relations advocates searched for new ways of influencing human behavior to attain the greatest efficiency. They developed their own principles of group support, happiness of the worker, leadership, and supervision standards. The approach strove for harmonious relationships without recognizing that such a situation is not always possible or desirable. The norms of human behavior became the important standard, and any variance from those norms was viewed as dysfunctional. Thus, there developed a need for controlling variances through manipulation of the informal group. During the 1940s and early 1950s, a challenge to the basic foundation of the Classical and Human

Relations approaches arose in the form of more "scientific" Decision Making approaches.

Decision Making

Although the Classical and Human Relations approaches focused on the same outcomes, they had very different orientations regarding how to achieve the most efficient operation of an organization. The Classical approach's focus on the need for rational behavior and the Human Relations' concern with the social and psychological needs of organization members placed the two approaches at opposite extremes in terms of how to accomplish the goals of the organization. The tension between the rational needs of the organization and the nature of the individual gave rise to a new perspective represented by the Decision Making approach. This approach recognized that there were conflicts between individual and organizational needs. Although the perspective was new as applied to public administration, it had its foundation in the work of Mary Parker Follett (1924), who recognized the need for some mechanism other than traditional organization structure to coordinate human effort. She argued that cooperation and coordination of effort could not be directed or coerced, but that they come from the adjustments individuals make as they interact. Chester Barnard (1938) also recognized that subordinates had "zones of indifference" whereby they would accept the authority of supervisors over them. Workers and managers engaged in a form of exchange where each would benefit. The worker accepted managers' authority to direct work in exchange for pay as long as what managers asked for did not violate workers' basic values. Follett and Barnard serve as a bridge between Classical perspectives and Decision Making approaches.

Herbert Simon is most closely identified with the Decision Making approach. In his *Administrative Behavior*, he developed a model of decision making that takes into account the inability of individuals to have complete information or even to use it if it were available. His model suggests organizing to enhance the flow of information and thus improve decision making. Because individuals have incomplete information and limits to their ability to perform (Simon, 1997), they satisfice. *Satisficing* refers to doing what is acceptable given the ability of the individual and the information available. The organization member operates within the limits set by the organization and on the basis of individual skills, abilities, information, and understanding. The process of satisficing was further elaborated in Charles E. Lindblom's discussion of "muddling through" (Lindblom, 1959). *Muddling through* is another name for the incremental approach in which decisions or actions occur as the result of limited comparison of alternatives that build upon past activity. As new needs or demands develop, administrators make adjustments to their decisions or policies. Rarely is there any full-scale change in direction or approach.

The Decision Making approach still relies upon a characterization of human beings as rational. While satisficing or muddling through, individuals were viewed as having a particular goal in mind and then making decisions relative to achievement of that goal. The underlying assumption remains that the members of the organization will strive to accomplish its goals. The difference from earlier approaches, however, is that individuals are also viewed as having differing understandings of the goals and as being limited in their ability to act in concert with them. Limits to individual abilities lead to scaling down of goals and looking to short-term accomplishments. Indeed, these short-term and scaled-down goals may be consistent with the organizational goals, but there also may be sidetracking and conflict.

For Simon, it was necessary for individuals to lose autonomy if they were to function well in the organization. *Losing autonomy* means that the individual accepts authoritatively made decisions of the manager and organization as legitimate. As with Chester Barnard (1938), members of organizations are viewed as accepting the authority of superiors for differing reasons, among them what the individual perceives to be rational. Authority is thus based on the consent of subordinates to have power exercised over them by the superior within a particular range or zone. The organization sets the limits for individual action, and members are expected to accept rationality in terms of organizational needs. This point set the stage for a spirited debate between Chris Argyris and Herbert Simon over what they term "rational man organization theory" (Argyris 1973a, 1973b; Simon, 1973). This debate reflects many of the concerns that emerged with the Neo-Human Relations Approach.

Neo-Human Relations

Neo-Human Relations (sometimes referred to as Organizational Humanism) has its roots in the Human Relations School, but it goes much further. While the Human Relations School attempted to make the worker happy so as to serve the organization's needs, the Neo-Human Relations approach concerned itself with the needs of the individual as well as the needs of the organization. Both should be addressed, according to the Neo-Human Relations approach, but the health of the individual is given primacy.

The writings of Abraham Maslow (1954, 1962, 1965) provide the basic inspiration to the Neo-Human Relationalists. His *hierarchy of human needs* (physiological, safety, love, esteem, and self-actualization) became the basis on which many organization theorists examined the relationship of the individual to the organization. Douglas McGregor (1960) usually is credited with adapting the hierarchy to an understanding of individuals in organizations. Basically, McGregor viewed the needs of the *self-actualizing* individual as being in conflict with the needs of the traditionally managed organization. Self-actualization is the realization of one's inherent potential and creative abilities. The needs of the traditional organization often inhibit creativity and individuality implicit in self-actualization.

While McGregor examined the general relationship of the hierarchy of human needs to organizational needs, Chris Argyris went further and analyzed specific elements of the human personality relative to traditional organizations (1964). His analysis focuses on the need of the mature human personality to move from passivity to activity, dependence to independence, and subordination to superordination. Further, he indicates that as individuals mature, they move from limited capacity to a wide range of capabilities, from shallow to in-depth understanding of things, from short-range to long-range perspectives, and from a lack of to a sense of self-awareness. Argyris argues that the demands of traditional management are inconsistent with these tendencies of the mature human personality. Instead, traditional organizations require people to be dependent, passive, subordinate, and short range in perspective. Traditional management also provides very limited discretion to employees; therefore, they use limited capabilities, have little understanding of the larger implications of what they do, and subordinate their own identity to the needs of the organization. The conflict between mature personality needs and organizational needs results in various modes of accommodation, including the intellectual separation of work and nonwork life, alienation from the organization, and possibly sabotage. The traditional approach also discourages individuals from taking responsibility for their work and fosters using rules, regulations, or policy as excuses for continuing old practices or for not doing something.

The conflicts between individual and organizational needs led to a great deal of study of matches between particular personality types and organizations. Typologies of individuals and the ways they adjust to organizational environments and demands became popular. Robert Presthus (1978) characterized individuals as upwardly mobiles, indifferents, and ambivalents, whereas Anthony Downs (1967) viewed them as climbers, conservers, zealots, advocates, and statesmen. Other typologies include what Maccoby terms the craftsman, jungle fighter, company man, and gamesman (Maccoby, 1976) and what Gouldner refers to as cosmopolitans and locals (Gouldner, 1957).

These typologies are based upon the ways individuals seek power and success in the organization, their views and understanding of organizational activities, self-interest, cause orientation, their approach to authority, or other modes of behavior that differentiate one person from another. Some people (upward mobiles, climbers, and company man) are so intent upon succeeding in the organization that they completely buy into the organization's values. Others (indifferents) accept the demands of the organization as necessary to earn economic security or the like, though they may not agree with all that they are asked to do in the organization. Still others (ambivalents and zealots) have strong values that often are in conflict with the organization's norms, but they attempt to work within the organization, often with great frustration. Although these typologies are interesting and helpful for characterizing behavior, there has been very little rigorous analysis to substantiate their existence. Thus, it is best to use them as guides to understand types of behavior rather than molds into which every member of an organization can be fit neatly.

These typologies have called attention to the fact that people respond differently to organizations and their demands upon the individual. As a result, organization theory has moved to formal consideration of the individual as a variable within the organization. The Neo-Human Relationists were concerned with humanizing the organization because of their concern with the integrity of the individual as much as for the interests of the organization. The tone of the Neo-Human Relationists actually suggests that the well-being of the individual is most important and that organizations reap benefits through the greater productivity of healthy individuals.

More importantly, Neo-Human Relationalists accept the idea that there are consistencies between the objectives of the organization and the needs of the individual. The key is to recognize that there are ways of organizing work to capitalize on the compatibility of organizational and individual needs. Because the Neo-Human Relations approach views work as a natural part of the human condition, people are viewed as interested in it. They are motivated by factors intrinsic to the work itself. They are achievement oriented and thus respond positively to opportunities to experience a sense of accomplishment. Further, positive work incentives are available: delegating responsibility, allowing discretion, independence of judgment on the job, and the opportunity to participate and be creative (Bennis, 1973; Blake & Mouton, 1994; McGregor, 1960).

The Neo-Human Relationists stressed democratic values within the organization, including full and free communication among individuals regardless of rank or power. Consensus rather than coercion should govern decision making because it fosters compromise as a means of managing conflict. Influence is based upon competence and expertise rather than the possession of formal power. Although Neo-Human Relationalists recognize that human needs and organizational needs may be in conflict, they emphasized the rational resolution of these conflicts while maintaining the dignity of the individual person (Bennis & Slater, 1998). Concerns of the Neo-Human Relationists are primarily internal to the organization.

In later years, the New Public Administration, while accepting the Neo-Human Relationalists view about relationships among members of an organization, expanded the concern with democracy to include external factors. The New Public Administration developed from a conference at Syracuse University's Minnowbrook Conference Center in 1968. In the New Public Administration, organizations are viewed as instruments for increasing societal as well as internal democracy. Public administrators are expected to change from neutral and impersonal bureaucrats to become advocates for social equity in all that they do (Marini, 1971). Interested scholars have met every twenty years since to examine trends in the field and renew the commitment to the values of the first Minnowbrook Conference.

Eugene McGregor (1960) uses the concepts of Theory X and Theory Y to explain the differing assumptions about human nature used by traditional and more contemporary organization theory. Theory X outlines the basic assumptions about human nature according to Classical management approaches. In this system, people are assumed to be inherently lazy and to shun work whenever possible. Further, people fear punishment and deprivation. These fears impel people to work and are used by management as a means of directing, controlling, and motivating workers. Theory X also assumes that people prefer to be dependent and want security most of all; thus, incentives are those things that contribute to security.

McGregor's Theory Y assumes that the expenditure of physical effort is a natural part of human nature and that punishment and external control are not the only or even necessarily the best motivators. People will work toward a goal to which they are committed. A sense of achievement engenders personal fulfillment and further commitment. Additionally, the average person learns to accept and seek responsibility and, given the opportunity to be creative and use initiative, will demonstrate a wide range of abilities. For Theory Y, which is the basis of the Neo-Human Relations approach, the organization ought to take advantage of these characteristics of people. More democratic and humane organizations are the result.

Systems

Systems theory is used by many as a focal point for understanding organizations and their activities. Systems theory views organizations as being composed of interrelated parts which affect one another and adapt to environmental changes. Daniel Katz and Robert Kahn (1978) articulately examined the organization as a social system that interacts with its environment and is affected internally by elements from the environment. Although not always explicitly acknowledged, the open systems approach provides the basis for much of the current analysis of organizations.

Systems theory treats organizations as complex units in which a variety of relationships exist. Those relationships are affected by formal, structural aspects of the organization as well as by informal, behavioral factors. Furthermore, the organization cannot be understood without reference to the larger system in which it operates.

James Thompson (2003) carries systems theory forward by using it in both closed and open forms for understanding organizations. *Closed systems* have clearly identifiable boundaries and highly structured and predictable activities. *Open systems* are much more complex, with constantly changing interactions within the organization and with the environment. Thus, open systems are much less predictable. By focusing on the closed system, it is possible to analyze organizations in their rational approach to goals from an internal perspective. For some purposes, it is possible and important to understand that organizations act without reference to their environment. At other times, it is necessary to understand environmental influences on organizations in order to have a complete picture of the organization. Some of its activities are accommodations to environmental influences. Particularly when it comes to survival, public sector organizations develop strategies to accommodate the environment. Even within the organization, the open systems approach is important in understanding *informal organizations* (those networks and interactions developed by organization members on their own) and their relationship to the formal organization. According to Thompson, management would like to operate as a closed system, but reality makes it impossible to do so (Thompson, 2003).

Bureaucratic Politics

Concerns of contemporary theorists differ from earlier theorists in that the individual is viewed in a dual role as part of the organization and as part of society as a whole. The organization also is viewed as part of the society as a whole. There are conflicts between organizational and social roles, some of which become centered in the individual. As a result, contemporary theory often examines the struggles individuals have in making those roles compatible. Alienation of the worker from the organization is often emphasized along with efforts to eliminate alienation and conflict. Organization Development theorists (Argyris & Schon, 1978; Golembiewski & Eddy, 1978; Harmon, 1981; Senge,

2006) view conflict as natural and search for ways to manage it to the advantage of the organization. At the same time, there exists a mutual interdependence between the individual and organization. Contemporary theorists recognize this interdependence. Each needs the other for certain purposes. By reducing the barriers to communication, organizations can create better understanding among their members and through participation in the management process, members become committed to organizational goals. Organization Development techniques are viewed as ways of integrating the needs of the individual and the organization.

The New Public Administration (Frederickson, 1974; Harmon, 1981; Marini, 1971) took the position that public agencies ought to foster social justice; thus, they have explicitly political roles. Their argument is that traditional public administration favors those who have access to power and politics; thus, those who most need government protection and service are left out of the system. This perspective raised questions about whom organizations are designed to serve. Examining these issues, Michael Harmon (1981) uses action theory, the idea that we need to look at the meaning, intent, and values of administrators to understand them and their organizations. Although the New Public Administration has sensitized academics and public administrators to social equity issues, it has not revolutionized the public administration community in the way its advocates might have expected.

Internal democracy was also a major tenet of the New Public Administration. Frederick Mosher (1982) considered the tenet a noble one, but he also noted that it could lead to a more fundamental problem for democracy. Carried to its fullest extent, internal democracy could lead to the bureaucrats deciding what the purpose of the organization is, thus conflicting with the idea of democratic control by those elected by the citizens to establish purposes for governmental organizations. Advocates of the New Public Administration concede the point but also note that they have forced the field to confront the issues, thus stimulating a continuing examination of the purposes of public organizations.

During the 1980s and 1990s, public organization theory was dominated by discussions of the New Public Management, often with an emphasis on reinvention, entrepreneurship, and managerialism. The emphases in these approaches have been the use of the market as a model for public administration and the idea that government could be run like a business. Citizens are viewed as customers, and government agencies are encouraged to adopt business approaches as much as possible. Privatization is advocated as an efficient way of providing government services. Critics claim that this approach tends to ignore the citizens who are supposed to be served by the agencies (Denhardt & Denhardt, 2007; King & Stivers, 1998). Janet and Robert Denhardt suggest a new emphasis, "The New Public Service," as a way of looking at public organizations (Denhardt & Denhardt, 2007). The major themes of their New Public Service are:

(1) Serve rather than steer—help citizens articulate and meet their shared interests.

(2) Make shared public interest the aim.

(3) Use collective and collaborative processes and efforts.

(4) Recognize that public interest is best served by dialogue about shared values, not by aggregation of individual interests.

(5) Recognize that accountability is not simple; there is no one measure.

(6) Value people, not just productivity.

(7) Value citizenship and public service above entrepreneurship (Denhardt & Denhardt, 2007, p. 410).

The varying expectations of public agencies lead them to engage in politics to reach decisions. Bureaucratic politics is inevitable because public organizations participate in the political system and help make decisions affecting society as a whole. Members of the organization bring many different values and perspectives to the organization, and they affect the way the organization interacts with the rest of the environment. As Nancy Grant notes, public organizations play a welfare maximizing role in our society, meaning that government provides for the needs that are not met by the market system (Grant, 1989).

When looking at organizations, it is clear that all these approaches to organization theory and behavior are in use. All organizations adapt elements of the various approaches. Even the most democratic and humane organization is unlikely to have the liberty to be concerned only with the needs of its members. The issue often becomes how humane and democratic the organization can be while still accomplishing its purpose.

The empirical evidence on the effectiveness of different organization approaches is difficult to evaluate (Latham & Pinder, 2005; Wright, 2001). Not surprisingly, successful experiments of companies or government agencies using a particular approach often receive a great deal of media and case-study attention. Failures of innovative approaches seldom get widely reported. However, there have been some in-depth studies, however, that shed light on the applicability of the more contemporary approaches. Dubin (1959), for example, concludes that some people work well in organizations where discretion and self-direction are paramount, whereas others prefer to have clear directives from management. Every worker has different needs and values; consequently, no one form of or approach to organizing work is appropriate for everyone. In his own study of an industrial organization, Dubin found that only 10 percent of industrial workers preferred independence.

Similarly, Kaplan and Tausky (1977) reviewed the research on Organizational Humanism and found that many of its precepts had to be accepted cautiously, if at all. Their evaluation of studies suggested that whereas professional employees were likely to benefit from the application of humanistic management approaches, manual labor and lower-salaried workers were not. Manual labor and lower-salaried workers tend to derive satisfaction off the job and not at work. People have widely different reasons for working and seek different things from work; the evidence does not support the idea that people view work as inherently interesting. Many of the other tenets of Organizational Humanism are challenged by Kaplan and Tausky. James Marcum also questions some of the fundamental assumptions about motivation theory based on fulfilling needs and suggests that we need to rethink how we get people engaged in the work of the organizations (Marcum, 2000). Despite the questions about the tenets and empirical validation of the humanistic approach, it has an impact on the way public sector agencies conduct their affairs (Rosenbloom, Kravchuk, & Clerkin, 2008).

Motivation and Management Styles

Motivation

As the previous discussion indicates, different things motivate different people. Organizations attempt to encourage particular types of behavior. In order to do so, it is necessary to address the great variation in human motivation. Our discussion of major organization theories focused upon assumptions about human nature. From those assumptions, theorists and those applying the theories also made assumptions about what would motivate people to do what the organization desires. For the Classical theorists, people could be motivated by addressing economic needs; thus, the primary motivator was believed to be money. Increased pay for increased productivity was the mechanism used.

For the Human Relations School, social and psychological factors were used to motivate people. Social needs were viewed as the key to productivity and were satisfied by social interaction. Therefore, Human Relations managers relied upon creating a sense of social support by appearing to care for the employee and by encouraging group activity.

Contemporary motivation theory usually pays homage to Maslow's hierarchy of needs. Each need is a motivator as long as it is unfulfilled. Once fulfilled, it no longer motivates, and the next higher need becomes a motivator. Though Maslow's hierarchy has provided the foundation of much of the contemporary literature on motivation, it also has led to some confusion. Many theorists suggest that each need has to be satisfied in order, whereas others stress that the level of needs of any one individual varies over time. Among those building upon Maslow's hierarchy is Frederick Herzberg (1966), who believed that motivation comes from within and that organizations need to use positive growth factors to encourage employees to produce. He claims that organizations tend to focus on "hygiene" factors such as physical surroundings, status, salary, and administrative rules and regulations, which all members of the organization expect anyway and thus are not effective motivators. Instead, opportunity for advancement, achievement, and increasing responsibility, job satisfaction, and recognition are factors that motivate workers. Organizations are encouraged to design work so as to emphasize the motivators.

According to *expectancy theories*, regardless of what motivates individuals, their expectations of a valued outcome are important. Expectancy theories are based on the idea that people will do things to gain some desired outcome (Vroom, 1995). As a motivator, the organization promises something in return for the contribution of the individual to the work of the organization. In order for it to be a motivator, the organization must fulfill the promise once the individual performs. If the organization does not come through, the individual becomes demotivated. Equity theories are related as well. They suggest that people's motivation is dependent upon whether they perceive that the reward for effort is equitable, both in terms of whether it is worth the effort and whether it is fair compared to what others receive for their levels of effort (Adams, 1965). If rewards are perceived as fair, they can be motivators, but they can have the opposite effect if they are perceived as unfair.

Employees come to organizations socialized to particular attitudes and values that also affect motivation (Denhardt, Denhardt, & Aristigueta, 2009; Eddy 1981; Van Wart 1998). Some people develop a strong work ethic and are satisfied with nothing less than their best effort; others may feel the need to do no more than is necessary to get by. Many employees need to be stroked and have a need for approval, whereas others have a need for independence and the opportunity to achieve on their own terms. Some have a need for exercising responsibility and discretion and a sense of accomplishment. Others may want money or symbols of success such as titles and accoutrements of office. Clearly, one approach to motivating employees is not going to be successful with these and other needs that characterize members of every organization. Even if managers had all the information about the variety of individuals in the organization and their needs, it would be hard to imagine how they could act on the information. The time and resources, to say nothing of the capabilities of the manager, required to use all of this information for motivating individuals make it a daunting task. Clearly, the humanistic approach identifies many factors important to the manager in dealing with individual employees. The key for management is in linking individual needs and action to the achievement of organizational goals. Understanding what motivates individual employees is the major first step.

Management

Management refers to the ability of supervisors and managers to obtain the cooperation of the members of their organization in the accomplishment of organizational goals. Many factors affect management, including leadership, formal authority, persuasion, interpersonal activities, the situation, and communication. Furthermore, managers have a number of tools such as decision making, information processing, budgeting, planning, and personnel systems to assist them in management. How effectively managers use these tools may well determine their success.

Much of management depends upon the ability of managers to get employees to suspend their own judgment and accept the manager's leadership (Barnard, 1938). Employees act on the basis of habit, their own self-interest and values, and what they believe to be rational. In order to get employees to change or comply with management directives, it is necessary to make management desires as consistent as possible with those of the individual employee. A key to such effort often is assumed to be the leadership abilities of the manager.

Moral codes are also important to the acceptance of a manager's directives (Barnard, 1938). All individuals have a moral code that delimits their behavior. When management or the organization demand activities in conflict with the subordinate's moral code, the individual is not likely to accept authority. The strength of commitment to the moral code will affect whether the subordinate will accept the authority as legitimate. Furthermore, the subordinate's views of the manager's moral code are also important in that we expect managers to provide moral leadership.

Managerial styles vary greatly and generally are assumed to influence the success of organizational activity (Eddy, 1981). Styles range from autocratic/authoritarian to democratic/participative. Ralph White and Ronald Lippitt (1968) conducted some of the most exhaustive studies of leadership and management syles. They experimented with adult leaders of boys clubs using three different leadership styles—authoritarian, democratic, and laissez-faire. In their experiments, the authoritarian style appeared to be most effective in the short run and as long as the leader was present. The democratic style appeared to be more effective in the long run, as people continued to perform even in the absence of the leader. The laissez-faire approach, in which the leader provides no real guidance, seemed to be ineffective.

Another approach to leadership styles arose from path-goal theory, focusing on the compatibility of the needs of the individuals in the organization and the leader behavior (House & Mitchell, 1974). In this theory, leadership is characterized as directive, supportive, participative, and achievement-oriented. Directive leadership focuses on the subordinates' acceptance of the need to get particular tasks done and the leader's legitimacy in organizing and directing the activity. Supportive leadership focuses on building relationships with subordinates so that they are willing to accept guidance. Participative leadership involves consultation with subordinates and consideration of their input. Achievement-oriented leadership means that the leader sets high expectations and provides encouragement to the subordinates, but the leader allows much discretion to the subordinates in organizing the work.

Situational and contingency leadership styles have many similarities to the path-goal style. Situational leadership is based on the idea that different situations require different styles (Hersey, Johnson, & Blanchard, 2007). Thus, leaders need to understand their organizations and members and then adapt their behavior to fit the situation. Leadership in this approach is highly dependent upon the readiness of subordinates to be led. Contingency theory also suggests that the style of leadership that will be successful is that which relates to the situation (Fiedler, 1967). Path-goal, situational, and contingency styles all are based on selecting the style that meets the needs of subordinates.

Yet another variation is the managerial grid that examines management on two axes emphasizing tasks and people (Blake & McCanse, 1991; Blake & Mouton, 1994). The task emphasis refers to focusing on the technical, operational aspects of goal accomplishment, whereas the people emphasis focuses on human relations and motivation based on Neo-Human Relations. Research suggests that the most effective leadership approach is one that is built on a combination of the two emphases. Individuals with high scores on both dimensions tend to make the best managers and combine the task orientation with good people skills. Sandra Blem (1977) developed a two-dimensional typology based on similar orientations. Calling hers the androgyny concept, Blem views managers as tough and assertive or as nurturing and relationship oriented. As with the Blake and Mouton grid, evidence suggests that a combination of the two styles is most effective (Sargent, 1978). Nonetheless, managers often have difficulty combining styles. It is difficult to consciously override one's natural style and replace it with a combination. At the same time, if a manager suddenly changes style, employees are likely to be suspicious and untrusting.

There are many variations on styles of leadership and management available in the literature, and consultants make good money training according to their approach. The lesson for managers is that they must be very adaptable. They need to adjust to different types of employees with differing needs. The research suggests that managers also need to combine a rational goal orientation with concern for their employees. Thus, it is necessary to be task oriented but also to understand employees and actively listen and allow participation. These combinations of efforts seem to lead to the greatest success. There is, however, no magic formula for good management, and different styles may have varying effects depending upon the situation in which they are used.

Administrative Communication

As Simon notes, communication is the instrument for linking behaviors of individuals in groups and thus is important in eliciting cooperative effort. There is no question that effective communication is critical to the ability of managers to manage. Nonetheless, communication is often taken for granted and therefore ineffective.

Communication may be characterized in a variety of ways. It may be examined as formal or informal (organizational or interpersonal), by direction of flow, internal or external, and by problems associated with it.

Formal and Informal

Formal communication refers to communication that is based in some particular organizational purpose. Some authoritative member of the organization attempts to communicate with a particular audience through appropriate channels, to accomplish the goals of the organization. *Informal communication*, on the other hand, is likely to be interpersonal and less structured. It also is likely to derive from many different sources, and its intended audience and purpose are not necessarily consistent with organizational goals. Although many managers concentrate on formal communication and pay little attention to the informal, they probably do so at their own peril. Informal communication, often through social networks, is important because it promotes good relations among people who have to work together. It often helps facilitate the work of the organization by speeding up the communication process and building a sense of community among workers.

Informal communication can also be destructive to the organization when it undermines managerial authority. Effective managers normally accept the inevitability of informal communication and utilize its channels when possible for furthering organizational goals. The Human Relations School placed a great deal of emphasis on informal communication and networking.

Communication Flow

Traditional management approaches usually assumed that the only really important communication in an organization is that which flows downward through the hierarchy. Downward communication is important for managers to let the rest of the organization know policy and what to do. Thus, downward communication is often in the form of information sharing and directives on how to comply with new policy and rules and regulations. It serves to keep members throughout the organization informed.

Upward communication is just as important as downward. Through upward communication, it is possible for managers high in the hierarchy to find out what is going on below. It is an important channel for learning about problems with policy or other aspects of the organization. Some upward channels are created for collecting particular kinds of information, others encourage employees to voice their concerns and suggestions. Effective managers normally encourage open channels of communication from every level of the organization.

Lateral (horizontal) communication also is very important because it cuts across authority lines and fosters voluntary coordination. Lateral communication permits people in one part of the organization to know speedily and at low cost what those in another part need or are doing. Usually, parts of organizations are interdependent and rely upon other units to accomplish certain tasks. Communication across unit lines permits units to learn what they can do to facilitate the other's work. Consider the needs of police and fire departments in emergency situations. In such situations, lateral communication among the responding services is crucial. However, the result is often the opposite with units working at cross-purposes or refusing to cooperate.

Lateral communication is also significant in building a sense of community in the organization. By learning about other elements of the organization and the ways specialized tasks fit into the complete picture, employees may identify more closely with the organization. They may also develop an attachment to the members of the organization as a group pursuing the same purposes.

All organizations have communication flow in all three directions. Some flows are encouraged more than others. In some organizations, managers attempt to open lines of communication as much as possible, whereas in others there are tendencies to maintain very formal channels with limited access. Contemporary organization theorists normally suggest expanding channels as much as possible as a way of involving members in the organization.

Internal and External

Normally when organizational communication is discussed, we think in terms of internal communication. In most organizations, the vast majority of communication is internal with management using it to hold the organization together and on track in pursuit of its goals. External communication is important because it keeps those outside the organization informed of what is happening. This form of communication is particularly important in the public sector, where citizens and clientele depend upon the services of the public agency.

Some external communication may be interpreted as public relations and is often handled officially by a public information office in the public sector. The purpose of external communication is to keep the public informed of services and programs. Often, however, the process is used to generate understanding and good will toward the organization. When the purpose is more to ensure the survival of the agency or program than to provide a needed service, external communication is abused. Another abuse may be the use of external communication to generate public support for larger budgets and the like. Such efforts take place in many ways. The friendly military base does not provide open house, fly municipal and state officials to meetings, and encourage civic involvement of its offices only out of a commitment to service. Rather, there are likely to be payoffs in the form of important support for its facilities and programs as a result of these activities. The military also offers free use of bases or operations in movies that put the military in a positive light. Other public agencies have different things to offer members of the public and utilize them for the same types of purposes.

External communication has also become problematic in many government agencies because of attempts to withhold particular information. It is only natural that an agency would not want to release information that is detrimental to its cause. Because the agency is also likely to be the only one knowing what information is available, there is a lot of control implied by this power over information. The experience of the FBI in not wanting to publicize some of its lapses in communicating information it had relating to the activities of individuals involved in the attacks on the World Trade Center and the Pentagon on September 11, 2001 is instructive. Freedom of information acts at the national and state levels, along with open-meetings legislation, have opened information up to a great extent, but there are still many problems.

In reality, top-level management often is unaware of many aspects of external communication (Moore, 1995). People within the organization, especially at middle-management levels, communicate constantly with counterparts in other similar organizations. Often the communication occurs between and among organizations within the same governmental jurisdiction. At other times, similar units in different cities or different states exchange information. Managers in the Department of Corrections, for example, deal with managers in counterpart organizations in other states on a regular basis. Associations of professionals in similar jobs (e.g., library associations) also provide ample opportunity for lateral communication of information. Such communication is often very effective in facilitating the work of the organization, enabling managers to take advantage of the experiences of others with similar situations or problems. At the same time, however, this form of communication has the potential for undermining the authority of top-level management. Middle-level managers have the opportunity to present strong cases for their perspectives from the experience of fellow professionals, and there is no assurance that the information is representative of all or most similar organizations.

Methods of communication constantly change. *Electronic communication* now pervades society and makes communicating with vast numbers of people very easy. Managers now send electronic communications to all members of the organization through various forms. The use of the electronic communication opens the world to communication from anyone who wants to use it. Thus, organizations no longer have to send information through hierarchical channels; everyone in the organization can be reached at the same time. Information technology is a great tool for organizations and managers (Barrett & Greene, 2001). Electronic communication also permits members of the organization to communicate with everyone else, including those higher up in management. As discussed later in the book, access to electronic communication creates some issues for organizations and requires policies guiding and controlling its use.

Communications Problems

Among the most important problems with communication are lack of clarity and access to information. For managers, it is important to state things clearly so that everyone understands the communication in the way it was intended. Virtually everyone has played the game where a statement is passed around the room by whispering in the ear of the person sitting in the next chair; by the time the statement gets around the room, it is very likely to be changed and often communicates something completely different from the original statement. The same happens in organizations. If a message is not stated in simple, straightfoward language, it is likely to mean many different things as it is passed from one level or unit to another. This is the problem of interpretation. People respond differently to the same words, and as they translate messages, they give those messages new meaning.

Access to information is another major problem. When channels of communication are limited and information is kept under wraps, members of the organization have a difficult time knowing what is going on. More importantly, very limited channels of communication have the potential for screening out information. The manager at the top of the organization may receive incomplete information if it goes up only through specified channels. At each level, it is possible that some information will be screened out, especially if it puts the one screening it in a bad light. At times, some managers may also assume, as well, that certain information is not important to pass along. This screening of information can place upper-level managers in the awkward position of not having complete information for making decisions. Similar screening can occur in downward and lateral communication. On the other hand, if too much information is communicated, channels become overloaded and people ignore some of the information.

With electronic technology, organizations now are able to collect, store, analyze, and disseminate information at amazing speed. E-mail represents the predominant method of disseminating information electronically, but many administrators now use other technologies, including social networking sites. Of course, organizations use Web pages to communicate much important information to employees and others. Along with these advantages come problems as well. Privacy of information is problematic, given the large amount of information stored on any individual or topic in many different places. Access to information is not always secure, and people who have ulterior motives can obtain it.

Democratic Administration

The New Public Administration and Organizational Humanists proposed an administrative system that would incorporate democratic values and practices into the operation of organizations. In suggesting change, they advocated participative management, democratization of the decision-making process, and humanization of the work situation. They also proposed that clients have the opportunity to help define and implement programs. Many organization theorists were very optimistic that bureaucracy would become increasingly democratized because of its increasing level of professionalization, education, and socialization among its staff (Bennis & Slater, 1998; Berkley, 1971). Although their expectations have not been met, there have been many attempts to democratize organizational life in the public sector. The traditional, hierarchical structure still dominates but changes constantly.

Most advocates of democratic administration start with a discussion of participative management. Participation by employees in the management process follows the Neo-Humanists' suggestion that individuals have the capability and desire to assume responsibility. Michael Smith (1976) notes that there are many reasons that organizations should adopt participative approaches. Among these reasons is that participative management facilitates the interpersonal social and political skills of employees, resulting in better interaction with the public. Members of an organization are also more likely to assume responsibility for their actions if they participate in the decisions leading to them. They are less likely to attempt to avoid the responsibility and accountability for them. Smith also believes that participative management decreases the amount of time and energy wasted resenting the boss. Because decision-making and responsibility are diffused, contacts with the public also are diffused, and there is the potential for greater responsiveness. Additionally, participation by members of the organization may result in better decisions. For example, in selecting people for promotion, member participation is likely to result in choices based on competence, ability, and merit. Of course, a negative effect may be that only those who conform to organizational norms get chosen, resulting in stagnation.

Although these are all persuasive arguments for adopting democratic administration, they have not resulted in dramatic change in organizations (Kim et al., 2005). Smith (1976) attributes the lack of success to the resistance of management to give up their power and independence, and the strength of their standard operating procedures. Top-level administrators perceive themselves to be elites (public guardians) and balk at the idea of sharing power with the rank and file. Moreover, there is a tendency among administrators to attempt to protect the organization from the uncertainty of the outside world, and that tendency reinforces traditional ways of doing things. Smith recognizes that some accommodations are made through the introduction of some democratic practices but does not find evidence of full participative management in public sector organizations.

Vasu, Stewart, and Garson (1998) suggest three other, albeit overlapping, impediments to participative management. They indicate that public organizations' accountability to the political environment breeds protectionism and thus reliance on traditional approaches. Additionally, the fact that the goals of public sector organizations are often unclear and difficult to measure makes it difficult to demonstrate that participative management or any alternative is effective. Finally, they suggest that public agencies resist participative management because of the general belief that elected political leaders are supposed to make policy decisions. Employees of bureaucracy are supposed to be implementing policy and not deciding what the policy should be.

Participative management approaches have been more common in the private sector than in public agencies. Nonetheless, there are a few approaches that have been used in government bureaucracies. Among the prominent approaches is management by objectives (MBO), which has been used by agencies at all levels of government. Basically, MBO involves participation by members of the organization in the establishment of goals with plans for accomplishing them (Drucker, 2006). In complete MBO programs, employees also participate in deciding how best to use resources and in seeing that activities are kept on track. MBO also implies evaluation of results for consistency with organizational purposes and effectiveness. Ultimately, the evaluation process is used to provide feedback to the decision-making process. As Newland (1976) indicates, however, most MBO experiments in the national government have been streamlined versions of the process involving only the setting of objectives, monitoring progress, and evaluating results.

Zero base budgeting (ZBB), which gained a great deal of popularity during the late 1970s, is a variation on the same theme. It permitted participation at the lower levels of the organization in the creation of decision packages that were the building blocks of the budget and thus policy for governmental units. Strategic planning, now common in most government agencies, also draws from basic MBO processes. Studies at the municipal level suggest that MBO has had many successes (Poister & Streib, 1995).

Total Quality Management (TQM), sometimes called Total Quality Initiatives, is yet another version of participative management. TQM focuses on examining the processes within an organization to ensure that they work toward the best quality outcomes (Deming 1993; West, 1995). Everyone in the organization is involved in constantly examining what the organization is doing so as to avoid errors that could lead to problems in attaining the goals of the organization with the highest level of quality possible. The idea is to build quality into the process all the way through rather than testing for quality at the end of the process.

Another effort at democratizing the workplace is the use of *Organization Development* (OD). Organization Development is a process that attempts to break down organizational barriers to effective work (Golembiewski & Eddy, 1978). In particular, OD focuses on opening up the communication process and encouraging participation by all members of the organization in decisions. The approach is based upon the assumption that if all members participate in an open problem-solving atmosphere, they will be better employees. By open communication, people are supposed to develop greater self-awareness and awareness of others, resulting in greater trust and commitment to the group's activities. Many public sector organizations do use OD, but there are practical limits to its use because of external politics and fiscal constraints that hurt any innovation. There are also many disagreements about the utility and ethics of such programs, thus causing many managers to be cautious.

Theory Z is yet another approach to organizing based upon Organizational Humanism (Ouchi & Jaeger, 1978). Essentially, it is the same as Theory Y in its basic assumptions and attempts to improve organizational performance through the same mechanisms as OD. The basic difference from OD is that Theory Z adds the concept of permanent rather than short-term employment and career path considerations. As far as the internal processes are concerned, however, Theory Z follows the same type of guidelines as OD.

Another form of participative management that is used very extensively in public as well as private sector organizations is bargaining. Collective bargaining, or labor management relations, as it is often called, allows for democratic participation to the extent that it provides for the representation of the interests of the worker. These interests are legitimized by a formal process in which employee representatives negotiate and reach agreement with management over issues of importance to both. Additionally, procedures are developed for preventing arbitrary action against individual employees and for the resolution of grievances brought against either party to the bargaining table. Grievances are usually handled by outside neutral parties, thus increasing the protections against arbitrariness. Although many managers complain that the bargaining model undermines their authority, it also may aid them in communicating with employees because the union leadership becomes the channel for communication. Although considered a form of democratization of the workplace, bargaining can also become very ritualized, and individual participation can get lost in the shuffle. Oftentimes, individual members feel that the union is taken over by the leadership and loses touch with the interests of the rank and file.

Codetermination has developed as another instrument for employees to have a formal voice in work organizations. Basically, it involves equal representation of workers and management on boards of directors. Work councils of employees are created. The boards and work councils have a great deal of power over working conditions. While codetermination is popular in Germany, it is not used in the United States at the present time; although, it is becoming increasingly common to have labor representatives on boards of directors of private firms.

Administrative democracy is a popular concept in the literature, but research indicates that it is rather limited in application. Most public bureaucracies continue to be dominated by hierarchical organizations with limited employee participation in the decision making. Nonetheless, organizations have become increasingly sensitive to employee needs and behavioral concerns over the past two or three decades. There are much greater opportunities for participation, and many employees find it possible to exercise discretion, independence, and creativity as parts of their jobs.

During the 1960s and 1970s, democratic administration was extended to include the general public in the decision-making process. Many of the War on Poverty and other social programs required participation by recipients of services or members of neighborhoods affected by the programs. Committees and councils of interested persons became partners in the implementation of policies. Although the experiments have worked well in many places, they also generated a lot of abuse and opposition from local elected officials who felt that they were being bypassed in the process. Nonetheless, citizen participation remains a goal of decision makers and, advocates continually suggest ways of improving it (Robbins, Simonsen, & Feldman, 2008; Schachter, 1997).

By the 1980s and 1990s, the New Public Management, with an emphasis on reinvention and faith in the market model, changed the focus once again. Democracy came to be defined in terms of process and procedural rights. With the emphasis on the market model, efficiency and running government like a business were emphasized. The National Performance Review, headed by Vice President Al Gore, was a symbol of this approach (National Performance Review, 1993). Many scholars challenge the New Public Management as not having substantive democracy at its core (Box, 2006; Box, Marshall, Reed, & Reed, 2001; Carroll, 1995; Denhardt & Denhardt, 2007; Frederickson, 1996; Moe, 1994; Riccucci, 2001; Rosenbloom, 1993). They argue that public administration needs to refocus its attention to substantive democratic issues such as social justice, citizenship, responsiveness, economic inequality, and the relationship of government to those issues and democratic accountability. Some scholars focus on allowing citizens to actually govern through discourse with little constraint on their ability to decide for themselves about public purposes and actions (Box, Marshall, Reed, & Reed 2001; Catlaw, 2007; Miller & Fox, 2007). Others see civic virtue, citizenship, and concern for public interest as important issues. They believe that government exists for citizens and should not view citizens as customers but as owners of the system (Schachter, 1997). Government needs to be responsive and build trust with its citizens (Denahrdt & Denhardt, 2007; King & Stivers, 1998).

Public Administrators conduct their activities through organizations, and the public and elected representatives expect results from those organizations. In order to produce results, public agencies need resources (other than employees) and processes to assist them. The next chapter turns to an examination of those resources and processes.

Review and Study Questions

1. How do individuals' values affect the way they behave in organizations? Provide an example and explain it.

2. What approach to organization theory do you find most helpful for understanding organizations? Explain your choice.

3. How did the Hawthorne Studies refine the way theorists looked at organizations and their members? Do those studies have any meaning for organizations today? Explain.

4. What importance is the concept of rationality to organization theory and behavior?

5. Explain the concept of satisficing and its importance for organizations.

6. What is the hierarchy of human needs, and why would it be of interest to organization theorists?

7. Distinguish between closed and open systems. Explain how each is useful in understanding different aspects of organizations.

8. What are the differences between the New Public Management and the New Public Service?

9. What do you think motivates people? How does your position relate to the different approaches to motivation theory?

10. What factors affect the success of managers in managing their organizations? How should managers use information about those factors?

11. What are the barriers to effective communication within the organization? How can they be overcome?

12. How do managers have to approach internal and external communication differently? What are the roles of each type of communication?

Exercises

1. Make an appointment to interview a city manager. Ask the manager what he or she considers most important about getting people to perform well. How does he or she get recalcitrant employees to do their work? Explore the manager's responses to be sure you understand what is meant by them. After the interview, evaluate the responses and explain what assumptions about human nature the manager's responses imply. What do the manager's responses imply about his or her views on motivation? How do they relate to motivation theories?

2. Interview the director of a public works department. Ask for the organization chart, and ask the manager to go over it with you. Discuss with him or her what kind or reporting relationships there are. From the explanation of the organization structure, is it possible to suggest anything about the department's theory about organizations?

3. Make an appointment with an employee union leader for a city. Ask the union leader about his/her perceptions about how the city and its managers manage people. Ask about how they involve employees in making decisions. What do the responses suggest about the city's style of management?

4. Attend a city council meeting or a school board meeting. Pay particular attention to the way the council or board members talk to staff people or citizens making presentations or commenting at the meeting. Do the council or board members show respect for the staff or citizens? Comparing council or board member responses to staff and citizens. Discuss which they give more deference to. Compare the responses of the staff and citizens. How clear are the council or board members, staff, and citizens in making their points? How could they have communicated better?

References

Adams, J. S. (1965). Inequtiy in social exchange. In L. Berkowitz (Ed.), *Advances in Experimental Social Psychology, vol. 2* (pp. 267-299). San Diego, CA: Academic Press.

Argyris, C. (1964). *Integrating the individual and organization.* New York: Wiley.

Argyris, C. (1973a). Some limits of rational man organizational theory. *Public Administration Review, 33,* 253-267.

Argyris, C. (1973b). Organization man: rational and self-actualizing. *Public Administration Review, 33,* 354-357.

Argyris, C., & Schon, D. (1978). *Organizational learning: A theory of action perspective.* Reading, MA: Addison-Wesley.

Barnard, C. I. (1938). *The functions of the executive.* Cambridge, MA: Harvard University Press.

Barrett, K., & Greene, R. (2001). *Powering up: How public managers can take control of information technology.* Washington, DC: CQ Press.

Bennis, W. (1973). *Beyond bureaucracy.* New York: McGraw-Hill.

Bennis W., & Slater, P. E. (1998). *The temporary society* (rev. ed.). San Francisco: Jossey-Bass.

Berkley, G. E. (1971). *The administrative revolution.* Englewood Cliffs, NJ: Prentice Hall.

Blake, R. R. & McCanse, A. A. (1991). *Leadership dilemmas: Grid solutions* (4th ed.). Houston, TX: Gulf.

Blake, R. R., & Mouton, J. S. (1994). *The managerial grid: Leadership styles for achieving production through people.* New York: Elsevier.

Blau, P. (1973). *The dynamics of bureaucracy: A study of interpersonal relationships in two government agencies* (2nd ed., rev.). Chicago: University of Chicago Press.

Blau, P., & Mayer, M. W. (1987). *Bureaucracy in modern society*, (3rd ed.). New York: McGraw-Hill.

Blem, S. L. (1977). Psychological androgyny. In A. G. Sargent (Ed.), *Beyond sex roles* (pp. 319-324). St Paul, MN: West.

Box, R. C. (Ed.). (2006). *Democracy and public administration*. Armonk, NY: M.E. Sharpe.

Box, R. C., Marshall, G. S., Reed, B. J., & Reed, C. M. (2002). New Public management and substantive democracy. *Public Administration Review, 61,* 608-19.

Brown, J. A. C. (1987). *The social psychology of industry*. New York: Penguin.

Carroll, J. D. (1995). The rhetoric of reform and political reality in the National Performance Review. *Public Administration Review, 55,* 302-12.

Catlaw, T. J. (2007). *Fabricating the people: Politics and administration in the biopolitical state*. Tuscaloosa: University of Alabama Press.

Deming, W. E. (1993). *The New economics for industry, government, education*. Cambridge, MA: MIT Center for Advanced Energy Study.

Denhardt, R. B. (2007). *Theories of public organization* (5th ed.). Florence, KY: Cengage.

Denhardt, J. V., & Denhardt, R. B. (2007). *The new public service, Serving not steering* (expanded ed.). Armonk, NY: M.E. Sharpe.

Denhardt, R. B., Denhardt, J. V., & Aristigueta, M. P. (2009). *Managing human behavior in public sector and nonprofit organizations* (2nd ed.). Thousand Oaks, CA: Sage.

Downs, A. (1967). *Inside bureaucracy*. Boston: Little, Brown & Co..

Drucker, P. F. (2006). *The practice of management* (reissue). New York: HarperCollins.

Dubin. R. (1959). Person and Organizations. *Proceedings of the 11th Annual Meeting of the Industrial Relations Research Association*. 1969, 160-163.

Eddy, W. B. (1981). *Public organization behavior and development*. Cambridge, MA: Winthrop.

Fielder, F. E. (1967). *A theory of leadership effectiveness*. New York: McGraw-Hill.

Follett, M. P. (1924). *Creative experience*. New York: Longman, Green.

Frederickson, H. G. (Ed.). (1974). A symposium: Social equity and public administration. *Public Administration Review, 34*, 1-51.

Frederickson, H. G. (1996). Comparing the reinventing government movement with the New Public Administration. *Public Administration Review, 56*, 263-270.

Freud, S. (1955). *The origin and development of psychoanalysis*. Chicago: Regnery.

Golembiewski, R., & Eddy, W. B. (1978). *Organization Development in public administration*. New York: Marcel Dekker.

Gouldner, A. W. (1957). Cosmopolitans and locals: Toward an analysis of latent social roles. *Administrative Science Quarterly, 2*, 281-292.

Grant, N. K. (1989). *"Response to Kirk Hart," Public Administration Review, 49*, 106-107.

Gulick, L., & Urwick, L. (Eds.). (1937). *Papers on the science of administration*. New York: Institute of Public Administration.

Harmon, M. M. (1981). *Action theory for public administration*. New York: Longman.

Harmon, M. M. (1994). *Organization theory for public administration*. Burke, VA: Chatelaine Press.

Hersey, P. H., Johnson, D. E., & Blanchard, K. H. (2007). *Management of organizational behavior: Leading human resources* (9th ed.). Upper Saddle River, NJ: Prentice-Hall.

Herzberg, F. (1966). *Work and the nature of man.* Cleveland, OH: World.

Homans, G. C. (1951). The Western Electric research. In S. D. Hoslett (Ed.), *Human Factors in Management* (rev. ed) (pp. 210-241). New York: Harper & Row.

House, R. J., & Mitchell, T. R. (1974). Path-goal theory of leadership. *Journal of Contemporary Business, 3,* 81-97.

Kaplan, H. R. & Tausky, C. (1977). Humanism in organizations: A critical appraisal. *Public Administration Review, 37,* 171-180.

Katz, D., & Kahn, R. L. (1978). *The social psychology of organizations* (2nd ed.). NewYork: Wiley.

Kim, P. S., Halligan, J., Cho, N., Oh, C. H., & Eikenberry, A. M. (2005). Toward participatory and transparent governance: Report on the sixth global forum on reinventing government. *Public Administration Review, 65,* 646-654.

King, C., & Stivers, C. (1998). *Government is us: Public administration in an anti-government era.* Thousand Oaks, CA: Sage.

Latham, G. P., & Pinder, C. C. (2005). Work motivation theory and research at the dawn of the twenty-first century. *Annual Review of Psychology, 56,* 485-516.

Lindblom, C. E. (1959). The science of muddling through. *Public Administration Review, 19,* 79-88.

Maccoby, M. (1976). *The gamesmen: The new corporate leaders.* New York: Simon & Schuster.

Marcum, J. (2000). Out with motivation, in with engagement. *National Productivity Review, 19*(4), 57-60.

McGregor, D. (1960). *The human side of enterprise.* New York: McGraw Hill.

Marini, F. (Ed.). (1971). *Toward a new public administration: The Minnowbrook perspective.* Scranton, PA: Chandler.

Maslow, A. (1954). *Motivation and personality.* New York: Harper & Brothers.

Maslow, A. (1962). *Toward a psychology of being.* Princeton, NJ: Van Nostrand.

Maslow, A. (1965). *Eupsychian management.* Homewood, IL: Richard D. Irwin.

Mayo, E. (2003). *The human problems of an industrial civilization: Early sociology of management and organizations, vol. 6* (reprint). Boca Raton, FL: Taylor & Francis.

Metcalf, H. C., & Urwick, L. (Eds.). (1940). *Dynamic administration: The collected papers of Mary Parker Follett.* New York: Harper & Row.

Miller, H., & Fox, C. J. (2007). *Postmodern public administration: Toward discourse* (rev. ed.). Thousand Oaks, CA: Sage.

Moe, R. C. (1994). "Reinventing Government" Exercise: Misinterpreting the problem, misjudging the consequences. *Public Administration Review, 54,* 111-22.

Moore, M. H. (1995). *Creating Public Value.* Cambridge, MA: Harvard University Press.

Morgan, G. (2006). *Images of organization* (updated ed.). Thousand Oaks, CA: Sage.

Mosher, F. C. (1982). *Democracy and the public service* (2nd ed.). New York: Oxford University Press.

National Performance Review. (1993). *Creating a government that works better and costs less: The report of the National Performance Review.* Washington, DC: U.S. Government Printing Office.

Newland, C. A. (1976). Policy/program objectives and federal management: The search for government effectiveness. *Public Administration Review, 36,* 20-27.

Ouchi, W. G., & Jaeger, A. M. (1978). Type Z organization—stability in the midst of mobility. *Academy of Management Review, 3,* 305-314.

Poister, T. H., & Streib, G. (1995). MBO in municipal government: Variations on a traditional management tool. *Public Administration Review, 55,* 48-56.

Presthus, R. (1978). *The organizational society* (rev. ed.). New York: St. Martin's Press.

Riccucci, N. M. (2001). The "old" public management versus the "new" public management: Where does public administration fit in? *Public Administration Review, 61,* 172-5.

Robbins, M. D., Simonsen, W., & Feldman, B. (2008). Citizens and resource allocation: Improving decision making with interactive Web-based citizen participation. *Public Administration Review, 68,* 564-575.

Rosenbloom, D. H. (1993). Have an administrative rx? Don't forget the politics! *Public Administration Review, 53,* 503-7.

Rosenbloom, D. H., Kravchuk, R. S. & Clerkin, R.M. (2008). *Public administration: Understanding management, politics, and law in the public sector* (7th ed.). New York: McGraw-Hill.

Sargent, A. (1978). The androgynous blend. *Management Review. 67* (October), 60-65.

Schachter, H. L. (1997). *Reinventing government or reinventing ourselves: The role of citizen owners in making a better government.* Albany: State University of New York Press.

Senge, P. H. (2006). *The fifth discipline: The art and practice of the learning organization* New York: Broadway Business Books.

Simon, H. A. (1997). *Administrative behavior: A study of decision-making processes in administrative organizations* (4th ed.). New York: Simon & Schuster.

Simon, H. A. (1973). Organization man: Rational or self-actualizing. *Public Administration Review. 33,* 346-353.

Smith, M. P. (1976). Barriers to organizational democracy in public administration. *Administration and Society, 18,* 275-317.

Taylor, F. W. (1913). *Principles of scientific management.* New York: Harper.

Thompson, J. (2003). *Organizations in action.* Pscataway, NJ: Transaction.

Thompson, V. (1961). *Modern Organization.* New York: Knopf.

Van Wart, M. (1998). Changing public sector values. New York: Garland.

Vasu, M. L., Stewart, D. W., & Garson, G. D. (1998). *Organizational behavior and public management* (3rd ed.). New York: Marcel Dekker.

Vroom, V. (1995). *Work and Motivation.* San Francisco: Jossey-Bass.

West, J. P. (1995). *Quality Management Today: What Local Government Needs to Know.* Washington, DC: International City/County Management Association.

White, R., & Lippitt, R. (1968). Leader behavior and member reaction in three social climates. In D. Cartwright & A. Zander (Eds.), *Group dynamics: Research and theory* (pp. 585-611). New York: Harper & Row.

Wright, B. E. (2001). Public-sector work motivation: A review of the current literature and a revised conceptual model. *Journal of Public Administration Research and Theory, 11,* 559-586.

Selected Web Sites

International Public Management Association for Human
 Resources (Membership organization of governmental
 personnel/human resources departments and individuals
 working in the field.)
 http://www.ipma-hr.org

National Center for Public Productivity (Research and public
 services organization devoted to improving productivity in
 the public sector.)
 http://newark.rutgers.edu:80/~/ncpp

National Public Employer Relations Association (Association of
 public professionals in labor management relations.)
 http://www.npelra.org

Public Administration Theory Network (International membership organization of professionals interested in public administration theory.)
 http://www.patnet.org/

Section on Democracy and Social Justice (Section of the American Society for Public Administration devoted to exploration
 of administrative and political alternative to promote social
 change and social justice.)
 www.aspaonline.org/dsj

Section on Professional & Organizational Development (Section
 of the American Society for Public Administration dedicated
 to professional and individual growth and development.)
 www.aspanet.org

5

Allocating Resources:
Planning, Budgeting and Evaluation

Careful allocation of resources under swampy conditions presents difficulties. It is challenging to plan what to do and to allocate resources to diverse actions amid conditions of uncertainty. Nonetheless, some administrators try to account for the larger picture and longer term as they allocate scarce resources to various activities of their organization. No matter how uncertain the environment, it is useful to keep an old Army saying in mind: "Supervisors fight alligators, administrators drain the swamps."

The metaphor reminds us that managing the swamp under increasingly complex conditions is categorically a different kind of activity than fighting alligators. Fighting alligators is reactive, has a short-time horizon, and seems frantic. In contrast, preserving the swamp, restoring the swamp, or making the swamp a better place in which to live, requires a more active stance. This necessitates longer time frames and a cooler perspective toward rapid change. Budgeting and performance evaluation activities can, if done strategically, equip administrators to spend less time fighting the beasts and more time creatively dealing with the total environment (Friend & Hickling, 2005; Friend & Jessop, 1977; Koteen, 1997).

In the process of becoming more proactive, strategic, and adaptive managers, public administrators must give special attention to some key management functions. *Management functions* are those activities that administrators carry out as they implement public policy. Allocation of fiscal and human resources to various tasks represents a primary management function. Evaluation of agency and program performance has become a primary strategic management function that complements resource allocation to promote high performance organizations (Friend & Jessop, 1977; Popovich, 1998).

Planning is a process by which schemes are devised to accomplish a given set of future goals. *Strategic planning* requires administrators to translate the organizational mission into measurable goals and performance objectives. Then they promote their choices of the preferred strategies to achieve those goals and objectives

Budgeting allocates resources among various competing purposes. Usually too many needs chase too few resources. Experiences in the recession of the 1980s and recent mega-recession in the early years of the 21st century suggest that resource shortages are likely to continue. Such shortages pose a major barrier to policy implementation and to budget planning and execution.

Under the best of conditions, budget planners expect the resultant mix of activities to satisfy agency goals. They assume that the services produced will serve important community needs, and that political authorities will continue to appreciate and support the agency's activities (Rubin, 2005; Shick, 2007). Under the most trying of fiscal and financial times, budget planners struggle to produce a satisfactory mix of activities that meet public needs and secure political support. This is no mean feat.

Evaluation deals with performance measurement and assesses the effectiveness of funded activities to meet service indicators (Wholey, Hatry & Newcomer, 2004; Wye, 2005). Evaluation helps administrators discover whether performance goals are accomplished, and if those activities positively benefit the community. Further, evaluation information may be used in "speaking truth to power" (Wildavsky, 1987) and in encouraging "authentic participation" of citizens (King, Felty, & Susel, 1998) by convincing authorities and the public of agency program accomplishments. Fiscal hard times increase the need for accurate evaluation of agency and program performance. Administrators must be armed with the facts needed to describe and defend the actual performance of agencies.

During the past thirty years, more emphasis has been placed on the development and use of performance measures in the evaluation of programs and services (Gore, 1993; Hatry, 1978;

Hatry et al., 2006). Performance-oriented measures often are hallmarks of excellence in private and public sector organizations (Hatry, 1978; Kamensky & Morales, 2005; Osborne & Gaebler, 1992; Peters & Waterman, 1982; Rossi, Freeman, & Lipsey, 2003). As David Ammons (2001) notes, "How are we doing?" is a question that citizens, elected officials, and managers need to be able to answer. Answering this question depends on how well agencies and jurisdictions are able to measure the efficiency, effectiveness, and productivity of their services qualitatively and quantitatively.

Limits to Strategic Management Planning

In a perfect, rational world, some kind of careful, long-term *strategic management planning* would unite budgeting and evaluation. John Bryson (2004) defines *strategic planning* as "a disciplined effort to produce fundamental decisions and actions that shape and guide what an organization (or other entity) is, what it does, and why it does it" (p. xii). Strategic management planning sets out long-term goals, various intermediate objectives leading to these goals, and strategies for attaining each of the objectives. Budgeting and financial management could allocate resources to support the strategic activities pursued in trying to reach timely objectives. Evaluation, in turn, could help managers, especially top managers, to close the loop joining performance (attainment of objectives), use and allocation of resources, and goal setting. Evaluation could provide accurate information (feedback) that would permit managers to alter the use of scarce resources over time to produce better results (Koteen, 1997; Osborne & Hutchinson, 2006).

A substantial minority of public agencies use strategic management planning to launch organizational direction, consider priorities, and steer decision making (Poister & Strieb, 2005). Additionally, evidence is emerging regarding growing sophistication of strategic planning, as demonstrated by the connection to performance activities (Kamensky & Morales, 2005). However most public agencies respond to the vagaries of the swamp one-day at a time. Since nearly all public managers are intelligent, well-intentioned persons, the lack of management planning is a perplexing problem. Why do so many experienced managers neglect the long-term?

Planning is by definition *rational*. Managers as planners attempt to apply their rationality to making proposals for the future. They hope to make things better. Often their hopes and expectations are dashed on the hard rocks of reality. Several general reasons account for why rational planning is limited and why planning often fails.

First, human frailty limits rationality. Daniel M. Wegner (2003) argues that what appears to be the conscious exercise of human intent is largely illusionary. People think that they will things to happen. That is, they think their pre-action thoughts lead them to systematically take steps that produce desirable results. Wegner's research, in contrast, indicates that we most often reason things out *after* we have started to act. He maintains that we usually explain what we have done after the fact rather than plan to do it before we act. Thus, rationality is a post-action conditional explanation or rationale for what we have done.

Thus, thinking ahead may rarely occur. And when it does, the capacity to make rational choices is further limited. Herbert Simon (1997) suggested that humans live in a world of "bounded rationality." Human capacity to be fully rational is limited or bounded by three things: values, skills, and knowledge. The values of managers color and bias their capacity to perceive reality and to assess potential impacts of alternative courses of action. The range of personal or collective skills in an organization may be insufficient to sort out options and assess them. Likewise, the knowledge base possessed may be inadequate for completion of the steps required in fully rational planning. Although education, training, and improved management practices may, in part, help overcome these limits, all decision-makers struggle with these constraints. They still can try to systematically set out, review, and select among options, but it is impossible for them to select the best option.

Second, managers are action-oriented persons (Denhardt & Denhardt, 2006; Webber, 1972). They want to get things done. Their rewards accrue from specific accomplishments, usually in a short time frame. As a consequence, many managers tend to live in the present. Planning, however, requires contemplation and a long time frame. Thus, many managers are not natural planners and often resist devoting time and effort needed to do a good job of planning (Berkley, 2008).

Third, uncertainty and ambiguity surround administrators. As we have stated before, the external environment changes so rapidly and unpredictably that the capacity to get a fix on it is elusive. Planning under these conditions must be fluid. This observation at first seems a contradiction. Planning pursues preferred futures. How can the pursuit of a preferred state of affairs be fluid? It is fluid because of the need to adapt and to adjust plans continuously during their implementation. Thus, plans are best viewed as "strategic guides" rather than fixed paths to the future (Koten, 1997). Even so, the swampy environment means that most plans will not produce the results originally expected of them.

Fourth, planning is concerned with individual and community values (Bolan & Nuttall, 1975; Simon, Smithberg, & Thompson, 1991). Plans propose to change the current distribution of public resources. Any recommendation to change the status quo engenders controversy and resistance based upon self-interest. Managers find it difficult both inside their organizations and in dealing with the public to secure basic agreement on goals, alternatives, and which alternatives are most promising. In short, planning always produces conflict.

The general lack of a planning perspective limits the effectiveness of managerial activities. Ironically, however, the dependence of public agencies and administrators on tax-based revenues forces many administrators to engage in planning-like activities when seeking and using financial resources. The need to secure continuous financial support for agencies leads many if not most public chief executives to apply rationality to the budgeting system.

Budgeting as Resource Allocation and Planning

Some people consider the development, allocation, and use of resources (financial resources in particular) to be the heart of the management system. No agency could last for long without an annual intake of fiscal calories. Since most public agencies live a long time, most successfully secure a relatively abundant diet of public funds. In popular opinion, public agencies consume a fat-rich diet.

Certainly, control of the allocation of resources to various uses is a central concern of elected officials and public managers. Legislators, particularly at the state and local levels, experience angst regarding "over-funding" and "reducing governmental waste." Few national, state, and local officials run for office on the promise that they will increase taxes and public spending. Yet they usually argue for more resources for programs supplying public goods for their constituents.

The bureaucratic concern often is the lack or potential loss of resources. Managers, especially top-level administrators, expend much energy and time on efforts to maintain or to increase levels of budgetary support for agency activities. If money is the life-blood of political life, budgeting is the means of getting life-supporting supplies.

Budgeting represents as much an internal as an external political game. Management competition between top-level, central managers and their mid- and lower-level counterparts in various departments, bureaus, and programs concerns who gets how much to do what. As we discussed in previous chapters, many reforms (particularly budgetary reforms) strive to give central administrators more influence over governmental bureaucracies. Top administrators such as the president, governors, mayors, city managers, county executives, and school superintendents all try to use allocation activities as a means of executive influence and conflict control (Nice, 2002). At the next organizational level, agency and department heads—such as park and recreation directors, police chiefs, secretaries of state, directors of human resources, and the like—engage in a dual struggle: to gain a measure of fiscal independence from superiors and to maintain a measure of fiscal control over subordinates. And so it goes down the line to the street level.

Despite the natural limits on rational planning, budgeting is the principal "planning" effort of many public agencies. Since the budget cycle in most jurisdictions focuses on a definable fiscal year, budget planning seldom engages long-term planning. Budgeting is also inherently a political process. This means that political values rather than administrative values often dominate budgeting (Rubin, 2005; Wildavsky & Caiden, 2004). Finally, most budget decisions involve incrementalism and marginal modifications rather than rational and fundamental changes to the swamp.

Nonetheless, it is in the early steps of budget planning that governmental organizations often come closest to adapting and examining their goals and performance. Budgeting secures for a program or an organization the resources needed to continue and perhaps improve its public service activities. Public organizations continue to reform and experiment with attempts to make budgeting more effective as a system of resource allocation (see Rubin, 2008).

In some public agencies, productivity assessments and the outcomes and impacts of public policy implementation have come to be intimately tied to resource allocations through the budget process (Kamensky & Morales, 2005; Osborne & Hutchinson, 2006). As public managers employ more quantitative measures of employee performance, regular assessments of agency activities, and research-based evaluations of policy impacts, they will use the resulting data sets in the budget process (Bland, 2007; Light, 1999; Myers, 1999).

Money, along with other agency resources such as human capital, organizational structure, and technology, support day-to-day activities such as educating our citizens, addressing national security issues, and providing quality of life amenities in local communities. Since the funds that support public budgets come mostly from involuntary taxes, the size of budgets and public service deliverables generate controversial political considerations. Budgets are political documents, budgeting is a political process, and management of budgeting brings administrators and pressure-groups face to face (Rubin, 1998, 2005; Shuman, 1992; Wildavsky & Caiden, 2004).

Three Views of the Budget

Public budgets may be characterized as records of community values, as plans laying out goals and resource allocations for a given time period, and as management tools. All three views are useful, and together they suggest why budgeting commands so much attention by chief administrative officers such as mayors, school district superintendents, city managers, governors, and the president.

Record of Community Values. The final, adopted version of a budget represents the results of months (and at times years) of political negotiation, compromise, and logrolling. The appropriations among competing interests and demands represented in the final budget and later supplemental appropriations tally the winners and losers in the political processes. Under conditions of severe economic recession and large reductions in tax revenues that result from these tough times, state and local administrators often find their agency or programs as major losers as the economy contracts.

Under normal conditions, an annual municipal budget comprises a formal statement of the city's current public policy values and priorities. Under conditions of severe stress, the budget is a formal statement of what is worth saving. Because budgets often represent the accumulation of incremental changes evolving from decisions over many years, good times and bad times, it serves as an historical record of community values for a local polity.

Working Plan. The budget documents, especially in the early stages of preparation and review, embody working plans of proposed resource allocations and performances promised. Agencies or departments typically are asked by the executive to submit their budget plans in advance of the actual formal consideration of the budget document. In this process, administrators lay out "wish lists" of actions they would like to take and goals they would like to accomplish. They must indicate what each task will cost. Often, they must document both the need for proposed levels of services and the expected achievements.

Levels of budgetary sophistication and budget preparation practices vary among governmental jurisdictions, but at times, budget preparation puts administrators into a classical planning mode. In this mode, administrators as planners develop their proposed budgets, set out goals, arrange these goals and objectives in priority, select ways to achieve these objectives, indicate resources needed to reach them, and project performance levels.

Budget preparation frequently is much less complete and provokes more conflict than suggested above. Furthermore, the plans made by the administrators are often not part of their written budget proposals. Nonetheless, even in relatively small public organizations, administrators tie budget preparation and managerial planning together. In large cities, most states, and the national government, administrators embrace managerial planning as part of the budget process.

Management Tool. Chief executive officers (mayors, city managers, governors, and presidents) try to use the budget-making process as a tool to influence and control administrative agencies and departments. They set the broad guidelines and constraints to which they hope the administrators and agencies will adhere. Insofar as the chief executive can direct the budget-planning activities and resist changes to the executive budget, budgeting allows some degree of central control over agencies and departments. Executives try to constrain the resource-hunting forays of administrators into the legislative processes by centrally vetting proposed changes and new requests. Further, the chief executive usually presents a completed budget plan to the council or legislature with a statement of executive goals, limits, and principles. Many presidents, governors, mayors, and city managers are surprised at the extent to which departments and agencies successfully resist central control in the budget process. Many a reformer has seen dreams of centralized fiscal management dashed upon the realities of the extent to which the budget process rests in the hands of administrators, legislators, and interest groups composing the Iron Triangle.

The Budget Process

Budgets are implemented or executed in time periods called *fiscal years*. The fiscal year (*FY*) should not be confused with the ordinary calendar year, which runs from January 1 through December 31. The typical state or local government's fiscal year is July 1 through June 30. The national government's fiscal year currently is October 1 through September 30. In a given fiscal year, administrators typically work on several steps of the budget process for different years at the same time.

Despite its complexity and variety, the budget cycle represents a critical component of the overall governance process. It consists of five basic steps: (1) research and database management, which provides the basic information used by budget planners; (2) preparation of a draft or proposed budget; (3) submission and adoption, which translates the proposed budget plan into policy; (4) implementation, which turns the budget appropriations into services; and (5) evaluation, including audit, program evaluation, and policy assessment.

Budgeting is continuous, and each of the five steps overlaps. Commonly, administrators work on two or three years' budget plans at the same time. The overlapping stages and long lead time not only make the job difficult for administrators in handling two or three budgets at a time, but bring them back into continuous contact with the other participants of the budget-making process. Furthermore, the role and stance of a given organization's administrators change in different stages of the budget cycle and in response to policy-makers and the external environment. This may be illustrated by a more detailed consideration of budgeting in a municipal setting.

Research and Database Development. Organizations build a budget upon the budgets of past years. The changes from one year to the next are seldom so great that past budget experience becomes irrelevant. Even with the past as a foundational, a certain amount of new information and knowledge is needed in subsequent years to support improved budget planning.

Local administrators normally estimate needs and proposed expenditures *before* they recommend appropriate tax increases (if needed). In local governments, most states, and the national government, forecasting future revenues is a key preparatory step. In a large city, the estimate of revenues may reflect the combined efforts of the finance or budget director, city manager's office, and planning department. These estimates of revenues from various sources are sometimes based upon demographic and economic developments and trends rather than on straight-line projections of past revenues. At best, however, these estimates provide rough guides and frequently miss the mark.

When the estimates miss the mark, small problems become large ones. Inherent incrementalism may result in dicey revenue estimates. Few governmental agencies, for example, foresaw the collapse of fiscal institutions during the decade of 2000-2010. Neither public administrators nor their private counterparts forecast the burst of the mortgage/lending bubble. Incrementally, this led budget planners to overestimate revenues.

Preparation. Budget preparation begins with the establishment of general guidelines by the chief executive. Departments are expected to stay within these guidelines. A department begins its internal preparation with an assessment of policy and program needs. The current fiscal year's budget generally serves as the base. Each unit asks for some increment above the amount needed to continue the current year's operations. Using these assessments and requests, departmental administrators develop proposed budget plans and supporting documentation. In small towns and cities, these estimates may be informal, but in larger cities, the budget documents may be rather large and elaborate. In larger jurisdictions, this step may include scenarios relating to different levels of available revenues and allocations. It also may reflect promises made by governing policy-makers and departments in terms of service and performance levels.

The departmental proposals are reviewed next by the central administration. This is a period of intense negotiation between the department heads and the chief executive. The department budget proposals are modified and compiled into a single budget document by the budget director. Frequently, the draft of the executive budget is distributed to department heads for review and comment before formal distribution to the city council.

Adoption. The city council members already will have information about the proposed executive budget before it is formally transmitted to them by the chief executive officer. Often, departmental administrators already will have begun their appeal for support or additional increments or restoration of cuts before completion of the budget preparation. Clientele or support groups also will have gotten into the act. Council members may be aggressive participants in the preparation stage. They are usually informed about departmental proposals by the time the formal executive budget reaches them.

Formal council consideration of the budget *follows* presentation of the executive budget. The council usually modifies the proposed budget. Political negotiations continue with the chief executive trying to defend and protect the proposed budget and the council challenging it. The council holds public hearings, receives public comment, questions administrators, and makes additional changes in the budget, sometimes radically altering it. During this time, departments and interest group allies often influence budget amendments. These changes may be with or without the blessing of the mayor or city manager. Although the mayor or city manager may try to enforce central control over the budget, departments and interest groups often can secure changes even in the face of opposition from the chief executive. Finally, at a public meeting, the council adopts the modified budget.

Implementation of the Budget. Administrators implement the budget as they attempt to manage their organizations in such a manner as to reach planned performance objectives. This often requires modification of the adopted budget and changes in proposed activities and services as the organizations adapt to environmental changes. During budget implementation, the council may be asked to make supplemental allocations upon the recommendation of the executive, assuming revenues are available. In fiscally constrained conditions, departmental administrators may be required to reduce expenditures. In any case, the budget implementation step is also a political process in which administrators continually struggle to protect their organizations and basic budget allotments.

Audit and Assessment. State law usually requires a formal financial audit. It consists of a review of the accounting records made during the implementation of the budget. The completed audit verifies that financial transactions conducted by the city were done according to legal requirements and followed generally accepted accounting practices. It typically also testifies to the accuracy of the records and financial reports by stating that they present "fairly" the financial position of the city (Rousmainiere, 1979). In past decades, this was the primary form of assessment of the use of budget resources for local governments. Today, in some governmental jurisdictions, additional assessments of performance occur. The performance audit looks more closely at how well the agency met its goals, objectives, and promised performance level. These assessments provide information to feed into the next budget cycle. This is also a policy assessment stage that helps tie a budget cycle into another by providing information for the databases used in the future. As part of the next cycle's research effort, the assessment of past performance provides a feedback loop and assists managers in shaping and adapting to change.

The steps of the budget cycle resemble planning. This is particularly true of the portions of the activities that engage administrators. In some organizations, research and preparation for the annual budget start well in advance of the announcement of principles and guidelines by the chief executive. The more sophisticated the management approach of an administrator or an organization, the more the budgeting exercise contributes to administrative policy planning.

Budget Reform: Search for Planning in Budgetary Systems

Major attempts to reform budgeting in the United States started at the beginning of the Republic, but the 20th century was notable for attempts to alter budget forms and practices to improve the managerial aspects of the budget process. We will discuss only a few such efforts here. Students who wish to pursue more complete discussions of budget reform might want to consult Jesse Burkhead, *Public Expenditure* (2009); Robert Lee, *Public Budgeting Systems* (2008); John Mikesell, *Financial Administration* (2006); Allen Schick "The Road to PPB: The Stages of Budget Reform" (1966), and Irene Rubin's edited classic *Public Budgeting* (2008) for excellent interpretations of budget reforms.

Budgeting as planning has high demands for information. Administrators use two kinds of information in budgeting: resource data and program data (Lee, 2008). *Resource data* refers to information regarding inputs (resources) such as money, equipment, and human capital used in producing services. *Program data* refers to what the organization does and the accomplishment of those activities. Financial planning requires that both kinds of information be considered in combination. Neither kind of data alone will answer the questions posed in a systematic planning process. If budgeting is to assist managers in making good planning decisions and to help them adjust to a changing environment, then the budgetary system must produce and use both kinds of data. As Lee (2008) suggests, much of the change in budgetary practices and forms may be viewed as an attempt to develop program data and to link it with resource data.

There are two general kinds of budgets and supporting systems in use today: line item and performance/program. A third system, zero based budgeting, is a variation of the performance/program approach and is used in some local governments. They deal with resource and program data differently, and each provides a different environment for budgeting.

Line Item Budget Systems. The line item budget is the more common form used today. Even jurisdictions that use a version of performance/program budgeting systems usually use line item information somewhere in their budget-making processes.

The conventional line item budget details the expenditures of each department by objects of expenditure and amount. There is a "budget line" for each expenditure item such as salaries, health insurance, travel, telephone usage, expendable materials, and energy costs. Line item budgets were originally designed around detailed expenditure control so that the chief administrator and the legislature could get a detailed set of fiscal information for each department or agency. The idea was to increase administrative and legislative oversight of draft budgets. The mountains of detail contained in contemporary line item budgets make oversight a tedious task and often lead to nitpicking and micromanagement from elected policy makers. Line item budgets have, however, fostered universal use of financial audit as a major accountability mechanism.

Line item budgets focus attention on the allocation of resources to specific purposes. They permit the auditor, legislator, or executive to know for what specific items departments and agencies spend funds. In contrast to the detailed information provided about specific uses of resources, line item budgets provide little, if any, information about the overall accomplishments of the departments supported by the resources. They do not provide any information about the relationships among various expenditures or about what happens as a result of expenditures. Reformers long have criticized the line item approach to budgeting for encouraging *incrementalism* in budgeting and for failing to promote the development of information useful in program planning (Lee, 2008).

Incrementalism in budgeting is the process whereby this year's appropriations become the *base* for next year's budget. In the preparation of their budget proposals, departments and agencies tend to take what they currently have as a given and ask for some additional increment above it for the next fiscal year.

By the 1930s, it became clear that traditional budget formats and practices did not make sense to those administrators interested in program planning and more central control of budgeting. (See Caiden, 1987 for a discussion of the executive budget.) The national, state, and most local budgets were not comprehensive documents that reflected the overall annual plans of the jurisdiction but rather were a compilation of hundreds and thousands of individual requests and allocations to specific units to do specific tasks. The budget and the budget process were elegant summaries of the politics of interest group-agency-legislative interaction with the agency playing the key role as protector of the public budgetary base of their operations (Shuman, 1992; Wildavsky & Caiden, 2004). As Wildavsky and Caiden have shown, public agencies tend to treat last year's budget as the "base" upon which to ask for this year's increase. Thus, the agency tries to protect this base in negotiations with the legislature regarding increases or cuts.

Program/Performance Budgeting. Although some authors discuss program and performance budgeting separately (Turnbull, 1981), they are variations on a theme (Lee, 2008) and will be treated as one approach here. Support for programmatic approaches to budgeting in the 1930s and 1940s grew out of the need to permit managers more flexibility in allocating resources to organizational activities (Burkhead & Miner, 2007). At the national level, the 1949 Hoover Commission report stressed the advantages of the "performance" budget and recommended that it be adopted throughout the national government (Commission on the Organization of the Executive Branch of the Government, 1949). A sophisticated version of program/performance based budgeting called Planning Programming Budgeting Systems (PPBS) was introduced at the national level in the 1960s. Although PPBS lasted only a few years at the national level, a few states and some local governments now use some form of program budgeting.

Program budgeting differs from line item budgeting in three important ways: (1) more attention is given to specification of program goals and objectives, (2) funds are distributed on the basis of program results, (3) departments are expected to demonstrate quantitatively the expected achievements at different levels of funding.

Administrators prepare program budgets differently from line item budgets. Instead of proposing budgets on the basis of line items, managers preparing program budgets usually do the following:

1. Define the major programs of the organization. In a municipal police department, these might be traffic control, crime prevention and control, investigation, internal affairs, training, and community relations.

2. Specify a set of goals and objectives for each program and develop measurements for each objective. Such measures often use baselines or benchmarks (Zhu, 2003).

Benchmarks are goal-related performance standards against which the actual performance of the program or activity is assessed. A goal of the police crime prevention and control program is to prevent crimes by patrolling residential neighborhoods. Typical objectives might be to decrease crimes against property by 5 percent, reduce the number of persons injured in the commission of crimes by 4 percent, and increase the percentage of homicides solved by arrest by 5 percent. Measures for the first objective, the decrease in the number of crimes against property, probably would be the number of crimes reported per 1,000 population and the per capita value of property loss by theft.

3. Identify the various inputs (resources) to be used to produce the desired results. Using the program structure and the measurement systems, the policy budget analysts then prepare a budget that shows what level of service the department proposes for each program and the resources required to support these programs.

In subsequent years, the departmental administrators, the chief executive of the city, the council, and even the public can tell if the department is meeting its objectives. This information is part of the evaluation of departmental performance and ties together planning, budgeting, and evaluation.

Zero Base Budgeting. Zero base budgeting (ZBB) is a variation of program/performance budgeting. Although seldom used in pure form, variants are used in many city-manager systems. Zero base budgeting was developed in the private sector (Pyhrr, 1977), briefly used by the U.S. Department of Agriculture in 1964, adopted by several states including Georgia, and implemented at the national level in the Carter administration in 1977.

ZBB is defined as a budgeting technique that generally attempts to analyze budget requests without an implicit commitment to sustaining past levels of funding. Under this system, programs and activities are organized and budgeted in a detailed plan that focuses review, evaluation, and analysis on all proposed operations—rather than on increases above current levels of operation, as in incremental budgeting. Programs and activities are analyzed in terms of successively increasing levels of performance and funding, starting from zero, and then evaluated and ranked in priority order. The purpose is to determine the level, if any, at which each program or activity should be conducted (General Accounting Office, 1979).

According to Berkley (2008), the ZBB approach has three steps:

1. *Identification of decision units.* In this first step, the organization's activities are clustered into separate decision units. In a university, such units could be academic departments, research centers, or administrative offices. The key is that all the activities of the organization must be assigned to some decision unit.

2. *Preparation of decision packages.* Each decision unit prepares budget proposals for that unit called "decision packages." All of the unit's activities and programs could operate at various levels, depending on how fully they are funded. The administrators of each unit develop a plan that shows several different gradations of activities, each with its own quantity of resources and outputs. These program and resource data form the decision package for a given level of activity. The different decision packages collectively may range from zero to some high level of requested resources. If the variation in levels of resources requested is well scaled, the differences between them show the relative impacts on programs of various levels of funding.

3. *Ranking decision packages.* Once the organization has prepared its decision packages, it ranks them in order of its priorities. After the originating unit completes its rankings, the decision packages are passed up to the administrative level above it. If the original unit were an academic department, then the dean's office would be the next level. Here the decision packages of one unit compete with those of another with all re-ranked. They then go to the next levels—academic vice president, president, and board of regents—where they are combined with all other decision packages and re-ranked at each level. ZBB principles suggest that in each successive re-ranking decision makers consider how well the decision package fits into the larger scope of priorities at that level. Often, decision packages experience modification as they pass through the levels of review and re-ranking. In the end, the continual reuse of program and resource information

supports increased rationality of the budget preparation, review, and compilation processes.

ZBB is flexible and permits adjustment to changing conditions because it is based on program evaluation (Pyhrr, 1977). Nonetheless, it did not work well in the national government and was abandoned by the Reagan administration in 1981. Its critics find that ZBB requires excessive effort in research and budget preparation, creates mountains of paperwork (Hammond & Knott 1980), does not overcome incrementalism (Lauth, 1978), and focuses too narrowly on the process of ranking decision packages to the detriment of considering external influences (Mikesell, 2006).

ZBB is similar to program/performance budgeting in three important ways. First, they both stress goal setting and assessing results. Second, they cluster expenditures into program or activity groups. Third, they require quantitative measures of outcomes. ZBB is best seen as a variation of the general program/performance approach to budgeting in which the development of information for program planning plays such an important role.

Formal ZBB is dead at the national level, rarely used in the states, and occasionally used in cities. Although it provides the chief executive with considerable control over budgeting, program budgeting is hard to do and cumbersome. Despite its limits and failures, some of its principles and practices are part of budgeting and program evaluation. The effort to provide program information through the identification and measurement of objectives continues. There is much more emphasis at all levels of government on the use of program information in budget preparation and adoption.

Evaluation

Organizational performance information is crucial to administrators coping with the uncertainty of life in the swamp. Adjustment to rapidly changing conditions requires a steady diet of information about how well things are going. Evaluation studies increasingly provide needed information about the relationship between organizations and their uncertain, ever-changing environment (Hatry, 2007; Koteen, 1997; Myers, 1998; Wholey et al., 2004).

Performance-oriented budgeting encourages public administrators to pay attention to the consequences of the way their organizations use resources (Osborne & Hutchinson, 2006). Although PPBS and ZBB approaches to budgeting are now seldom practiced in their pure forms, many local governments use some variant of them. Even in organizations that have moved away from performance-based budgeting, there continues to be considerable emphasis on evaluation of organization and program performance. The complexities of pure performance-based budgeting generally have led to more streamlined practices, but a lasting contribution of PPBS and ZBB is the continued development and use of evaluation information in the planning and allocation activities of many public organizations.

Budget reform is just one of the roots of evaluation research. Applied research for evaluation of the performance of public organizations and programs dates at least from the 1940s. The social reform programs of the 1960s spawned widespread evaluation research as social scientists renewed their interest in such topics as crime, poverty, education, and urban development. Practicing public administrators were slower to move toward use of evaluation research for assessment of their organizations and programs. By the mid-1970s, however, efforts to promote the use of *evaluation research* by public administrators were found at all levels of American government (Fukahera, 1977; General Accounting Office, 1976; Wholey et al., 2004). Today, a growing body of literature flourishes regarding program evaluation and performance measurement (Ammons, 2001; Hatry, 2007; Hatry, et al. 2006; Kamensky & Morales, 2005; Moynihan, 2008; Rossi, Freeman, & Lipsey, 2003).

What is evaluation research? It is similar to but different from ordinary "hypothesis testing" social inquiry. In hypothesis-testing research, the inquiry is directed toward testing a set of empirical propositions to see if they are valid. The validation process usually leads to the development of a theory that explains social phenomena. Evaluation research is applied research that uses theory, research design, and methods to provide evaluation information about the performance of organizations and their programs. It may lead to refinement of social theory, but its main purpose is to aid assessments of how well organizations and programs perform.

Program Evaluation

Program evaluation refers to research conducted to assess the programs implemented by public organizations. Program evaluation in the United States probably dates from the early 1900s but came into common practice only in the 1980s and the 1990s. Public administrators need to know more about the consequences of the use of organizational resources in order to increase their effectiveness. Program evaluation provides part of the feedback that encourages organizations to adjust to a changing, uncertain environment (Rossi, Freeman, & Lipsey, 2003).

Major Purposes of Program Evaluation. Program evaluation has three major purposes. First, it provides information about the degree to which a program achieves its objectives. Second, it informs administrators and other policymakers about the unintended consequences of program implementation. Often, programs have unanticipated negative or positive consequences. If the unintended consequences cause harm and outweigh the positive results of the achievement of the nominal objectives of the program, then policymakers have reason to alter or abolish the program. Third, it often provides information about the level of public satisfaction with the outcomes of the program and the degree of public support for the program. This is vital information in the politically charged environment of most programs and important to surviving in the swamp.

Carefully prepared program evaluations often provide administrators with useful information (Hatry et al., 2006). On the other hand, the very administrators and organizations for which they are prepared sometimes disregard program evaluations. This suggests some serious problems with program evaluations.

Problems with Program Evaluation. Like most innovations, the actual practice of program evaluation differs from theoretical expectations about it. Major problems may be clustered into three groups of related issues. First, program evaluations often reflect tensions between the evaluators and the administrators of the programs. Second, measurement of program outcomes and impacts can be challenging. Third, program evaluations may not produce much usable information.

Members of the organization may do program evaluation, but it is often done by someone outside of the organization. This may produce a kind of doctor-patient relationship in which the evaluator treats the organization and its administrators as "sick" and in need of "therapy" (Archebald, 1970). In this situation, little trust develops between the evaluator and those evaluated. The resulting tension not only weakens the evaluation itself but also, in the long run, reduces the probability that the organization will make use of the recommendations of the evaluation report. Even if the evaluator develops a more positive relationship with the organization and its members, some administrators view with some suspicion any evaluation reports that pose serious questions and provide negative feedback.

A fundamental issue for program evaluation is the extent to which the evaluation actually measures and assesses the performance of an organization and program. Two key aspects of this problem plague evaluators. First, can the effects of the "treatment" (the program) be assessed separately from all of the other factors that may have contributed to the actual outcomes? Good research design and use of appropriate statistical tools, especially time series analysis, enhance the possibility of successfully isolating the effects of the program. Yet it is frequently difficult to tell if the treatment produces positive results. Second, measurement of outcomes and impacts is difficult. Inputs such as units of resources—money, time, energy—used to implement the program are relatively easy to measure, but outcomes and impacts, which are the consequences of the program for the external environment, are much more difficult to assess.

Using a traffic control program as an illustration, we can demonstrate some of the key problems with measuring and assessing the outcomes and impacts of public programs. *Outputs* might include the number of hours and the number of warnings or citations issued. These items are accepted "measures" of traffic control outputs, but do they measure well the consequences of the program? Probably not.

Let us turn to "outcomes." A major outcome of good traffic control is more orderly traffic flow over streets and freeways. Yet how much of the orderly or disorderly flow of traffic on the streets or freeways is attributable to police efforts and how much to other factors such as mechanical breakdowns, weather, driver habits, and the physics of traffic? As much as the police chief would like to take credit for those few mornings when traffic on surface streets and freeways flows well, the department usually has little data to show the consequences of traffic control on flow.

Assessments get even less distinct when we turn to impacts. Impacts are the long-term social consequences of public programs. Impacts may be intended or unintended. They also may be positive or negative. An intended positive impact of traffic control is possible reduction in the number of fatalities resulting from traffic accidents. Fatalities in automobile accidents result from unsafe vehicles, careless driving, poor weather conditions, or drunk drivers. Insofar as the outcome of more orderly traffic flow contributes to safer driving and fewer chances for vehicles to collide, it could contribute to reduced fatalities. Other examples of intended impacts from better traffic control include energy savings and cleaner air. Unfortunately for the police, we have little capacity to show the impact of traffic control on these things.

The current quantity and quality of the feedback available to most organizations is insufficient. We do not measure productivity well enough or frequently enough to provide hard information to the managers and staff who produce the goods and services. Traditional measures such as numbers of persons on patrol, response time, and number of accidents are, at best, indirect or at worst, measures of the use of resources rather than real outputs, outcomes, and impacts. This issue becomes complicated further because many of the community-oriented policing duties performed, as well as social worker support, do not lend themselves well to unit measurement. Much of the effort of the police officer and the social worker involves handling domestic relations. Measuring such things as stopping a quarrel or keeping a family together, except in terms of frequency of occurrence, is difficult.

Usefulness of Program Evaluations. Unfortunately, many governmental officials make little use of evaluation research. There are a number of reasons for this. First, academicians compile much evaluation research that addresses problems in such a way that the results often have marginal use to administrators and other policymakers (Lindblom & Cohen 1979). Second, life in the swamp with its pressure for survival does not entice administrators to make careful use of evaluation reports (Daily, 1983).

Third, the findings of evaluation studies often are threatening and harsh, at least in the eyes of the administrators (Greer and Greer, 1982; Weiss 1982).

On the positive side, there is more emphasis on formal, data-driven evaluation than ever before. In the past thirty years, all levels of governments have made strides in the use of performance measures. For example, Donald Monynihan (2008) outlines the "performance management doctrine" assumptions applied to the federal government in recent years that demand performance measures. First, inefficiency arises in government. Second, governments may transform themselves to minimize inefficiencies. Third, tackling sub-par performance supports fiscal health and promotes trust in government. Fourth, program evaluation and performance management advances the abilities of government to act rationally. And, fifth, program evaluation can improve decision making and advance accountability.

More broadly, benchmarking is a major innovation in performance assessment borrowed from the private sector and shared across public agencies (Ammons, 2001; Hatry, 2007). *Benchmarks* are performance standards used as comparison points for assessing the current program results (Ammons, 2001). Municipalities that monitor the results of their departmental programs have traditionally used departmental past performance as their benchmarks.

A library typically might measure its performance in terms of total circulation (a workload measure), circulation per employee (a productivity measure), circulation per capita (a program effectiveness measure), or circulation per $1,000 (production cost measure) (Ammons, 2001). Using these four measures, the library managers might gather the data annually and show trends over time. The gross trends over five or ten years might show increases or decreases in any or all of the four measures. These trends would be internal measures of how well the library system performs.

As interesting and useful as these measures may be for the library's internal management purposes and for justifying next year's budget requests, such vertical measures based solely on past agency experience are insufficient. Agency managers need more objective measures. Horizontal comparisons anchored in the experiences of respected municipalities or well-developed professional standards are more useful (Ammons, 2001). Fortunately for libraries and librarians, their national organizations, (American Library Association and Public Library Association), have long offered professionally developed standards and measures for many library functions. Further, as Ammons, (2001) and Hatry and associates (2006) show, many municipal libraries use creative, client-oriented measures of performance such as client satisfaction, usefulness of staff, quality of holdings and services, physical accessibility, hours of operation, availability of parking, and safety of parking lots and premises. Thus, librarians and libraries may use many experiences and measures to make performance comparisons over time.

Further, as Carol Weiss (1977) argues, the very act of conducting an evaluation carries importance to the organization. The process of conducting the research, though it may be unnerving, promotes a sense of introspection in the organization. Members of the organization refresh their concern with program goals and become concerned with how well things are going. As a consequence, though the organization may not formally respond to the recommendations of the evaluation report, it may alter its behavior in response to being studied.

Overall, is program evaluation worth the effort? This kind of question led to the rapid decline of PPBC and ZBB. The experience appears to be more mixed with regard to program evaluation. Some program evaluation is not done well. Program evaluation is finding its way into the policy stream and organizational practice. This is especially true as the federal government ratchets up historic levels of debts while most states and local governments shift into cutback mode. Localities that use modified forms of program budgeting often use simple program evaluation studies to provide information for use in budgeting. Some programs have regular assessments mandated by governing bodies. Impact statements, most often required for assessing environmental consequences, are widely used. Some localities and states have "sunsetting" provisions that make use of program evaluations. Sunset laws require automatic review of agencies and programs by the legislature. These laws force assessment of ongoing programs by both legislators and administrators and encourage use of program evaluations. Although program evaluations are seldom fully used by administrators and others, when they are, they provide information useful in adjusting organizations to a changing environment.

Organizational Performance

The assessment of whole organizations also is uncertain. Even with the use of benchmarking, performance budgeting still focuses assessments of organizations on degrees of achievement of specified goals or objectives. It sounds sensible to say that we should judge organizations in terms of goal attainment. This assumes that the goals are known, reachable, agreed upon, and measurable. Should a prison be assessed in terms of how many prisoners it handles per month, the number of persons it passes through, the number of prisoners rehabilitated, the occurrence of recidivism in its ex-inmates, the lack of riots, or by some other criteria? What about libraries? How can we accurately measure goal achievement? Should it be by such measures as numbers of books circulated, number of special reading classes for the young, impact on literacy, quality of the collection, number of fines levied, books lost or recovered?

Notice that we come back to a struggle with one of the most serious problems we face in deciding what to plan. What are some good measures of outputs, outcomes, and impacts? Better overall performance requires more agreement about good measures (Kamensky, Morales, & Abramson, 2005). Even with the recent successes of benchmarking, public agencies mostly opt for indicators of input measures such as number of dollars expended, gallons of fuel used, and numbers of faculty available to teach. Sometimes output measures such as cases handled, books circulated, citations issued, and gallons of water delivered are used in planning, budgeting, and assessment.

One of the most positive spin-offs of programmed budgeting and productivity assessments has been the increased awareness of the public, elected officials, interest groups, and managers about the issues of performance measurement and the need for more objective, valid measures and assessment systems. One can argue that much of the program evaluation and policy analysis done in the past six decades has been flawed, but an equal argument can be made that a new subdiscipline of public administration has emerged. Unquestionably, the surveys of community satisfaction, program analysis, and cost-effectiveness studies done for some programs and in some governmental agencies have served the public well. The public is becoming more aware and better informed about the performance of public agencies.

Officials demonstrate more responsiveness and sensitivity to community values. Managers pay more attention to final outcomes. Organizations strive a bit harder for better internal and external feedback.

It is important to remember that public agencies are at the beginning of the development of systematic assessment rather than at some mature point. Much remains to be explored in the study and practice of program evaluation and policy assessment. Among the more important strategies is to increase the use of time series analysis to better show the long-term successes and failures of policies. Benchmarking is a step, but only a step, in that direction. A considerable amount of comparison over time has occurred in applied science and engineering, but the social sciences, especially public administration, require more.

The balance sheet on how well organizations develop and make use of evaluation information still unfolds. As suggested several times, public administrators need considerable evaluation information to perform well in the swamp. Public administration practice is getting better at developing the needed information and some implementation progress is apparent. In the next chapter, we examine the effectiveness of organizational response to environmental change and uncertainty. The rate of successful adjustment is an open question, but the processes of planning, budgeting, and evaluation assist organizations in developing capacity to handle change.

In the next chapter, we consider how public managers and agencies can better manage their organizations. Ironically, the political swamp today is even more tenuous than it was in the 1980s when we wrote the first edition of this book. Managers need to be even more aware of and more skilled in strategic activities that permit them to tie together internal management of agencies with increased and more effective linkages with the public and better communications and relationships with external authorities.

Review and Study Questions

1. Why do some public administrators do so little planning?

2. Public administrators are action-oriented persons. What are some of the advantages and disadvantages of being action oriented? Would you expect your local fire chief to be especially action oriented? Why or why not?

3. In what ways is a municipal budget a working plan? What kinds of actions does the typical municipal budget promise to take? Why?

4. Many critics of American budgeting argue that it is inherently incremental. What do they mean by this? In your opinion, is the incremental nature of budgeting good or bad? Why?

5. Which, in your opinion, is the most important step in the five-step budget process from the point of view of the city manager? Why?

6. Zero-base budgeting (ZBB) was largely a failure at all levels of government. What characteristics of the Administrative Swamp and the Iron Triangle led to the demise of zero-base budgeting?

7. Performance assessments and program evaluation research are key elements in strategic management. Yet, agencies often resist evaluations and ignore information from evaluations. Why?

8. Programmed budgeting, often used in local governments, depends on performance assessments for information about how well programs are doing. What kinds of performance assessments are likely to be most useful to (1) elected officials, (2) citizens, and (3) top-level managers? Which of these are most likely to want outcome and impact measures of programs and departments? Why?

9. Most scholars writing about the budget process think that political values always outweigh administrative values in budget making. Why do they think this? Do you agree? Why or why not?

Exercises

1. Go to the Web site of the largest city in your region. Look up the most recent budget information you can find on the site.

   a) Use it to answer the following questions:

   b) Which departments get most of the resources?

   c) Which departments get the fewest resources?

   d) What does this tell you about the values and priorities of this city?

2. Use the public document section of your campus library or your state government's website to locate copies of the past three state budgets. Use these documents to find out the following:

   a) What kind of budget format and system does the state use?

   b) Which players in the budget process does the state budget system favor?

   c) What have been the biggest changes (increases or decreases) in amounts budgeted to specific departments and programs?

   d) What trends do these data suggest?

   e) Can you tell why these increases or decreases have taken place?

   f) Were you surprised by any of these changes? Why or why not?

3. Pretend that you are the sitting governor in your state. It is probably true that there is a projected revenue shortfall in your state, but even if there is not one projected, please assume that revenues will be down 12% in the next fiscal year. What strategy will you use to handle this shortfall? Will you spread the reductions across the board? Will you, instead, target certain agencies or programs to take the brunt of the cuts? Which strategy is more politically safe? Why? If the shortfall were 25%, would your strategy change? Why or why not?

4. Get a copy of your state legislature's most recent budget bill (the actual legislative act). Get a copy of the governor's proposed budget and compare it with what the legislature passed. What are the major differences between the two? What accounts for these differences?

5. Use newspapers, the Internet, and state documents to find out what kinds of data and statements your state's director of the department of corrections used in the justification to defend and perhaps increase the department of corrections' most recent budget. Overall, would you say the director used political data and values more than administrative data and values to make the case for the departmental budget? How objective or subjective were the arguments and information? What buttons did this person try to push? How politically effective were the arguments and information? What lessons can you derive about the state budget process?

References

Ammons, D. N. (2001). *Municipal benchmarks, assessing local performance and establishing community standards* (2nd ed.). Thousand Oaks, CA: Sage.

Archebald, K. A. (1970). Alternative orientations to social science utilization. *Social Science Informant, 9*, 7-35.

Berkeley, G. E. (2008). *The craft of public administration* (10th ed.). New York: McGraw-Hill.

Bland, R. L. (2007). *Budgeting: A budgeting guide for local government* (2nd ed.). Washington, DC: International City/County Management Association.

Bolan, R. S., & Nuttall, R. L. (1975). *Urban planning and politics.* Lexington, MA: Lexington Books.

Bryson, J. (2004). *Strategic planning for public and nonprofit organizations* (3rd ed.). San Francisco: Wiley.

Burkhead, J., & Miner, J. (2007). *Public expenditure* (reprint). New Brunswick, NJ: Transaction.

Caiden, N. (1987). Paradox, ambiguity, and enigma: The strange case of the executive budget and the United States constitution. *Public Administration Review, 47*, 84-92.

Commission on Organization of the Executive Branch of Government (1949). *Budgeting and accounting.* Washington, DC: U.S. Government Printing Office. Referenced in R. D. Lee, Jr. (2008), *Public Budgeting Systems* (8th ed.). Sudbury, MA: Jones & Bartlett.

Daily, J. H. (1983). Overcoming obstacles to program evaluation in local government. *Policy Studies Journal, 12*, 287-294.

Denhardt, R. B., & Denhardt, J. V. (2006). *The dance of leadership: The art of leading in business, government, and society.* Armonk, NY: M. E. Sharpe.

Friend, J. K., & Hickling, A. (2005). *Planning under pressure* (3rd ed.). Newark, NJ: Butterworth-Heineman.

Friend, J. K., & Jessop, W. N. (1977). *Local government and strategic choice* (2nd ed.). St. Louis, MO: Elsevier.

Fukahera, R. S. (1977). Productivity improvement in cities. *1977 municipal yearbook.* Washington, DC: International City/County Management Association.

General Accounting Office (1976). *Evaluation and analysis to support decision-making*, PAD-75.9, September 1.

General Accounting Office (1979). *Streamlining zero-based budgeting will benefit decision making.* Washington, DC: U.S. Government Printing Office.

Gore, A. E., Jr. (1993). *From red tape to results: Creating a government that works better and costs less.* Report of the National Performance Review. Washington, DC: U.S. Government Printing Office.

Greer, T. V., & Greer, J. G. (1982). Problems in evaluating costs and benefits of social programs. *Public Administration Review, 42*, 151-156.

Hammond, T., & Knott, J. (1980). *A zero-based look at zero-base budgeting*. New Brunswick, NJ: Transaction.

Hatry, H. P. (1978). The status of productivity measurement in the public sector. *Public Administration Review, 38*, 28-33.

Hatry, H. P., Fisk, D. M., Hall, J. R., Jr., Schaenman, P. S., & Synder, L. (2006). *How effective are your public services? Procedures for Performance Measurement* (3rd ed.). Washington, DC: ICMA Press/Urban Institute.

Hatry, H. P. (2007). *Performance measurement* (2nd ed.). Baltimore, MD: Hopkins Fulfillment Services.

Kamensky, J. M., & Morales, A. (Eds.). (2005). *Managing for results, 2005*. Lanham, MD: Rowman & Littlefield.

Kamensky, J. M., Morales, A., & Abramson, M. A. (2005). From "useful measure" to "measures used." In J. M. Kamensky & A. Morales (Eds.), *Managing for results, 2005* (pp.1-14). Lanham, MD: Rowman & Littlefield.

King, C. S., Felty, K. M., & Susel, B. O. (1998). The question of participation: Toward authentic participation in public administration. *Public Administration Review, 58*, 317-326.

Koteen, J. (1997). *Strategic management in public and nonprofit organizations, managing public concerns in an era of limits* (2nd ed.). Westport, CT: Praeger.

Lauth, T. P. (1978). Zero-based budgeting in Georgia state government: Myth and reality. *Public Administration Review, 38*, 420-430.

Lee, R. D., Jr. (2008). *Public Budgeting Systems* (8th ed.). Sudbury, MA: Jones & Bartlett.

Light, P. (1999). *The new public service*. Washington, DC: Brookings Institution.

Lindblom, C. E., & Cohen, D. K. (1979). *Usable knowledge: Social science and social problem solving*. New Haven, CT: Yale University.

Mikesell, J. L. (2006). *Financial administration: Analysis and applications for the public sector* (7th ed.). Florence, KY: Cengage Learning.

Moynihan, D. P. (2008). *The dynamics of performance management: Constructing information and reform* (2nd ed.). Washington, DC: Georgetown University Press.

Myers, R. T. (Ed.). (1999). *Handbook of governmental budgeting.* (Jossey-Bass nonprofit and public management series). San Francisco: Jossey-Bass.

Nice, D. C. (2002). *Public Budgeting.* Florence, KY: Cengage Learning.

Osborne, D., & Gaebler, T. (1992). *Reinventing government.* New York: Addison-Wesley.

Osborne, D., & Hutchinson, P. (2006). *The price of government: Getting the results we need in an age of permanent fiscal crisis.* Jackson, TN: Basic Books.

Peters, T. J., & Waterman, R. H. (1982). *In search of excellence: Lessons from America's best run companies.* New York: Warner Books.

Poister, T. H., & Streib, G. (2005). Elements of strategic planning and management in municipal government: Status after two decades. *Public Administration Review, 65,* 45-56.

Popovich, M. G., (Ed.). (1998). *Creating high-performance government organizations.* San Francisco: Jossey-Bass.

Pyhrr, P. A. (1977). The zero-base approach to government budgeting. *Public Administration Review, 37,* 1-8.

Rossi, P. H., Freeman, H. E. & Lipsey, M. W. (2003). *Evaluation: A systemic approach* (7th ed.). Thousand Oaks, CA: Sage.

Rousmainiere, P. F. (Ed.). (1979). *Local government auditing, a manual for public officials.* New York: Council on Municipal Affairs.

Rubin, I. S. (1998). *Class, tax, and power: Municipal budgeting in the United States.* New York: Chatham House.

Rubin, I. S. (2005). *The politics of public budgeting: Getting and spending, borrowing and balancing* (5th ed.). Washington, DC: CQ Press.

Rubin, I. S. (Ed.). (2008). *Public budgeting: Policy, process, and politics*. Armonk, NY: M. E. Sharpe.

Shick, A. (2007). *The federal budget: Politics, policy, and process* (3rd ed.). Washington, DC: Brookings Institution Press.

Schick, A. (1966). The road to PPB: The stages of budget reform. *Public Administration Review, 26,* 243-258.

Shuman, H. E. (1992). *Politics and the budget: The struggle between the president and congress* (3rd ed.). Englewood Cliffs, NJ: Prentice Hall.

Simon, H. A. (1997). *Administrative behavior* (4th ed.). New York: Simon & Schuster.

Simon, H. A., Smithburg, D. W., & Thompson, V. A. (1991). *Public Administration*. New Brunswick, NJ: Transaction.

Turnbull, A. B., III. (1981). The budgetary process and decision making in public agencies. In T. Vocino & J. Rabin (Eds.), *Contemporary public administration* (pp. 231-239). New York: Harcourt.

Webber, R. A. (1972). *Time and management*. New York: Van Nostrand.

Wegner, D. M. (2003). T*he illusion of conscious will*. Cambridge, MA: MIT Press.

Weiss, C. H. (1977). Research for policy's sake: The enlightenment foundation of social research. *Policy Analysis, 3,* 352-545.

Weiss, C. H. (1982). Measuring the use of evaluation. *Evaluation Studies Review Annual, 7,* 129-145.

Wholey, J. S., Hatry, H. P., & Newcomer, K. E. (Eds.). (2004). *Handbook of practical program evaluation* (2nd ed.). San Francisco: Jossey-Bass.

Wildavsky, A. (1987). *Speaking truth to power: The art and craft of policy analysis*. New Brunswick, NJ: Transaction.

Wildavsky, A. & Caiden, N. (2004). *The new politics of the budgetary process* (5th ed.). New York: Pearson.

Wye, C. (2005). Performance management for career executives: A "start where you are, use what you have" guide. In J. M. Kamensky & A. Morales, (Eds.). *Managing for results* (pp. 17-82). Lanham, MD: Rowman & Littlefield.

Zhu, J. (2003). *Quantitative models for performance evaluation and benchmarking*. Norwell, MA: Klumar Academic.

Web Sites

American Association for Budget and Program Analysis. (Organization that serves federal, state, and local governments, as well as corporate executives and academics in the fields of budgeting and program analysis. Co-sponsor of the journal *Public Budgeting and Finance*.)
http://www.aabpa.org/index.html

Association of Budgeting and Financial Management. (Association affiliated as a section of the American Society for Public Administration. Co-sponsor of the journal *Public Budgeting and Finance*.)
http://www.abfm.org

Congressional Budget Office. (Federal agency that provides objective and non-partisan analysis of economic and budgetary decisions.)
http://www.cbo.gov

Government Accounting Standards Board. (Independent organization that develops standards of accounting and financial reporting for U.S. state and local governments.)
http://www.gasb.org/main.html

Government Finance Officers Association. (National professional association for government finance officers at all levels. Publisher of *Government Finance Review*.)
http://www.gfoa.org

National Association of Counties. (Organization that represents county governments and promotes good governance.)
http://www.naco.org

National League of Cities. (Organization that represents municipal governments and promotes good governance.)
http://www.nlc.org

National Association of State Budget Officers. (Organization that serves state finance officers.)
http://www.nasbo.org

National Tax Association. (Organization that serves tax professionals. Supports *The National Tax Journal*. Has links to major economic, finance, and tax data bases.)
http://www.ntanet.org

Public Agenda. (A nonpartisan, nonprofit organization devoted to bridging the gap between governmental leaders and the public.)
http://www.publicagenda.org

State of California, Legislative Analyst's Office. (Example of budget, financial, and policy analysis at state level.)
http://www.lao.gov/laoapp/main.aspx

The Dismal Scientist. (Journal and Web site supporting economic data bases and links to additional major economic databases.)
http://www.economy.com/dismal

U.S. Office of Management and Budget (OMB). (The main budget planning and coordination arm of the Executive Office of the President. Responsible for management of the administration's performance assessment system.)
http://www.whitehouse.gov/omb

U.S. Government Accountability Office (GAO). (The main financial and program analysis arm of the U.S. Congress.)
http://www.gao.gov

6

Managerial Work in the Swamp

Management is a tough job. Leading an organization through the swamp challenges even the most able practitioners. As Mintzberg (1973) notes, the manager has often been seen as a folk hero in America. Continuing experience with rascals in top management positions in both the private and public sectors has tarnished this image. Yet, effective top-level managers are heroic. None are more heroic than public managers who accomplish their public trust year after year. We must understand the nature of managerial work in the swamp to appreciate how difficult the job is and how well most public managers balance the competing demands and pressures of their jobs.

Public administrators try to manage their organizations to be helpful to the communities they serve. "The aim of managerial work in the public sector is to create *public* value just as the aim of managerial work in the private sector is to create *private* value" (Moore, 1995, p. 28). *Private value* usually refers to the products firms produce to sell to customers and the income derived from these products. The goods and services produced by private firms improve the quality of life of those who purchase and use them.

Public value is harder to define, but it involves improving the quality of life of individuals and communities through the provision of goods and services by public organizations. Often public value, such as environmental quality, accrues to the community at large. The concept of public value may become clearer if we consider an example of the public value provided by a contemporary public agency. The Metropolitan Atlanta Regional Transit Authority (MARTA) manages a large public transit system in Atlanta, Georgia. This bus and rail system contributes value to individuals and the community by providing publicly subsidized, low-cost public transportation. About 500,000 people ride MARTA buses and trains each day (www.itsmarta.com; accessed July 26, 2009). The subsidized fares mean that low-income persons can use it. Insofar as MARTA encourages riders to use their automobiles less it also provides public value as it indirectly contributes to a reduction of pollution from auto exhausts. Thus, MARTA contributes two overlapping public values: low-cost, reliable transit to its riders and improved air quality to the community at large.

Mark Moore (1995) and Mark Popovich (1998) argue that public managers must strive to make their agencies into *high performance organizations*. "High performance organizations are groups of employees who produce desired goods and services at higher quality with the same or fewer resources" (Popovich, 1998, p. 11). Managers cannot rest on past performance and historic patterns of accomplishment, but rather, should help employees and citizens create *additional* units of public value (Moore, 1995). Creation of additional units of public value such as cleaner air, safer streets, better-educated children, and increased community pride requires managers to overcome the considerable limitations and challenges of the administrative swamp.

Effective management of individual organizations is not enough. "Today's public manager must do more than be the effective manager of an agency's internal operations. Effectiveness is a necessary but not sufficient condition for success; today's manager must be a creative innovator as well" (Cohen & Eimicke, 1998, p. xiii). Being innovative and creative in a complex, confusing, and changing managerial realm is not easy.

Challenges and Constraints

Public administrators face new challenges daily. Mark Twain is reputed to have said, "History is just one damn thing after another." Not all change is damnable, but it often seems that way to the hard-pressed director of corrections, city manager, or liaison officer for the Department of State. Public managers at all levels feel pressures. The innovative and adaptive manager strives to create additional public value under considerable constraints.

Among those conditions that make executing public policy so trying are:

(1) the demanding and risky political environment within which the public organization and manager operate

(2) the intractability of the organization and its members

(3) the executive's comprehension of management functions

(4) the need for inter-organizational linkages and relationships.

Line staff, supervisors, middle managers, and top-level managers all operate under these constraining conditions. All of their jobs are more difficult and, at times, more rewarding because of trying circumstances. High-level administrators such as city managers, heads of state-level departments, and directors of large municipal, county, or school district offices and programs are more likely than line staff, supervisors, and middle managers to be under the spotlight of public opinion and political accountability. They bear most of the political risks in leading public organizations. They are the subjects of most of our discussion of innovative and adaptive management.

A Demanding and Risky Political Environment

Administration always plays out in a political environment. Historically, such provisions as the national Hatch Act and its state and local variations have sheltered individual public administrators from direct involvement in electoral politics. Nonetheless, as noted in Chapter 2, the political exchange system always constrains the world of administration. Today, politics impinge forcefully and directly into the day-to-day life of top-level administrators. Elected officials demand more and offer less support to the bureaucracy. Bureaucrat bashing now is a refined art. Furthermore, politicians feel free to try to intervene directly into the day-to-day activities of agencies at all levels.

Public managers and organizations often manage boundary conditions to protect themselves from the outside world. Agencies typically include clientele groups inside their spheres of influence and receptivity but try to keep the communication system under their control. The Iron Triangle noted in Chapter 2 is as much a defense system as an attempt to promote reciprocity.

At the same time as they cultivate their Iron Triangles, managers often endeavor to keep outsiders out of agency affairs. Outsiders may include political actors with nominal authority over agency matters. At the national level, for example, members of Congress, cabinet members, and presidents are amazed and dismayed at the capacity of federal agencies to resist outside authority. Similarly, governors, state department heads, and state legislators often find that state agencies can skillfully resist outside and downward pressures. Things are little different at the local level. In council-manager cities, for example, council members often find that they have minimum direct influence over city departments and programs. City managers frequently make themselves and their immediate staff the center of political communication (Nalbandian, 1991).

More active citizen groups, more demanding customers, increasingly effective interest groups, more aggressive media, and actively questioning elected officials, however, make it difficult for administrators to insulate public organizations from political pressures. The tradition of impermeable boundaries and controlled political communication is giving way to attempts by high-level administrators to foster external political support and allies. Effective managers often blur boundaries and openly court two-way lateral and vertical political communication with outsiders (Ammons & Newell, 1989).

Carolyn Ban, (1995) in her study of federal administrators, found that managers whose work preferences lead them toward an *open systems* approach are either innovators or brokers or a combination of the two. Open systems refers to organizations that have permeable boundaries (Harmon, 1994) and to administrators that are open to others (Farmer, 1995). Openness, in its most profound form, would engage administrators in democratic dialogue and exchange with all political participants from the least visible citizen to the most obvious authorities (King, Felty, & Susel, 1998). "*Innovator[s]* focus on creative approaches, being at the cutting edge, managing change, [and] involvement in broad policy issues. *Broker[s]* focus on acquiring resources and on external interactions with clients, constituents, other agencies, [and] Congress" (Ban, 1995, p. 73).

Most public organizations are semi-open systems. It is difficult to fully isolate an organization from politics. Not all managers, however, are open to political action and political communication. Some would prefer to be left alone so that they could do an effective job of internal management. Management theory, ideology, and practice, however, favor the top-level manager who innovates, sees the big picture, develops external resources and support systems, and is deeply involved in the policy system. The current emphasis on entrepreneurial behavior mandates a combination of innovator and broker at the top of the organization (Abramson & Littman, 2002; Johnston, 2008; Moore, 1995; Popovich, 1998). Innovating and brokering are high-risk behaviors. Stepping purposefully and forcefully into the political arena may lead to considerable accomplishment and a short administrative tenure.

Innovations, according to Moore (1995), create political risks. The media often initially support the innovation and administrator because the efforts are newsworthy. When the project falters, however, the fickle media and political leaders seek to fix blame. Recently, the city manager of a fast-growing suburban bedroom city joined with his colleagues in the metropolitan area to push for support for and adoption of a fixed rail transit system. This system would have tied the suburban city with the downtown corridor of the central city, regional airport, and regional mult-campus university. When completed during the 2010s, commuters in the suburban city would have had inexpensive, rapid, and convenient transportation to work, play, shopping, entertainment, and education. And, like MARTA in Atlanta, the transit system also promised to reduce air pollution.

The city manager worked closely with local business leaders, elected officials in several cities including the mayor and council members in the home city, regional and state transportation administrators and planners, the media, university officials, and other city managers and city planners. The manager and the manager's staff were proud that they ran an open process and touched all the bases.

When the regional transit agency revealed the location of the main route of the rail system, political support melted like snow in the Sahara. The selected route ran straight down the main street of the suburban city connecting its core businesses and city hall with key economic and service centers in the rest of the metroplex. It also ran down the middle of the home city's automobile row and threatened, during the construction stage, to thoroughly disrupt the thriving firms that depend on a regional market. Local and regional owners such as the auto dealerships and repair shops could see some long-run gains, but they wondered how many people would use the train to shop for automobiles. The potential for short-run loses quickly got their full collective attention and heated the political pot.

Shortly, the council and mayor bailed out, blaming the city manager and the city staff for not fully informing them of the options, the route, and the potential economic losses to local businesses. The media jumped in for the kill. The local chamber of commerce called for the city manager's resignation. Some rapid fence mending and smoothing actions saved the manager's job. The city withdrew its support for the preferred route and moderated its support of the whole system.

What are some lessons about political life that may be drawn from this example? First, the city manager was correct in taking the lead in this project. Without the manager's lead, the city would have been left out of the transit plan and could not have garnered any of its potential long-run benefits. Second, the manager probably played the game well. The manager and staff conducted a public inquiry into rapid transit. Public discussions considered the pros and cons of joining in the regional plan before developing support for the project. It was an open, inclusive process with the key stakeholders at the table. Third, everyone seems to have missed the issue of the trade-offs between short- and long-run benefits and costs to the politically significant automobile dealerships. Innovations may provide far-reaching and long-term values, but politics, it seems, is narrow-minded and has short-term vision. Fourth, scapegoats are found for political failures. In this case, the city manager became the scapegoat.

The ever-changing political environment leaves the administrator in a double bind. Actively engaging the political environment is a hallmark of innovative, adaptive management. Reconciling political conflicts with organizational objectives, however, is tough sailing. As distasteful as many managers find the vagueness, contradictions, and messiness of political life, they must participate in it. For many issues, there are few others willing to provide responsible political leadership (Ammons & Newell, 1989; Nalbandian, 1991).

The Intractability of the Organization

High-level public managers, whose traditional task is to accomplish organizational goals, lead organizations to produce results that fulfill public needs. Getting the members of the organization to cooperate, as we have discussed in Chapters Three and Four, is not an easy task. Keeping the organization on track and achieving even modest organizational goals challenges the most innovative and creative executives. Adaptive and innovative management requires executives to link the internal behavior of the organization to the fluid, confusing external environment.

Many management situations involve estimation of risk. Experience and training equip persons to handle risk situations. We have posited, however, that the manager lives in the swamp where it is even difficult to estimate the probabilities of occurrence of key events. Here managers face *uncertainty,* wherein situational conditions can be assumed to be random.

Warren Bennis (1969), both a practicing manager and an academic, has characterized these uncertain management conditions as the metaphor of the arrow (see Figure 6.1). The arrow represents the organization moving through time and space toward a target. Note that in our representation the arrow is not about to hit the target. Good managers will attempt to shift the movement of the arrow more toward the target but will have limited success. Why is this so?

First, the target is probably elusive. Initially, it may have been poorly defined and dimly perceived. Further, in a dynamic world filled with changing expectations, it may have moved or morphed in some way. Second, the main body of the arrow, which

Figure 6.1

represents the living organization, has momentum of its own. Most of the movement of the arrow through time-space is the result of hundreds of thousands, perhaps millions, of decisions made by the scores of individuals who comprise the organization. These decisions—which range from such mundane concerns as "Will I go to work today?" to such cosmic concerns as "There is a 6 percent shortfall in state revenue this year; where will I cut back?"—combine to push the arrow through time-space under its own momentum, not really under the control of anyone.

The bottom fletch (feather) of the arrow represents the efforts of the managers to manage. They push the arrow more toward a path that will cause it to come closer to the target (which may be moving). Note that the mass of the fletch, *managing efforts,* is smaller than the mass of the organization as a whole. This recognizes the fact that only a portion of the total work of the organization guides it to *direct* achievement of the formal goals of the unit.

The top fletch represents external *random shocks* to the organization that also alter its path. Note that as illustrated, the mass of this fletch is less than the mass of the main body. Yet it may vary in size under different circumstances. The external events are frequently more influential than the constructive efforts of administrators in determining motion toward goals.

Because the shocks are random, some push it more toward the target and others push it away. The problem is that at any given moment, at any given place in the journey toward or away from the target, managers are hard pressed to know just which shocks will affect the organization and in what direction they will push it.

Adaptive management is an interesting but chancy game. The organization tends to go its own way. Managers try to anticipate helpful external events and take advantage of them and to predict deleterious events and counter them. While they do this, they attempt to adjust the internal practices and behavior of their organization to overcome inertia and enhance organizational capacity to absorb negative shocks.

High-Level Management Functions

People inside and outside public organizations expect a lot from high-level public managers. Managers themselves have bought into the idea of high-powered executives leading high performance organizations. Much of the current emphasis in theory and in practice on entrepreneurial management feeds on the notion of organization Supermen and Wonder Women leading their organizations to higher and higher levels of performance. This raises the question of what may be the limits of managerial effort.

The Multiple Functions and Roles of Management

Organization and management theorists have long pondered what constitutes the *main* functions of high-level managers. Henri Fayol (1949), one of the founders of the Classical School of management and organization theory, laid out his five basic managerial functions as planning, organizing, coordinating, commanding and controlling. Frederick Taylor (1913), an exponent of the classical approach, and Mary Parker Follett (1924), a critic of the classical approach, were early prophets of American management. They contributed much to the understanding of the functions that managers carry out in guiding and sustaining their organizations. Although very different in their approaches to what constitutes effective leadership and good organizational management, Taylor and Follett shared Fayol's notion of multiple managerial functions. The effective high-level manager, whatever the management style and organizational model, carries out a wide range of functions.

Chester Barnard (1938) contributed to the idea of multiple management functions as he focused on what the chief executive must do to foster a positive organizational environment. He stressed that the executive's primary job is to maintain the organization in operation. According to Michael Harmon (1994), Barnard felt that certain "executive functions" are needed to ensure that the organization is well maintained over time. These included: (1) maintenance of organizational communication, (2) securing of essential services from individuals, and (3) formation of organizational purpose and objectives.

The conception of multiple executive functions found its most well known American expression in the *Papers on the Science of Administration* (Gulick & Urwick, 1937). Luther Gulick, the senior editor of the papers, expanded Fayol's model and coined the famous acronym POSDCORB to describe the main functions of the executive (Harmon, 1994; Mintzberg, 1973).

The following is a representation of Gulick and Urwick's summary statement about the work of the chief executive (1937, p. 13).
"What is the work of the chief executive?"
" What does he do?"
The answer is **POSDCORB**.

POSDCORB is a made-up word designed to call attention to the various functional elements of the work of a chief executive, because "administration" and "management" have lost all specific content. **POSDCORB** is made up of the initials of the following activities:

> *Planning*, that is, working out in broad outline the things than need to be done and the methods for doing them to accomplish the purpose set for the enterprise;

> *Organizing*, that is the establishment of the formal structure of authority through which work subdivisions are arranged, defined and coordinated for the defined objectives;

> *Staffing*, that is the whole body of bringing in and training the staff and maintaining favorable conditions of work;

> *Directing*, that is the continuous task of making decisions and embodying them in specific and general orders and instructions and serving as leader of the enterprise;

> *Co-ordinating*, that is the all important duty of inter-relating the various parts of the work;

> *Reporting*, that is keeping those to whom the executive is responsible informed as to what is going on, which thus includes keeping himself/herself and his/her subordinates informed through records, research and inspection;

> *Budgeting,* with all that goes with budgeting in the form of fiscal planning, accounting and control.

Gulick adds staffing, reporting, and budgeting to Fayol's model. He softens the notion of commanding and controlling to directing. Gulick's list is inclusive and contains most of the functions earlier theorists included; albeit in different terms.

Although some find **POSDCORB** quaint, the idea of multiple management functions underlies many discussions of management and leadership (Denhardt & Denhardt, 2008; Harmon, 1994; Van Wart, 2005). Henry Mintzberg (1973) notes this fact and finds that **POSDCORD** continues to live. Mintzberg says that the Classical School and **POSDCORB** "served to label our areas of ignorance, and may have [informed] managers what they should be doing . . . but too long served to block our search for a deeper understanding of the work of the manager" (1973, p. 11).

After reviewing eight schools of thought on managerial functions, Mintzberg finds most conceptions of managerial work wanting. He then summarizes the empirical literature and his own research. He develops the notion of Ten Working Roles and teases them out in his book *The Nature of Managerial Work* (1973). Although he focuses on private sector organizations and empirical work on managers in them, we can use his model to show the breadth and complexity of what is commonly expected of public executives.

The work of the manager consists of many overlapping and complementary roles. A *role* is defined as "an organized set of behaviors belonging to an identifiable office or position" (Sabin & Allen, 1968, as presented by Mintzberg, 1973, p. 54). The high-level manager, argues Mintzberg, links the organization and its environment. Every manager, as we have repeatedly noted in this book, must guide the organization within a complex, swampy environment. In doing so, the manager carries out various roles. Mintzberg specifies ten roles, common to all managers ranging from the city manager to the shop foreman in the vehicle pool, and divides them into three clusters as follows (pp. 58-94): **Interpersonal roles** (use of manager's status and authority in interpersonal relationships)

- Figurehead (the manager as a formal symbol of the organization)

- Leader (the manager as guide and motivator)

- Liaison (the manager as exchange agent with high-status individuals outside the organization)

Informational roles (service as the receiver and transmitter of information, inside and outside of the organization)

- Monitor (the manager as a seeker of information that enables her or him to understand what is taking place internally and externally)

- Disseminator (the manager as a primary sender of external information into the organization and internal information from one subordinate to another)

- Spokesperson (manager as transmitter of information into the organization's environment)

Decisional roles (make significant strategic decisions)

- Entrepreneur (manager as initiator and designer of systematic change)

- Disturbance handler (manager as the take-charge person; the person who makes corrections to handle the crises of the moment)

- Resource allocator (manager as the person in charge of strategic resources (money, time, materials, equipment, human resources, and reputation)

- Negotiator (manager as a participant in negotiation activity)

It is often said that managers are generalists. Certainly the lists of functions and roles considered thus far suggest that managers are generalists. They guide a group of specialists toward the completion of organizational goals, objectives, and strategies. But, as Mintzberg (1973) forcefully notes, managers are actually specialists in securing strategic efforts. He means that high-level managers should not deal with tactical issues, but rather take the broader and longer-term view. High-level managers need to strategically lead the organization through the swamp. When compared to the other kinds of work, successfully carrying out the five or ten functions and roles invites managers to invoke their own kind of specialization: getting others to work well together. Remember, however, that we have shown that getting others to work together is not an easy task.

Implications of the Multiple Functions and Roles

Society expects that high-level managers should excel continuously in carrying out all of the roles outlined above. This, however, is unlikely. The job is too complex for a single person to do well. Managers often take too much of the job on themselves despite its complexity and demands. As Mintzberg (1973) notes, the manager often feels compelled to perform a large amount of work at an unrelenting pace. Many managers never escape from the job. They work long hours, take few breaks, and take work home with them. It is difficult to convince high-level managers to take time off, relax, and recharge. In our own training work with high-level managers such as city managers, police chiefs, and planning directors, we often found them to be *micro-managers* deeply involved in the day-to-day affairs of the entire program, department, or organization. Most of them aspired to be top-level generalists early in their careers. Ironically, it is the attention to detail that drives many and earned them a shot at a high-level job in the first place. They are not really either generalists or specialists. Police chiefs, for example, should not try to be *top cops*, but rather strategic leaders of the department who link it with the external world. It is hard, however, to convince a person who has worked his or her way up from the ranks that management of the day-to-day affairs of the department are best left to others.

Many successful managers have found ways to reduce the pressing demands of the multiple functions and roles of management. Mintzberg suggests *job sharing* as one useful approach to reducing the scope and demands of high-level management (Mintzberg, 1973). Different managers have different interests, experiences, skills, and traits. A manager gravitates to certain tasks because of these differences and personal preferences, leaving to other members of the organization responsibility for other functions of high-level management. For example, it is common for U.S. presidents to pick certain themes and areas on which to concentrate and then let others take leadership in other areas. The second and third in command often carry out important roles and functions in lieu of the formal chief executive. City managers, for example, often divide the high-level functions among deputy and assistant city managers and deal with the outside political relationships with the city council and civic leaders themselves (Nalbandian, 1991; Vanacour, 1990).

The primary purpose of the public manager is to ensure that the organization—Executive Office of the Presidency, Arizona State Department of Administration, the New York Port Authority, the City of Pittsburgh, or the Director of MARTA—provides public value to its customers and citizens. In doing this, as Mintzberg (1973) and Moore (1995) suggest, the manager must actually do four things very well:

(1) Work with others, especially other members of the management system, to maintain stability of the organization's internal operations.

(2) Lead the organization's strategy-making system and work with others to adapt the organization in a systematic way to its changing, murky environment.

(3) Make sure that the organization serves the ends of outside authority and the public.

(4) Serve as a major communication link between the organization and its environment.

Successful managers who may wish to live to a comfortable old age will find ways to accomplish these four tasks and at the same time escape from the unrelenting pressures and time demands of the job. We shall turn to further discussion of these themes later in the chapter.

Inter-organizational Relationships

Public agencies do not govern alone. Public managers are increasingly aware that governance involves a convoluted set of relationships attending many of the activities of their organization. For example, the provision of such basic municipal services as fire and police protection involves those departments in relationships with many different organizations. The list of active participants includes at least the following: (1) neighborhood and homeowners associations, (2) other city departments, (3) comparable public safety departments in other cities and counties in the region, (4) state and sub-national public safety agencies, (5) federal agencies, (6) private firms and nonprofit organizations at all levels, and (7) unions and professional associations. Not every action by police and fire immediately involve all of these organizations, but most are sufficiently involved in the weekly activities of the municipal public safety departments that the fire and police chiefs are fully aware of these relationships. Capable managers find ways to cultivate, maintain, and use these interdepartmental, interagency, interjurisdictional, intergovernmental, and intersectoral relationships.

Inter-departmental linkages include communications and working relationships with other departments in the same organization. For example, fire prevention programs require the municipal fire department to cooperate and coordinate its efforts with those of the city manager's (or mayor's) office and with the municipal police, planning, housing, social services, transportation, and public affairs departments. These linkages, communications, and coproduction efforts occur at all organizational levels: line staff, supervisory, middle management, and top management. Key to our concerns in this chapter are the strategic relationships maintained by top-level managers such as the fire chief and the departmental management team with their counterparts in other city departments and programs.

Inter-jurisdictional relationships link the organization with similar roughly co-equal departments or programs in different locations. Such linkages may involve formal inter-agency agreements to share resources and efforts to co-produce improved services to citizens. Inter-library loan and exchange programs, for example, permit borrowers to tap into the resources of regional, national, and even international libraries. Although electronic systems have made inter-library programs more effective, such coordinated efforts require considerable contributions by all participating libraries. The administrative head of each participating library must use significant strategic resources including that leader's time and energy to keep the inter-library systems functioning well.

Intergovernmental relationships encompass the vertical and horizontal relationships with other governments in the American system of federalism. Strictly speaking, the inter-jurisdictional relationships discussed above are a part of the intergovernmental system. We treat them as separate and distinctive because local governments have so many inter-jurisdictional relationships. In this section, we focus on four intergovernmental relationships: the relationship between 1) the local governments and the state government to which they are beholden, 2) local governments and the national government, 3) state government and other state governments, and 4) state governments and the national government.

The intended functioning of the National Incident Management System (NIMS) versus its actual execution during Hurricane Katrina offers a useful example of intergovernmental relationships gone awry. The design of NIMS contemplates timely collaboration among public agencies and their constituent subunits. It is intent upon "establishing an Incident Command System, standardizing communication, working for joint preparedness (planning, training, qualifications, certifications), creating a Joint Information System to disseminate a unified message, and setting up a National Integration Center to guide the process of coordination" (Lester & Krejci, 2007, p. 84). Although training and inter-agency cooperation occurred before the hurricane's landfall, the response of public agencies revealed problematical communications (Garnett & Kouzmin, 2007) and inadequate and tardy coordination. Dealing with such emergencies as they unfold requires both management skills and improvisation (Somers & Svara, 2009).

Inter-sectoral relationships involve the public organization in working ties with private and nonprofit organizations. Pressure to move service provision to the private sector coupled with reduced public resources lead American governments more and more toward moving traditional public services to private firms. At the same time, communities increasingly depend upon nonprofit organizations to provide key social services. Clearly, public organizations charged with public safety, recreation, housing, health care, waste disposal, and a wide range of other goods and services work with and depend on private and nonprofit providers.

Even without the political and economic pressures to do more with less and to turn to the market, public agencies would still engage in inter-sectoral behavior. An example from air quality management programs will illustrate this point. The Clean Air Act of 1990 requires all states to develop and implement a State Implementation Plan (SIP) designed to bring the air quality in non-attainment areas into compliance with federal air quality standards within a prescribed period of time. Each state has a department charged with administering environmental laws. This agency usually is responsible for development, implementation, and evaluation of the SIP.

The actual implementation of the SIP and the attainment of air quality standards, however, require interaction among public, private, and nonprofit organizations. This amounts to inter-sectoral *coproduction*. In this application, coproduction means cooperative joint behavior among organizations to produce something of public value, in this example, cleaner air. Administrators of state-level abatement programs such as vehicle exhaust inspections must try to work cooperatively with

(1) managers of voluntary abatement efforts by private firms such as the operators of energy generating plants burning coal, and

(2) managers of efforts by nonprofit public interest centers that try to force compliance with federal and state air quality standards by regulated firms through litigation or the threat of litigation.

Relationships among the regulatory agency, private firms it regulates, and public interest organizations are often unfriendly. Trying to get all stakeholders to the table and enticing them to work together in implementation of the SIP challenges even the most creative and nimble public administrator. Nonetheless, environmental quality managers must collaborate and lead their agencies in complex webs of inter-departmental, inter-jurisdictional, intergovernmental, and inter-sectoral settings.

The combination of the major constraining forces outlined above—the demanding and risky political environment, the intractability of the organization, the executive's understanding of management functions, and the sets of networks—makes administrative life interesting and exacting.

Responding to the Constraints

Most societal pressures and management traditions equate growth with success and progress. Decline in resources and organizational size requires a new perspective. *Wicked* problems and swamp conditions also oblige a new perspective. Moving outside of the home organization into the messiness of wicked problems and complex networks is arduous. Dealing with the conflicted, murky political environment frustrates administrators. Not all managers adjust to the new direction or assumptions.

Public management continues to be one of the most challenging of all professions. The fluid environment produces a sense of urgency and uncertainty among managers. Life in the swamp creates stress. Fighting alligators is no fun; draining swamps is nearly impossible. Although administrators strive to cope as best they can, uncharted crises frustrate many.

Responses to the perceived chaos and darkness of the swamp vary. Some managers vote with their feet and move on to new jobs. Many leave the public sector and take positions with private firms. Others rotate to positions in other jurisdictions. Some continue to do what they have done in the past with the hope that things soon will return to normal. Changes appear to them as anomalous, and they hope that as things return to normal, they will become more comfortable. They try to wait out change. Others take a positive attitude and try to alter the way they manage and the way their organizations operate. This adaptive behavior of the last group promises to assist them in learning to manage in the swampy conditions of contemporary society.

All of these types of responses are reasonable. Change of location and position often refreshes the manager; it is a cure for burnout and tedium. Past experience applied to new situations also often works. Incrementalism makes sense, and, in the long run, some things move toward historical norms that appear familiar. More active responses also succeed by opening the organization to more input from the environment and thereby enhancing learning on the part of administrators.

Facing Up to the Swamp

Management is an interesting but chancy game. The organization tends to go its own way. Managers try to anticipate helpful events and take advantage of them and to predict deleterious events and defuse them. At the same time they do this, they attempt to adjust the internal practices and behavior of their organization to overcome inertia and enhance organizational capacity to handle negative shocks.

Taking clues from Moore (1995), Koteen (1997) and Popovich (1998), the following discussion of how managers may strategically face up to the swamp touches on five themes:

(1) Managers must make the organization more efficient.

(2) Managers must become more adept at building and using community support.

(3) Managers must ensure that the organization provides substantive value to authorities, citizens, customers, and other beneficiaries.
(4) Managers must explore and utilize new organizational approaches.
(5) Managers must actively mobilize political support for the organization and its goals.

Responding in the Organization: More Efficient Management

Nearly every agency and manager will say they can do a better job if they have more resources. Given resource constraints, the issue becomes one of being more effective with fewer resources. Meeting resource reduction is often called *cutback management* (Levine, 1978, 1979). The main strategy in cutback efforts is deciding which past activities are least essential to the agency's mission and reducing or eliminating these until expenditures equal available resources.

Under severe resource reduction, these kinds of responses may be the best approach. Most agencies, however, do not fully use the resources they have. A more enlightened response to resource reduction is to seize the opportunity to reform operations internally. This process often kicks-off with three piercing questions: What are we trying to do? How are we trying to do it? What is a better way? There are at least four strategies that may be pursued.

The first is a variation of the general cutback strategy. It requires administrators to ensure that as much as possible of what the agency currently does leads to attainment of its mission and goals. Over time, many administrators get sloppy in their resource allocation and performance assessment activities. Resources often are devoted to activities that do not directly support agency goals. Managers periodically need to do an internal inventory and performance audit to see if all activities are necessary and if they can be done in a more effective manner. This includes reviewing the organization's use of technology, equipment effectiveness, and appropriate facility design. Most managers will find activities to cut or reduce or change when conducting self-evaluations.

A second approach improves the information available at various decision points. Lazy, content organizations make nearly all decisions according to some fixed routine. This can be disastrous under tight resource conditions or in the face of a changing environment. More productive organizations strive to make a variety of information available. This usually involves some form of management information system. Such information-rich organizations often make use of some kind of multilevel, participatory planning and management. Although only some public bureaucracies practice participatory management, those that do are advantaged by tapping into the information and knowledge base of all employees.

A third option increases internal training. This sounds counterintuitive because training is often treated as a frill and is one of the first things cut in budget rollbacks. Yet many employees do not understand their roles in and contributions to the overall organization. Many lack appropriate skill levels for the positions they currently fill. Many also do not have commitment to and support for the goals of the organization. Training, which in the short run takes time and resources away from service activities, actually can save resources by making individual employees and work groups more effective. The challenge is to reserve some resources for these activities, even under resource constraints.

A final example, drawn from military organizations and defense contractors, is the establishment of mobile teams of "trouble-shooters." Trouble-shooters are available to move to different places in the organization to put out "fires," lend special support, or temporarily increase resources available for a given task. This is difficult to accomplish under resource constraint conditions, but every organization under stress needs a team that has good cohesion and that can be deployed for assistance to subparts of the organization.

Responding in the Community: Developing Support and Contributions

Bureaucracies in the ordinary course of events are good at developing support systems for their lobbying activities with the legislature, executive, and other agencies. Frequently they develop strong relationships with clientele groups, even to the detriment of the executive's attempts to control them. The same instincts and techniques may be used to enhance their capacity to respond positively to change.

Few bureaucracies make effective use of advisory boards and citizen groups. Yet they need a more broadly based information system and public support system to do well in the face of a rapidly changing environment (Needleman & Needleman, 1974; Yin & Yates, 1974). Some agencies, mostly among local governments, have learned that they can educate the public. Such efforts develop broader positive support and enhance public acceptance and compliance with public agency goals. Managers need to get out of their offices and meet with leaders and ordinary citizens in their native habitat. Regular solicitation of formal and informal input by private citizens and citizen organizations will provide administrators with valuable information concerning the performance of their agencies.

In addition to providing information or participating in decision making, in some instances, ordinary citizens are regularly involved in the production and delivery of public services by agencies. This has been termed *citizen coproduction* because citizens actually become part of the street-level bureaucracy in the sense that they join with the public bureaucracy in providing, producing, and delivering the service (Bish & Neubert, 1977; Rich, 1981; Wilson, 1982). In several municipal-type services such as police protection, recreation, education, and libraries, direct citizen involvement in the production stream of agencies has resulted in improved services, reduced costs, and greater understanding and support for the bureaucracy. In fact, coproduction has proven so effective that it is often a preferred option when localities face possible reduction in revenues.

Coproduction activities may take many forms. A few examples will illustrate the variety of contributions citizens make to the production of services. A common example is *Neighborhood Watch,* in which local residents form cooperative arrangements to watch over the property of their neighbors and to report any suspicious activities to the local law enforcement authorities. Another example is the voluntary teachers or teachers' aides who, without compensation, assist regular teachers in special math or reading sessions. This is a particularly interesting example, because it puts underused community resources to public use. The suicide hotline serves as a final example. It melds private and public resources into a communication center to which depressed and potentially suicidal persons may call for help. Every city and town has hundreds if not thousands of such examples of coproduction. What is new is that agencies under fiscal stress are seeking out new and expanded opportunities to secure direct private and voluntary contributions to bureaucratic production of services.

These efforts to involve bureaucracies more in community affairs and citizens more in production of services have beneficial effects exceeding cost reduction and improvement of services. They provide more joint understanding and public support. They tend to reduce public hostility toward government and bureaucratic cynicism toward the public. This contributes to the development of social capital.

Responding in the Community: Creating Additional Value

Complacent bureaucratic behavior is unethical. The manager must lead the organization into new arenas and new levels of service, even in the face of limited resources. Infusing a sense of public purpose is difficult, but it must be done if the typical public organization is to be worthy of its label of "public."

"How are we doing?" is the key question (Ammons, 2001). Managers who seriously ask the organization and its members to ponder and answer this question systematically help them go beyond the ordinary. Those who practice strategic management must regularly ask and answer this question for everything the organization does (Bryson, 2004; Koteen, 1997; Moore, 1995).

Seriously asking and answering this question requires the manager to develop and practice a collaborative management style. Koteen (1997, pp. 55-57) lists practices and commitments common to successful top-level collaborative managers. What follows builds closely on his presentation, but in some places uses different terms than he uses. Nonetheless, the basic framework and content were originally Koteen's.

Practice 1: *Challenge the process.*
The top managers who imbue organizations with strategic choices seek to change the current situation. In doing so, they commit themselves and the organization to searching for opportunities to change, grow, innovate, and improve. Further, they ask the organization and its members to join them in taking risks and learning from mistakes.

Practice 2: *Develop a shared vision.*
Strategic leaders help create the future by developing a vision of what needs to be done and getting others to share it. They seek out the aspirations of others and try to blend their vision with the interests of others.

Practice 3: *Enable others to act.*
Strategic leaders actively seek partners inside and outside the organization. They share power, responsibilities, and information. They expand the discretion and visibility of others.

Practice 4: *Model the way.*
Although this reads like a Zen saying, it is basically American. Good managers find ways to demonstrate high standards and moral leadership by the way they think and act. Managers must behave in ways consistent with the ethical values they espouse. They also must help others succeed by giving them choices and supporting what they do.

Practice 5: *Encourage the heart.*
Another Zen-like injunction, this means that managers must give recognition to every success. This supports the use of measurable performance standards that let people know when things are done well. It also requires the manager to develop teams and then celebrate team accomplishments through positive public recognition and rewards.

Responding to New Organizational Approaches: Entrepreneurship, Collaboratives, and Public-Private Partnerships

As life in the administrative swamp evolves, the intractability of some challenges and the complexity of some opportunities call for a wide range of organizational approaches. These new forms of governance impose new demands on public administrators for adaptive management. We will review the more common trends: entrepreneurship, collaboratives, and public-private partnerships.

    Entrepreneurship. Historically, the public sector is viewed as bureaucratic. It is considered overly conservative, change resistant, and slow moving. To the extent that it does adapt, Windrum (2008) claims that changes occur from forces outside of public agencies. External environmental turbulence motivates public organizations to adjust internally, re-evaluate strategy, and re-engineer operational practices (Morris & Jones, 1999).

Entrepreneurship has emerged as a prime organizational approach to the administrative swamp within the last two to three decades. Morris and Jones (1999) conceptualize *entrepreneurship* as a management practice undergirded by pillars of innovativeness and risk taking within a proactive stance. *Innovativeness* here conveys engagement in efforts to generate novel approaches to challenges and opportunities. *Risk-taking* necessitates reasoned calculation. It entails committing organizational resources toward addressing challenges and exploiting opportunities where failure is possible. *Proactiveness* involves implementation. It means energized leadership in taking the strategic steps necessary to achieve an objective in a timely fashion. Policy and service entrepreneurs arise and assume risk for public sector gains as "innovation champions" (Windrum, 2008). They create value for citizens by prompting unique combinations of resources to meet public priorities (Morris & Jones, 1999). The reality of public sector entrepreneurship contests the Weberian notion of public agencies as static bureaucracies where innovative ideas are smothered (Windrum, 2008).

Quite often, public sector entrepreneurship reflects the strong influence of market-based mechanisms to achieve public purposes. This trend is so prevalent that public sector entrepreneurship and market-based mechanisms are frequently referred to synonymously (Osborne & Gaebler, 1992; Osborne & Hutchinson, 2004; Kamensky & Morales, 2006). Kamensky and Morales identify and provide a broad range of examples of market-based mechanisms considered entrepreneurial in *Competition, Choice, and Incentives in Government Programs* (2006). They organize these under three subject areas: public services delivery, internal government services delivery, and regulatory standards or prices (see Table 6.1).

Table 6.1:
Market-Based Approaches Considered Entrepreneurial

Subject Area	Example
Public service delivery	Competitive sourcing Public-prvate partnership Vouchers Outsourcing Contracting out Privatization Divestiture or asset sale
Internal government service delivery	Government-operated franchises Performance-based organizations Pay for performance Competitive grants and loans
Regulatory standards or prices	Tradable permits Auctions Bidding User charges/fees Bartering Risk-based enforcement Deposit/refund systems Tax incentives Subsidies Taxes

Adapted from Kamensky and Morales (2006, p. 8).

Entrepreneurship does not emerge without public administrators cultivating it. They "play a key, pivotal role, setting priorities, undertaking interorganizational initiatives where appropriate, and encouraging and rewarding actors for their contributions" (Bernier & Hafsi, 2007, p. 494). They also perform in a symbolic role as they develop new organizational yardsticks and innovation goals. They promote proactiveness and calculated risks.

Borins (2000) finds that entrepreneurial innovation tends to arise from five conditions or challenges. First, initiatives can come from the political realm, either a legislative mandate or a special push from an elected policy-maker. Second, new administrative leadership for the organization may result in entrepreneurial action. Third, a crisis can spur the need for substantive change. Fourth, failure to adapt to organizational environmental pressures and dissatisfaction with current agency performance may motivate new initiatives. And fifth, new opportunities and technological advances may prompt a flourish of entrepreneurial activities.

Entrepreneurship is a widely used strategy for facing organizational change with differing perspectives. The National Performance Review (Gore, 1993) identifies four overarching principles of entrepreneurship. These revolve around (1) reduction of red tape; (2) promotion of customer, or citizen, satisfaction; (3) empowerment of employees, and (4) promotion of cost efficient performance.

Moon (1999, pp. 32-33) adds to this by labeling three dimensions of "managerial entrepreneurship." First, "product-based managerial entrepreneurship" underscores qualitative improvement of public services, often measured through some form of citizen feedback. Second, "process-based managerial entrepreneurship" encompasses streamlining procedures and internal communications and interactions. Euphemistically, this refers to elimination of "red tape" (Gore, 1993). Third, "behavior-based managerial entrepreneurship" involves taking risks in making organizational changes and decisions.

Relatedly, Morris and Jones (1999) view the so-called "reinventing government" perspective as revolving around three major entrepreneurial tenets popularized by Osborne and Gaebler (1992). First, *downsizing* calls for trimming down public agencies—focusing on the right public priorities and achieving those priorities in the right way. Second, *reengineering* refers to reexamining and redesigning work processes to get the results that citizens want at the lowest cost (this is akin to Moon's "process-based managerial entrepreneurship"). Third, *continuous improvement* marshals participative management and reform from within, and constantly inspires motivation and empowerment to ratchet-up quality.

Reflecting a life-cycle theory, Bernier and Hafsi (2007) say that entrepreneurship disappears as an organization matures, and greater emphasis is placed on operating in a more machine-like manner. The bureaucratic tendency to standardize dampens entrepreneurial ingenuity over time. However, as complexity and chaotic conditions return, especially due to turbulent environmental changes, public agencies attempt to make the most of intellectual capital throughout the organization. This encourages a revival of entrepreneurship to improve operational capabilities.

Public administrators must be sensitive to these cyclical patterns and differing perspectives. They need to bring out the best in others while traveling the swamp under changing circumstances. Further, Terry (1993) cautions that the concept of public entrepreneurship evokes a romanticized view of public administrators as extraordinary change agents that transform public agencies at will. Certainly that is not the case. Public agencies are susceptible to bad as well as good changes. Absent a market test for feedback, a bad change may persist for years (Wilson, 1989). Consequently, although entrepreneurship provides many tools to address public service issues, it also must be bounded by prudence and democratic values.

Collaboratives. Many public administrators serve as leaders of their organization and work with multiple organizations and citizens through some form of collaborative. As a consequence, they must be able to exercise autonomy and interdependence as well as know when to assert authority and to seek participation (O'Leary, Gazley, & McGuire, 2009). At the same time, they continue to face the traditional norms of efficiency, effectiveness, responsiveness, and accountability (O'Toole, 1997). This obligates them to balance technical needs for clarity about program authority with demands for inclusiveness and authentic participation (King, Felty, & Susel, 1998; O'Toole, 1997).

Collaboration involves two or more organizations working together to hunt for a "mutually determined solution" to common objectives (Sink, 1998). It tends to be a purposive relationship aimed at solving an issue for stakeholders by discovering a solution within a given set of constraints (Agranoff & McGuire, 2004). It may include sharing intellectual capital, systems learning, and consensus building.

Effort is voluntary in collaborations. Motivations usually surface from a desire to attain a synergy from increased capacity or resource sharing. Fosler (2002) finds that collaboration is characterized by the degree of mutual planning, alignment of objectives, approaches, agendas, and resources, with an equitable stake in risks and benefits. In the management arena, collaboration is contrasted with lower levels of cooperation by requiring four elements (Gray, 1989): (1) stakeholder interdependence, (2) constructive approaches to participant differences, (3) shared ownership of decisions, and (4) collective responsibility for the future success of the partnership. Some consider American federalism as a strong example of collaboration (Agranoff & McGuire, 2004).

Collaboratives refer to various modes of managing across traditional organizational borders (O'Leary, Gazley, & McGuire, 2009). They have come of age since O'Toole (1997) suggested their importance as an integral dimension of governance. Conceptually, collaborative public management describes the process of facilitating and operating in multiorganizational arrangements to solve problems that cannot be solved or easily solved by single organizations (Agranoff & McGuire, 2004). Collaborative means co-labor to achieve common goals, often working across boundaries and in multi-sector and multi-actor relationships. Such efforts have increased the latitude to approach public problems in creative ways (Page, 2004). They are based on the value of reciprocity and may include participatory governance: "the active involvement of citizens in government decision making" (O'Leary, Gazley, & McGuire, 2009, p. 3).

Although many scholars and practitioners use the terms on the continuum of collaborative services synonymously, research indicates qualitative differences exist based upon the intensity of various service relationships (Selden, Sowa, & Sandfort, 2006). Cooperation refers to support through informal and personal relationships between organizational representatives. Coordination involves deliberate strategic moves between organizations to advance mutual objectives. Collaboration engages close and mutual sharing of resources, authority, and benefits. Further, collaboration may extend to include joint planning, budgeting, and staffing. Service integration occurs when two or more organizations coproduce new public goods and services for common clients. Service integration usually represents significant service delivery improvements through greater efficiency, economy, effectiveness, or some combination of all three.

The potential downside of collaboratives concerns possible mission drift, real or perceived loss of institutional autonomy or accountability, cooptation of participants, fiscal instability, performance measurement difficulties, and costliness of involvement (Gazley & Brudney, 2007). Page (2004) finds that making colloboratives accountable for performance results is challenging. Accountability problems may arise from the legal, hierarchical, political, and professional realms.

Closely aligned with collaboratives, the term "networks" is also in vogue. In contrast to collaboratives, Mandell (1999) contends that networks arise as linkages among collaborating organizations become more formalized along mutual interests. "The institutional glue congealing networked ties may include authority bonds, exchange relations, and coalitions based on common interests" (O'Toole, 1997, p. 45). Additionally, the size of networks dwarfs the relative size of collaboratives. While a collaborative may include several local or regional agencies, networks, such as the Medicare program, can be national in scope. It functions across a nation-wide network of health professionals, insurers, and public agencies. Although networks may require sequential or concurrent activities by a host of actors, each action signifies movement of independent organizations.

Agranoff (2007) describes four general types of public networks. *Informational networks* permit stakeholder exchanges and education. *Developmental networks* go a step further than communication and engage in capacity building. *Outreach networks* focus on strategy to support information exchange and capacity building. *Action networks* involve information exchange and capacity building with planning and decision making superimposed.

Similar to collaboratives, just more formal and relatively larger, Agranoff (2007) observes that network activities revolve around several important functions. These include problem identification and clarification, mobilization and adaptation of resources, advancement of knowledge, building capacity, programming, and collaborative decision making. Public managers often find themselves operating in multi-organizational, networked arrangements to tackle projects and issues that cannot be worked out well by only one organization (O'Leary, Gazley, & McGuire, 2009). Networks are not replacing public agency management hierarchies but rather providing an alternative means to attack wicked problems. They nudge managers into working at the boundaries of public agencies to solve critical issues.

Public-Private Partnerships. *Public-private partnerships* denote initiatives financed and run through some alliance between government and one or more private sector enterprises. They attempt to combine advantages of both sectors or to cover for a disadvantage from one of the sectors. For example, public tax-exempt bonds may make a public-private partnership involving an infrastructure project fiscally viable (Koppenjan & Enserink, 2009). Public-private partnerships (sometimes called public-private or joint ventures) form to permit public and private organizations "to share the costs, risks, benefits, and profits" (Gansler 2006, p. 73). They may take shape in a wide variety of configurations to gain operational synergy from the partnership's activities. Common areas of mutual gain may include advantages achieved through intellectual capital, infrastructure, technology, financing, and operational capabilities. For effectiveness, Gansler suggests that such partnerships function in a competitive environment to keep the pressure on performance.

Public-private partnerships are institutional arrangements designed to mobilize the necessary resources for joint participation in a public and private mission. The relationships are grounded on shared responsibility, dialogue, cooperation, and management participation. In some instances, such collaboration facilitates better governance and more effective provision of services (Ysa, 2007). Often such a partnership may gain a competitive advantage, generate cost savings, enhance organizational learning, and produce superior services (O'Leary, Gazley, & McGuire 2009).

Peters (1998) suggests the following distinguishing characteristics for public partnerships: (1) two or more organizations involved, one of which is public; (2) representatives empowered to negotiate on their respective organization's behalf; (3) a long-term relationship independent of grants or contracts; (4) participant organizations bring valued contributions to the partnership; and (5) organizations share outcome responsibilities. Naturally, the over-arching benefit of public-private partnerships revolves around mutual mission accomplishment not otherwise reachable, or not reachable as readily, without the partnership. Gansler's (2006) examples include increasing productivity, asset use, revenue production, overhead reduction, and facility investment. Adaptive management must ensure that the potential weaknesses of public private partnerships do not tarnish these benefits. Management must be vigilant to avoid the blurring of sector roles while minimizing risks. Additionally, sometimes the private sector's short-term return on investment requirements clash with, or negatively influence, long-term public agency goals (Koppenjan & Enserink, 2009). Attentive public administrators prepare themselves to cope with this possibility.

Ysa (2007) identifies three ideal types of public-private partnerships. First, *instrumental public-private partnerships* strive to reach specific operational objectives shared by the participants (e.g., a building project). Second, *symbolic public-private partnerships* aim to increase control over joint collaboration and to allocate resources. Such partnerships usually seek favorable public relations while relying upon traditional hierarchies (e.g., a health fair for low-income seniors offered through a public hospital in partnership with private health care providers). And, third, *organic public-private partnerships* emerge as the result of negotiable boundaries and rely on trust among the parties. Typically, these are based on reciprocity, interdependence, and shared values and interests (e.g., establishment of a business improvement district that includes at least one public agency).

Responding in the Networks: Building Political Support

Organizations, to be successful, must be legitimate and politically sustainable (Denhardt, Denhardt, & Aristigueta, 2009; Koteen, 1997; Moore, 1995). The organization and its efforts must attract authority, support, and funds from its political authorizing environment to which it is accountable (Moore, 1995). The *political authorizing environment*, characterized as part of the Iron Triangle in Chapter 2, provides public organizations with a formal mission, legal authority, and their basic institutional and financial resources.

Insofar as the manager cultivates and strengthens the organization's linkages with legislators, lobbyists, executives, other agencies, clientele groups, interest groups, and the media, the organization will be able to function. This simple idea is the cornerstone of the principle that effective strategic management of external networks is largely political in nature.

"Strategic management in the public sector begins by *looking up toward politics* [emphasis added]. By politics, I mean not only the current expectations and aspirations of citizens and their representatives but also the older political agreements formally enshrined in the legislation that defines public manager's mandates for action" (Moore, 1995, p. 105).

One might quarrel about looking up since politics surrounds public agencies, but looking toward political power and authority merits attention. Managers must mobilize political support, cultivate legitimacy, and encourage political coproduction in all of the networks touching their job. Participating in politics lets managers know what politically powerful actors think is important. Political institutions and processes, as we have shown in Chapters 2 and 5, can grant or deny the basic resources organizations need to carry out their functions. Finally, politics and the political process are among the main means of holding organizations and managers externally accountable (Meier & Bohte, 2007; Moore, 1995; Popovich, 1998).

Thus, managers at all levels should be students of politics. Further, they should be effective political managers. Many are. Some are not. Effective political managers, according to Moore (1995), accomplish four interrelated political outcomes for their organizations:

(1) Secure political mandates from political executives and legislatures to act in the public interest.

(2) Build continuing political support for the organization and its actions.

(3) Develop authorization for making changes and innovations.

(4) Mobilize decentralized political coproduction relationships.

Successful managerial politics is similar to a kind of political banking. One develops political credit by helping others—politicians, interest groups, other agencies, private firms, nonprofit organizations, citizen groups, and members of the mass media—do their jobs better. Insofar as the managers lend support and credit to other actors in their networks, they have some expectation of support and other resources when they need them.

Engaging in such reciprocal behavior presents managers with an ethical fine line to travel. Managers need to exercise just the right amount of political communication and influence (Menzel, 2007; Moore, 1995; Popovich, 1997). Too little political exchange with persons in authority and in coproductive relationships will not secure sufficient authority, political support, and resources for the strategic changes desired by the manager. Too much political exchange is likely to surprise, offend, or threaten those in authority or coproductive relationships. A well-informed political leader is a likely ally, but prudence is important.

The right balance between too much and too little depends on person, time, place, and issue. No hard and fast rules exist to guide the strategic manager to politically safe ground. Nonetheless, managers must take some political risks in developing and maintaining usable political networks.

Popovich (1997) makes an analogy that managing change in a complex political environment is like playing in a large jazz ensemble. "You start with a tempo in mind. The players begin to lay down some melody based on it. But you must listen closely. As soloists let loose or the rhythm section hits a grove, there will be changes. You have the dual responsibility of keeping the beat moving forward while responding to the tempo changes" (p. 45). Good managers have soul.

Efforts by practicing administrators to improve the capacity of themselves, their staffs, and their organizations to live in the swamp will prevail in spite of difficulties. Managers must make their organization more efficient. They must build and use community support. They must ensure that their organization continuously provides substantive value. They must avail themselves of new organizational approaches. And they must mobilize political support for their organization and its goals.

Much has been done recently to bring public administration into closer harmony with its turbulent environment. It remains, however, a stressed profession and a rapidly changing field of study. The swamp is not getting any easier to manage. Crisis management prevails. In the next chapter, we explore the idea of a *new and improved public administration*. Public administration and public administrators must be able to make hard choices and provide moral leadership in a time when public regard for the public service has waned.

Review and Study Questions

1. What is public value? How does it differ from private value?

2. How might high-performance organizations differ from public agencies of the past?

3. Which of the following four major clusters of constraints do you think causes the most problems for the high-level public managers, and why? (a) the political environment, (b) the intractability of the organization and its members, (c) the executive's understanding of high management functions, or (d) the inter-agency, inter-jurisdictional and inter-sectoral linkages and relationships.

4. Does the relative importance of the constraints noted in Question 3 vary at different levels in the American political system? For example, think about the variations that may occur for the American president, governor of your state, a mayor, city manager, and superintendent of a local school district. What are the differences, if any?

5. Mark Moore argues that managing of political constraints is the most demanding and most important function for high-level managers. Do you agree? Why or why not?

6. What makes public bureaucracies intractable? What practical things might a manager do to overcome this intractability? Can managers successfully overcome this intractability? Why or why not?

7. What do you see as the value of collaborative and public-private partnerships in local government? What challenges do they raise for the public agency involved?

8. What kinds of practical things can a manager do to reduce the number and variety of roles he or she must carry out?

9. Intergovernmental and intersectoral constraints and opportunities are increasingly important to governance by local governments. What are the main reasons for this? What kinds of actions can local managers take to cope creatively with these constraints and opportunities?

10. What is coproduction? Why is it becoming more common? What are its implications for effective public management?

11. Why do managers vote with their feet? What are some implications for job security of voting with one's feet? What are some implications for stability and continuity in government?

12. What do you think of the jazz metaphor used by Popovich? Is it a good idea for public managers to have political soul? Why or why not?

13. Can anyone actually manage public agencies in such a manner as to effectively adapt to the multitude of constraints attending the job? Would you like to try? Why or why not?

Exercises

1. Select a local or state agency. Find out what are its main mission, goals, and objectives. (Hint: look at its strategic plan, annual report, budget document, and Web site). Think about the external roles of the head of that organization. Pick a recent controversial issue confronting that administrator and organization. Based on media accounts, try to describe a *political map* involving that administrator, organization, and controversy. Who are the main actors/stakeholders? What are their points of pressure and resources? What are their values and interests? What can the manager do to cope with their values, interests, pressures, and resources? Does it appear to you that the manager had thought these kinds of issues out before the controversy started? Does it appear that the manager is accomplishing the kind of jazz ensemble behavior recommended by Popovich?

2. Select some specific current policy issue for your region. Identify the lead agency, that is, the public agency that has primary public responsibility for dealing with that issue. Pretend that you are an advisor to the head of that agency. Think about the range of coproducers that the lead public agency might be able to join with in producing public value. Note that potential coproducers may be private, public, or nonprofit, individuals or organizations. Coproducers could be local, regional, state, national, or even international. What kinds of strategic interventions could the lead agency undertake to make fuller use of coproducers in handling this issue? Write a make-believe analytic memorandum to the head administrator in which you lay out the problem, some potential coproducer allies and what they could contribute, and suggested strategies that might bring them into a coproductive relationship with the agency for this issue.

3. Conduct an interview with a high-level administrator in your state government or a regional office of your state government. In this interview, try to discover whether or not this person thinks that development and maintenance of political support is an important part of his or her job. See if you can find out why this person thinks this way. In what way does this attention or inattention to political communication affect this person's job performance?

References

Abramson, M. A., & Littman, I. D. (Eds.). (2002). *Innovation.* Lanham, MD: Rowman & Littlefield.

Ammons, D. (2001). *Municipal benchmarks, assessing local performance and establishing community standards* (2nd ed.). Thousand Oaks, CA: Sage.

Ammons, D., & Newell, C. (1989). *City executives: Leadership roles, work characteristics, and time management.* New York: State University of New York Press.

Agranoff, R. (2007). *Managing within networks: Adding value to public organizations*. Washington, DC: Georgetown University Press.

Agranoff, R., & McGuire. M. (2004). *Collaborative public management: New strategies for local governments*. Washington, DC: Georgetown University Press.

Ban, C. (1995). *How do public managers manage? Bureaucratic constraints, organizational culture, and the potential for reform*. San Francisco: Jossey-Bass.

Barnard, C. (1938). *The functions of the executive*. Cambridge, MA: Harvard University Press.

Bennis, W. G. (1969). *Organizational development: Its nature, origins, and prospects*. Menlo Park, CA: Addison-Wesley.

Bernier, L., & Hafsi. T. (2007). The changing nature of public entrepreneurship. *Public Administration Review, 67*, 488-503.

Bish, F. P., & Neubert, N. M. (1977). Citizen contributions to the production of community safety and security. In M. S. Rosentraub (Ed.), *Financing local government: New approaches to old problems* (pp. 34-50). Ft. Collins, CO: Western Social Science Association.

Borins, S. (2000). Loose cannons and rule breakers, or enterprising leaders? Some evidence about innovative public managers. *Public Administration Review, 60*, 498-507.

Bryson, J. (2004). *Strategic planning for public and nonprofit organizations* (3rd ed.). San Francisco: Wiley.

Cohen, S., & Eimicke. W. (1998). *Tools for innovators, creative solutions for managing public sector organizations*. San Francisco: Jossey-Bass.

Denhardt, R. B., & Denhardt, J. V. (2008). *Public administration, an action orientation* (6th ed.). Florence, KY: Wadsworth.

Denhardt, R. B., Denhardt, J. V., & Aristigueta, M. P. (2009). *Managing human behavior in public and nonprofit organizations* (2nd ed.). Thousand Oaks, CA: Sage.

Farmer, D. J. (1995). *The language of public administration, bureaucracy, modernity, and post modernity.* Tuscaloosa, AL: University of Alabama Press.

Fayol, H. (1949). *General and industrial management* (Constance Storrs, Trans.). London: Sir Isaac Pittman and Sons.

Follett, M. P. (1924). *Creative experience.* New York: Longmans, Green & Co.

Fosler, R. S. (2002). *Working better together: How government, business, and nonprofit organizations can achieve public purposes through cross sector collaboration, alliances, and partnerships.* Washington, DC: Independent Sector.

Gansler, J. S. (2006). Moving toward market-based government: The changing role of government as the provider. In J. M. Kamensky & A. Morales (Eds.), *Competition, choice, and incentives in government programs* (pp. 35-120). Lanham, MD: Rowman & Littlefield.

Garnett, J. L., & Kouzmin, A. (2007). Communicating throughout Katrina: Competing and complementary conceptual lens on crisis communication. *Public Administration Review, 67,* 171-188.

Gazley, B., & Brudney, J. L. (2007). The purpose (and perils) of government–nonprofit partnership. *Nonprofit and Voluntary Sector Quarterly 36,* 389-416.

Gore, A. (1993). *From red tape to results: Creating a government that works better and costs less.* Washington, DC: Government Printing Office.

Gray, B. (1989). *Collaborating: Finding common ground for multiparty problems.* San Francisco: Jossey-Bass.

Gulick, L., & Urwick, L. (Eds.). (1937). *Papers on the science of administration.* New York: Institute for Public Administration.

Harmon, M. M. (1994). *Organization theory for public administration.* Burke, VA: Chatelaine Press.

Johnston, V. R. (Ed.). (2008). *Entrepreneurial management and public policy* (2nd ed.). Huntington NY: Nova Science.

Kamensky, J. M., & Morales, A. (2006). *Competition, choice, and incentives in government programs.* Lanham, MD: Rowman & Littlefield Publishers, Inc..

King, C. S., Felty, K. M., & Susel, B. O. (1998). The question of participation: Toward authentic participation in public administration. *Public Administration Review, 58,* 317-326.

Koppenjan, J. F. M., & Enserink, B. (2009). Public-private partnerships in urban infrastructures: Reconciling private sector participation and sustainability. *Public Administration Review, 69,* 284-296.

Koteen, J. (1997). *Strategic management in public and nonprofit organizations, managing public concerns in an era of limits* (2nd ed.). Westport, CT: Praeger.

Lester, W., & Krejci, D. (2007). Business "not" as usual: The National Incident Management System, federalism, and leadership. *Public Administration Review, 67,* 84-93.

Levine, C. H. (1978). Organizational decline and cutback management. *Public Administration Review, 38,* 316-325.

Levine, C. H. (1979). More on cutback management: Hard questions for hard times. *Public Administration Review, 39,* 179-189.

Mandell, M. P. (Ed.). (2001). *Getting results through collaboration.* Westport, CT: Greenwood.

Meier, K. J., & Bohte, J. (2007). *Politics and the bureaucracy: Policymaking in the fourth branch of government* (5th ed.). Florence, KY: Cengage Learning.

Menzel, D. C. (2007). *Ethics management for public administrators: Building organizations of integrity.* Armonk, NY: M. E. Sharpe.

Mintzberg, H. (1973). *The nature of managerial work.* New York: Harper & Row.

Moon, M. J. (1999). The pursuit of managerial entrepreneurship: Does organization matter? *Public Administration Review, 59*, 31-43.

Moore, M. H. (1995). *Creating public value, strategic management in government.* Cambridge, MA: Harvard University Press.

Morris, M. H., & Jones, F. F. (1999). Entrepreneurship in established organizations: The case of the public sector. *Entrepreneurship Theory and Practice, 24*, 71-93.

Nalbandian, J. (1991). *Professionalism in local government: Transformation in the roles, responsibilities, and values of city managers.* San Francisco: Jossey-Bass.

Needleman, M. L., &. Needleman, C. E. (1974). *Guerrillas in the bureaucracy.* New York: Wiley.

Osborne, D., & Gaebler, T. (1992). *Reinventing government: How the entrepreneurial spirit is transforming the public sector.* Reading, MA: Addison-Wesley.

Osborne, D., & Hutchinson, P. (2004). *The price of government: Getting the result we need in an age of permanent fiscal crisis.* New York: Basic Books.

O'Leary, R., Gazley, B., McGuire, M., & Bingham, L. B. (2009). Public managers in collaboration. In R. O'Leary & L. B. Bingham (Eds.), *The collaborative public manager: New ideas for the twenty-first century* (pp. 1-12). Washington, DC: Georgetown University Press.

O'Toole, L. J., Jr. (1997). Treating networks seriously: Practical and research-based agendas in public administration. *Public Administration Review, 57*, 45-52.

Page, S. (2004). Measuring accountability for results in interagency collaboratives. *Public Administration Review, 64*, 591-606.

Peters, B. G. (1998). "With a little help from our friends": Public-private partnerships as institutions and instruments. In J. Pierre (Ed.), *Partnerships in urban governance* (pp.11-33). New York: St. Martin's Press.

Popovich, M. G. (Ed.). (1998). *Creating high-performance government organizations, a practical guide for public managers.* San Francisco: Jossey-Bass.

Rich, R. C. (1981). Interaction of the voluntary and governmental sectors: Toward an understanding of the coproduction of municipal services. *Administration and Society, 13,* 59-76.

Sabin, T. R., & Allen, V. L. (1968). Role theory. In G. Lindzey & E. Aronson (Eds.). *The handbook of social psychology, Vol. 1* (2nd ed.) (pp. 488-567). Reading, MA: Addison-Wesley.

Selden, S. C., Sowa, J. E., & Sandfort, J. (2006). The impact of nonprofit collaboration in early child care and education on management and program outcomes. *Public Administration Review, 66,* 412-425.

Sink, D. W. (1998). Interorganizational collaboration. In J. M. Shafritz (Ed.), *The international encyclopedia of public policy and administration* (pp.1188-1191). Boulder, CO: Westview.

Somers, S., & Svara, J. H. (2009). Assessing and managing environmental risk: Connecting local government management with emergency management. *Public Administration Review, 69,* 181-193.

Taylor, F. W. (1913). *Principles of scientific management.* New York: Harper.

Terry, L. D. (1993). Why we should abandon the misconceived quest to reconcile public entrepreneurship with democracy. *Public Administration Review, 53,* 393-395.

Vanacour, M. (1990). *An examination of role relationships between assistant city managers and city managers* (Unpublished doctoral dissertation). Arizona State University, Tempe, AZ.

Van Wart, M. (2005). *Dynamics of leadership in public service: Theory and practice.* Armonk, NY: M. E. Sharpe.

Wilson, J. Q. (1989). *Bureaucracy: What government agencies do and why they do it.* New York: Basic Books.

Wilson, K. K. (1982). Citizen coproduction as a mode of participation: Conjectures and models. *Journal of Urban Affairs, 3,* 37-50.

Windrum, P. (2008). Innovation and entrepreneurship in public services. In P. Windrum & P. Koch (Eds.), *Innovation in public sector services: Entrepreneurship, creativity and management, 2008* (pp. 3-20). Northampton, MA: Edward Elgar.

Yin, R. K., & Yates, D. (1974). *Street level government: Assessing decentralization and urban services.* Santa Monica, CA: Rand Corporation.

Ysa, T. (2007). Governance forms in urban public-private partnerships. *International Public Management Journal, 10,* 35-57.

Selected Websites

American Society for Public Administration. (Public service organization dedicated to advancing teaching and practice of public and nonprofit administration.)
http://www.aspanet.org/scriptcontent/ASPAgeneral.cfm

Association for Public Policy Analysis and Management. (Organization dedicated to improving public policy and management by fostering excellence in research, analysis, and education.)
https://www.appam.org/home.asp

Congressional Institute. (A nonprofit corporation dedicated to helping Members of Congress serve their constituents and helping Americans better understand the operations of the national legislature.)
http://www.conginst.org/index.php?option=com_frontpage&Itemid=1

International City/County Management Association. (Professional and educational organization that serves chief appointed managers, administrators, and assistants in cities, towns, counties, and regional entities internationally.)
http://icma.org/main/bc.asp?bcid=60&hsid=1&ssid1=17

Metropolitan Atlanta Rapid Transit Authority. (Organization that serves the greater Atlanta regional transit system.)
http://www.itsmarta.com

National Academy of Public Administration. (Chartered by Congress, this organization is dedicated to improving performance of governance systems.)
http://www.napawash.org/about_academy/index.html

National Association of County Administrators. (Organization that encourages professional development for county administrators.)
http://www.countyadministrators.org/

National Association of State Chief Administrators. (National organization that serves state chief officials from administration and general services.)
http://www.nasca.org/

National League of Cities. (National organization representing municipal governments throughout the United States.)
http://www.nlc.org/

7

A New and Improved Public Administration

Many public managers reflect back to the Golden Age of public administration with considerable wishfulness. Even managers who matured in the 1980s often speak of better, past times when government and bureaucracy were more positively viewed by the public. Good public administration primarily meant effective management of an organization's internal affairs.

Politics, of course, was always a concern. Today, however, politics impinge more forcefully and directly into the day-to-day life of top-level administrators. Interest groups exhibit more sophistication. Elected officials are more demanding than before and often are less supportive of bureaucracy. At the same time, 24-hour news cycles tend to superficially skim public issues without supporting data analysis to educate the public.

As this book has demonstrated, public administration in the United States is characterized by tensions among numerous competing values. There is no reason to believe that the future will be any different. Social change and the increasing complexity of social organizations will continue to influence the relevant environment and dynamics of public organization. Though the specific issues vary over time, the fundamental issues identified in this text will continue to affect the adaptation of public administration to social reality.

An Adaptive Approach to Public Administration

Large organizations are a fact of life in our complex society. The efforts to organize government activities along bureaucratic lines assumed a need for rational approaches to accomplishing tasks. This rationality often stressed quantitative methods and empirical evidence at the expense of more qualitative concerns. Over time, a conflict developed between values associated with bureaucratic rationality and qualitative values such as social and environmental justice, participation, creativity, and innovation. These qualitative values attained high levels of visibility and importance in the post-World II era, especially since the 1960s. Bureaucratic traditions and organization theory often seemed at odds with these new values.

Even some of the base concerns of the traditionalists are at odds with the democratic values of our society. For example, accountability and responsiveness have always been major issues in public administration, but many of the features of rational bureaucracy work against responsiveness to democratic impulses. Rational bureaucracy is supposed to foster efficiency, but political democracy, especially as practiced under the United States Constitution, builds in high political costs and inefficiencies (Denhardt & Denhardt, 2007; Karl, 1987). Checks and balances were created in our government to assure that no one person, group, class, or part of government could exercise effective centralized control over the whole. Although American bureaucracy has long valued efficiency, values other than efficiency are extremely important to democratic polities. The emergence of social equity and other concerns associated with the civil rights movement of the 1960s are examples of democratic political values that get in the way of bureaucratic efficiency.

Many students of public affairs focus on responsiveness as the primary value that should guide all government activity. As a general principle, people favor responsive government. So long as political leaders who support their views are in power, they seem to want the bureaucracy to be responsive. However, when someone representing the opposite ideological stance attains a leadership position, the same idealists may want the bureaucracy to be less responsive and actually become obstructionist in their approach to the new leadership (Price, 1975). Thus, the fervor with which one wants bureaucracy to respond is determined, in part, by whether one's interests are likely to be served.

Perfect solutions to problems of organizations in a complex society are unlikely to be found, and organizations cannot solve most social problems (Gulick, 1987; Rittel & Webber, 1973; Sirianni, 1984). Many organization theorists attempted to develop a singular model to solve virtually all organizational problems. As students of organization theory are well aware, such approaches led to a large body of literature pointing out the inadequacies of each of the preferred models. Organization theorists need to accept the pluralism of modern society as a given and recognize its need for organization theory to accommodate many alternatives (Denhardt, 2007; Hall, 1999; Sirianni, 1984). Each situation or problem is likely to call for something different in organization approaches. Recognizing that fact can lead to efforts at developing alternative organization theories to meet varying needs. Among these alternatives, many will involve entrepreneurship, collaboratives, and public-private partnerships, as we have discussed in Chapter 6. Obviously, there still is need for some stability and boundaries, but flexibility and adaptability are important components in producing relevant organizations.

The tendency of organizations to emphasize particular norms to the exclusion of others constrains their adaptability. Bureaucracies go to great lengths to mute dissent or opposition when they would be more prudent to encourage such activities (Weinstein, 1979). Dissent and opposition to prevailing norms, within limits, can enhance the vitality and relevance of organizations.

On the Streets: Making Policy Consumable

President Truman was famous for a sign on his desk which says, "THE BUCK STOPS HERE." This sign is an object lesson about life at the top. What about life at the other end of the hierarchy? Some have argued that the final point of discretion is at the street level (Parenti, 2007; Riccucci, 2005; Vinzant & Crothers, 1998). The teacher, the police officer, the lifeguard, the social worker, the person at the reserve desk of the library, and millions of others are the final deliverers of goods and services. They are the last decision makers in the long chain of providers from policy recommendation through implementation.

In the daily delivery of public services, these holders of the lowest-level, service production-oriented jobs give meaning to public policy. Despite popular images of an unresponsive bureaucracy, the street-level bureaucrat is usually sensitive to the needs of the consumer of public goods and services and mediates against the sharp edges of rules meant to ensure a legal, rational order. Conversely, the street-level bureaucrat often is the last blank face and rule-bound decision maker in a long sequence of unfeeling responses to human needs.

The problem for democratic society is the trade-off between the pursuit of organizational, bureaucratic, and citizen needs. One may visualize the citizen-consumer as the last person bearing the costs of the bureaucratic state. For example, consider the older citizen who has specific health care, nutritional, and recreational needs and lacks personal means to pay fully for privately provided services. Many communities use public, nonprofit, and privately provided resources to provide special programs and facilities for the elderly. Meals-on-wheels, senior citizen centers, discount fares on buses, and health clinics for the elderly are common attempts to provide special care and services for older members of the community. Such efforts may effectively reduce the *consumption costs* that the elderly bear in their use of publicly provided services. The monetary, transportation, and psychological costs associated with consumption of normally distributed services are lowered for this sector of the population.

Making public services more consumable for the community in general and for specific target populations was a major goal for American public policy and public administration during the 1960s and 1970s. Many of the experimental programs of the 1960s and 1970s were attempts to repackage and redeliver public services to enhance their usefulness. A serious problem with reducing consumption costs is that it raises the average production costs of services. Both the producing agencies and the taxpayers must bear additional increments to reduce consumption costs. In many cases, an inverse relationship exists between reducing the costs borne by the final consumer and the costs borne by the producing unit and jurisdiction. The increasing costs to the agencies and governmental jurisdictions have resulted in efforts during the 1980s and 1990s to find ways of cutting government expenditures. The New Public Management, with its emphasis on efficiency and managerialism, has resulted in reduced levels of services and increased costs for the final consumer of the services through imposition of fees or sharing of the cost between the program and the ultimate recipient of the service.

Bilingual education programs may be used as an example to illustrate the inverse relationship between production and consumption costs. The recruitment and training of special teachers, the development of specialized curriculum materials, and the injection of bilingual programs into traditional classrooms all increased the production costs of education. The efforts to meet the particular needs of a special non-English speaking population raised the average cost of providing education in many local school districts. At the same time, it made the education offered to special populations more usable and more readily consumable. The non-English speaking students were able to make better use of the educational service provided. Partly in response to increasing costs, residents in some states (e.g., Arizona and California) passed referenda outlawing bilingual education.

If school districts cut back bilingual programs to save money, the production costs of education may be reduced. There is likely to be a corresponding rise in the consumption costs borne by the non-English speaking students. No longer will their development of English language proficiency be fostered through special programs. Instead, individual students and their families will be expected to pick up the psychological and material costs of learning English in the regular classroom setting or outside the schools. The personal acquisition of language skills becomes relatively more expensive for these special populations. In the long run, the reduction of bilingual education will result in citizens lacking skills in English. This could mean fewer opportunities for social development and advancement (Gerber, Lupis, McCubbin, & Kiewiet, 2001).

Although bilingual education is a special case, it illustrates a general point: efforts to reduce consumption costs often result in additional production costs. Conversely, decreases in production costs often carry with them increases in consumption costs. For example, red tape is the inverse of lowering consumption costs. It involves long lines, time delays, centralized delivery systems, special forms, rules and procedures, and rigid legal constraints. These tend to raise the costs borne by the citizen consumer. In the normal world of bureaucracy, more attention is given to production costs and less attention to consumption costs.

In this era of reduced public support for many services, there is the possibility of pricing many service consumers out of some publicly provided services. Recreation and fire services are timely examples. Both of these services are amenable to *user fees* in which potential users are asked to pay some out-of-pocket cost (in addition to the general taxes supporting the jurisdiction) to use such facilities as tennis courts, swimming pools, and basketball courts, or to pay a special charge for fire protection services. Although in most cases, the user fees are nominal, in many cases they are not, and they effectively raise the cost of services beyond the reach of poorer citizens. Efforts to economize through outsourcing, higher user fees, increased dependence on private market producers, and economies of large-scale production systems sometimes shift more and more of the actual costs of public services to the individual citizens.

The dilemma of bureaucratic behavior becomes the extent to which upper- and middle-level members of the social hierarchy can and will subsidize those less fortunate. The final arbiter of social justice is the last person who can increase or reduce consumption costs.

An Era of Limits

Through the 1970s, most administrators had high expectations that they would have plentiful resources to accomplish the many tasks they were given. The 1980s began a time of major limits that continue to this day. Not only do public managers fight swampy conditions, they now operate in an age of permanent fiscal crisis (Osborne & Hutchinson, 2006). Administrators often lack resources to do an adequate job of implementing policies and reaching specified goals. The public demands increasing amounts of services but often is not supportive, or insists that their current taxes should pay for the expanded services. Elected officials are no less demanding than the public, but often are much less supportive of the bureaucracy.

Today, a host of recent changes presents the administrator with an unpredictable environment, fewer resources, and a reduced menu of options. Among the most pressing changes are (1) single interest politics, which increase demands on administrators for specific responses to specific groups; (2) revitalization of conservatism, which constrains the resource base of governments and support for social welfare programs; and (3) slower economic growth, which reduces the resources available for use by public administrators.

Single Interest Politics

Interest groups increasingly target public agencies as the principal participants in the policy process. These groups typically have narrow focuses and strive toward getting administrators to do specific things in particular ways for target populations. Historically, the narrow focuses of these groups have been somewhat offset by the broader focuses of political parties, legislative bodies, and bureaucracies. More and more, candidates for and winners of public office at the state and local levels are *single interest candidates* (Phillips, 1982; Prewitt, 1970; Rozell, Wilcox, & Madland, 2005). They run their campaigns, make their commitments, and work toward the achievement of narrowly defined, often self-interested goals such as reducing property taxes, prohibiting abortion on demand, or establishing English as the official language of a state. These narrow focuses make specific laws, court decisions, and agencies the likely targets of their efforts.

Single interest politics diminishes the sense of community among citizens and reduces popular support for many social welfare and social justice programs. It puts public administrators in a severe bind. They have considerable incentive to narrow their efforts and to cater to supporters from a few interest groups and selected elective officials. Their role in representing third-party interests is diminished. As mentioned before, they tend to cultivate relationships with clientele groups for support and to act as lobbyists in their own interests.

Fiscal and Political Conservatism

Many states and localities have adopted institutional constraints in the form of revenue, tax, or expenditure caps that limit the availability and use of tax funds. This reflects a growing tide of fiscal conservatism that retards the capacity of states and localities to fully use the potential tax base. Coupled with reduced funds from the national government through intergovernmental programs and transfers, this has greatly limited the amount of funds available to localities.

Neoconservatism goes beyond fiscal issues (Dolbeare, 1986; Heilbrunn, 2009; Murray, 2006; Reich, 1983). There is less support for social reform policies than there was in the past. Although the Obama administration may reverse the long-term trend, the real gains made in the recent past have convinced many people that we no longer need a robust social service agenda. Many feel that less attention and public resources should be given to housing, poverty, education, civil rights, and environmental programs as we did in the 1960s and 1970s. It also may be that failures of past social policies have made people suspicious of such efforts and the agencies charged with their implementation. It probably is true that a history of waste and ineffectiveness in bureaucracy has convinced many Americans that government is not very efficient in dealing with social issues. Even liberals are much less optimistic about the capacity of governmental agencies to act. Whatever the roots, state and local bureaucracies must do their work in a much more critical, less supportive, and more conservative political environment (Lipset & Schneider, 1983).

Slower Economic Growth

It is axiomatic that the United States now has an information- and service-based economy (Atkinson & Court, 1998; Bluestone & Harrison, 1982; Devol, Klowden, Bedroussian, & Yeo, 2009). The fact that we lose more jobs annually than we produce in the industrial sector (Hall, 2007); that our industrial growth is very selective and that our agricultural, mining, and timber-cutting activities are in decline, have profound effects on our fiscal ability to support many government activities. Support for government is also affected by our reduced competitiveness internationally in many product and commodity markets, and by the fact that most of our real growth is in service, government, and information communication technology sectors. The Golden Age of public administration coincided with the period of our most profound national economic growth and dominance of many international markets. Even if we were not in a period of conservatism, the capacity of our regional and local economies to support government would be severely restricted. The rate of increase in the local and regional taxes is no longer as great as our appetite for services. Additionally, we now must cope with historic national debt brought on by the fiscal turmoil that started in 2008.

The Limits of the Welfare State and Liberal Market Economy

There is considerable debate about the effectiveness and lasting impacts of the social welfare policies, market control mechanisms, and environmental regulations of the past several decades. Some commentators believe that the policies based on the belief that government can protect citizens from all problems are part of the problem. They even blame widespread poverty, poor health care, high levels of crime, inadequate housing, drug addiction, and unstable regional economies on failed regulatory and welfare policies. Others argue that we have done too little and that we are in a period of regression brought about by cutbacks in governmental efforts. They fear that we will lose any gains made in income redistribution, improved opportunities for education, and environmental quality.

Part of the argument is ideological and simply shows that there are still strong conservative and liberal perspectives and factions in the United States. Part of the concern transcends political perspective and partisanship. On the one hand, we tenaciously cling to the idea of individualism, privatism, and a free market. On the other hand, our nation is dependent upon the rules, regulations, activities, and services of the welfare and regulatory state. This contradiction presents a philosophical and practical dilemma. People want a community composed of individuals working together, but lack the basic perspective and institutions to do this easily. Citizens thrive on the benefits provided by the welfare and regulatory state but push to reduce the size and impact of public institutions.

The public administrator is indeed in the middle. The special role, competence, and influence of the bureaucrat and bureaucracy suggest that if this contradiction can be solved, it will be solved by an even more enlightened, humane, and adaptive public service. Institutional and procedural reforms over the years have tried to balance individualism and community values. Such reforms as open meeting laws, requirements for citizen participation, ethics commissions, and equal employment opportunity requirements have caused the modern American state to adjust to new issues and crises. Yet, as suggested in the earlier discussion of organizations and organization behavior in Chapters 3 and 4, such reforms are marginal and only partially complete.

The hard fact remains that public power, like private power, cannot solve all problems. There are *wicked problems* (Rittel & Webber, 1973) that by definition are not easy to solve or cannot be solved at all. Crime is an example of a public problem that is wicked in more ways than one. Crime is wicked in the ordinary sense of the word. It is bad because it hurts people. It also is wicked because it is not clear how to prevent and control crime. Crime increases despite all our efforts to reduce it. At present, there is no rational solution to the problem of crime in our society.

There are large-scale problems that can only be partially solved because the causes and the external effects are so hard to manage. Air pollution is such a problem. Most of the causes or sources of typical urban air pollution are known. It is, however, a classic case of a problem fraught with externalities. It is hard to put a boundary around air pollution and prescribe a rational solution to it. Most air quality control strategies—testing of automobiles, emission caps and trade efforts, inspection of coal- and gas-burning facilities, regulation of the use of toxic materials, and conservation of fuels—handle only portions of the production of pollution. Even in coastal Southern California, which has perhaps the most complete air pollution control program in the nation, only parts of the problem can be handled. When dealing with smog, people have had to learn to live with partial solutions. There are hard choices and uncomfortable trade-offs. Nearly all efforts to focus on a problem or set of problems shift public resources from other problems. Thus, the menu may be large, but the options are limited.

The Golden Age of public administration is over. In that Golden Age, agencies often had sufficient resources to attempt many solutions to many problems. Most governmental jurisdictions no longer have sufficient slack resources to invest in a wide menu of issues. At least at the local level, this lesson is being driven home forcefully. Reductions in funds available from the national government, state and locally imposed taxing and spending limits, and weakened state economies all have reduced the amount of public funds available to localities. Many communities actively explore ways to reduce public services, make more use of private market providers, entertain collaboratives, and engage in joint ventures with private sector entrepreneurs. Traditional lines between public and private sectors are becoming blurred as governments increasingly partner with private sector organizations to carry out their functions.

The newest public administration may well be adaptive public administration as governments adapt and adjust to fiscal, institutional, and political limits. Local governments, for example, often lack the tax base or authority to tax the local economy effectively. Coupled with reductions in funds available from the state and national governments, they are fiscally squeezed. Institutional limits such as constraints on the ability to annex growing suburbs to established cities or to engage in joint private-public undertakings weaken the capacity of local governments to adjust to changing conditions. Political limits include unstable coalitions of interest groups and fiscal conservatism. Taken together, these limiting factors place local and state officials in a new world of public administration. In this new world of limits, administrators struggle to carry out much of the welfare state without adequate resources. The adaptation often is wholly pragmatic, unconscious, and not well thought out. Nonetheless, the role and function of public administration is being reshaped as managers try to overcome the considerable problems of administering the welfare and regulatory state.

Consequences of Limits

The consequences of these trends for public administrators are as contradictory as limiting. First, the resources available to public agencies, especially those at the state and local levels, are unlikely to increase at a rate commensurate with growth in the private sector and in the national public economy. Put another way, even when the national economy prospers, local public sectors cannot capture much of that new growth as public revenue. Unfortunately, when the economy is not prospering, demands for services increase while available resources decline. Political conservatism and slower growth in the public sector have not retarded the demand for selected public services. Single interest politics and politicians increase rather than decrease the demand for specific governmental activities. A list of high-demand services includes increased police protection, more roads and highways, better outdoor recreational facilities, improved social security and services for the aged, safer domestic water supplies, more effective elementary and secondary schools, national healthcare, and winning the war on terror. Demands for more services come at the same time as pressure for more deregulation, streamlining of regulatory processes, less social welfare, and less government in general. Most localities face the problem of doing more with less in an uncongenial setting.

This decline in available resources has been coupled with an increased demand for performance measurement and excellence in the public service. This has put increased cross-pressures on public administrators. In the 1950s and 1960s, most public agencies became accustomed to growing budgets, and much of the public administration literature seemed to be based on an assumption of growth. In the 1970s and 1980s, that growth assumption changed dramatically, bringing with it new demands on public managers. The change continued through the 1990s into the 21st century.

Under conditions of generous public budgets, it is taken for granted that as long as resources are expanding in an organization, things are easier to manage. Members of the organization can be given increased resources or at least are not likely to lose any of their resources. Subunits thus can be provided incentives to work together and accept guidance from the management of the organization. During times of decline in resources, however, the incentives are not there. Many stresses develop internally and externally (Levine, 1978, 1979; Rubin, 1985; Waldo, 1980). Trade-offs become necessary to provide better service in high demand areas while settling for less in other valued services (Pollitt & Bouckaert, 2004).

Today, public administrators have to deal with other bureaucrats, employee organizations (unions), clientele, the general public, and political leaders. They all expect the same or higher levels of service, even though the resources to provide services are diminished. Even if it is possible to convince these various interested parties that service levels have to be cut, establishing priorities is extremely difficult. Each actor tends to believe that the others should absorb the cut.

In social service agencies, cuts are especially difficult because resource reductions often mean that more people end up needing services. As fallout from other programs and employment losses climb, social service agencies are likely to see more clientele. With fewer resources, they are less able to serve the clientele, and frustration mounts for all concerned.

Within the organization, Levine (1979) argues that cutback management increases conflict among members of the organization and is detrimental to efforts to democratize organizational management. He also suggests that it reduces innovative and creative initiatives in organizations. Clearly, as fewer resources are available to managers, there are fewer for them to give their members. People are less likely to accept change and to work together when they are uncertain about their own job security and the maintenance of their organization's viability. The challenge to managers is immense.

In addition to the practical implementation of cutbacks, managers have to deal with their psychological impact. Most societal pressures and management traditions equate growth with success and progress. Decline in resources and organizational size requires a new perspective. Not all managers are able to adjust to the new direction or assumptions or to maintain the creative spark that spurs innovation.

Some Positive Trends

Not all change is confining. Some recent trends present public administrators with opportunities. Among the most promising trends are: (1) increased diversity in public life, (2) broader diffusion of humanistic management practices, and (3) widespread use of information technology by managers in the public sector. Managers and agencies need to seek out the positive side of these and other trends to maximize their capacity to perform in a socially and professionally credible manner in the face of an ever-changing environment.

Diversity in Public Life

The diversity of candidates running for public office and being elected has been increasing over the past two decades. Larger numbers of ethnic minorities and women are entering public service, reflecting a more representative bureaucracy (Dolan & Rosenbloom, 2003). Diversity also increasingly includes the idea that all aspects of the community should be reflected in the workplace and that diversity should not focus only on a few groups who have been underutilized in the past. This approach to diversity is referred to as *full-spectrum diversity* (Slack, 1997).

Diversity in the public service offers considerable opportunity for improved public management by expanding the range of values and ideas within which the bureaucracy operates (Ospina, 2001). Any trend that increases rather than reduces the variety of values expressed in governmental arenas is a gain.

Changes in the numbers of women and minorities in the public service have made it more representative of the whole society (Cayer & Sigelman, 1980; Choi, 2009; Dometrius, 1984; Huckle, 1983; McCabe & Stream, 2000). In some jurisdictions, the increases at the entry and middle levels are impressive (Naff, 1998; Sigelman & Cayer, 1986). Mobility to the higher levels, especially for women, has not kept pace with increases at the entry level, but the increase in the relative numbers of women and minorities in many jurisdictions is changing the mix of public service employees (Bayes, 1985; Dometrius, 1984; Huckle, 1983; McCabe & Stream, 2000; Sigelman & Cayer 1986). However, Riccucci (2009) suggests that "the glass continues to come up half empty . . . [and] white women and people of color continue to be disadvantaged" in the federal government (p. 379). Even though the overall representation of women has increased, women of different racial and ethnic groups are underrepresented and continue to experience inequality (Hsieh & Winslow, 2006). Starks (2009) adds that the lack of proportionate representation at senior federal levels may mean deficiencies in viewpoints when considering policies, regulations, and strategic planning.

Despite an imperfect trend, the overall changes are opening up bureaucracies and infusing alternative ways of accomplishing objectives. Some people see such adaptations as destabilizing and producing conflict. However, in the long run, this trend is likely to produce a more democratic governmental system and a more representative, less rigid and closed bureaucracy.

Humanistic and Democratic Management

One of the lasting contributions of the past three decades of management theory and practice has been the shift away from power-oriented practices, which stress dominance of top-level managers over their employees, toward those that empower lower-level employees (Bennis, 1969; Block, 1991; Conger & Kanungo, 1988; Garson & Overman, 1983; Mintzberg, 1979; Tjosvold & Sun, 2006). Increasing attention is given to the involvement of individual employees and groups of employees in the overall management of organizations (Denhardt, Denhardt, & Aristigueta, 2009).

The New Public Administration of the 1960s and 1970s included expectations of greater participation by members of the organization and the public in decision making (Denhardt, 2007; Frederickson, 1996; Marini, 1971). Reforms such as citizen involvement in bureaucracy, customer-based service values, participatory management, strategic management, program evaluation and benchmarking, have considerably altered and even improved the practice of public management in the United States (Frederickson, 1996; Hill & Lynn, 2009; Kettl, 2005; McNabb, 2009; Mosher, 1975; Waldo, 1980). Some of that improvement has been in humanizing the bureaucracy itself.

One cannot argue that fully participatory management has arrived or even that most public administrators buy into forms of participatory management. It is clear, however, that public administration practice is moving toward a human-relations, humanely expressive form of management. The new generation of public administrators seems to have a strong commitment to humanistic approaches to management.

Diffusion of Information Technology

The computer revolution has taken firm root in public administration (Fountain, 2001: Seneviratne, 1999; Warren & Weschler, 1999; White, 2007). As previously mentioned, much of the impact of mainframe computers and electronic data processing was negative and dehumanizing. A kind of mystique developed around the application of computers to management. A computer elite came to dominate the development and use of large computers in public agencies. Access to and use of computers was retarded by poor training, cliques of knowledgeable users, and poor equipment. Sometimes the adoption of a computer system appeared to the uninitiated administrator as a waste of resources that made the overall job of management more difficult.

Although there are residual negative feelings about computers in many agencies, the infusion of microcomputers into everyday life has made the computer one of the most widely used tools in the office. The personal, micro computer and the wide variety of software for it have dispelled much of the mistrust and mystique surrounding computers. Much of the use of microcomputers is for word processing, but increasingly managers use micro, mini, mainframe computers and computer networks for data management, problem solving, and production control activities. Access to the Internet and email has quickly become as common as word processing. In fact, email is now the most common use of personal computers. The Internet is the most used source of information for many people, and email is the preferred form of communication by many organization members.

Few technologies, except perhaps the telephone and copy machines, have had and are having such a pervasive impact as computers on the way people and organizations work. Impacts such as reduced time in record keeping and management, more timely communication, online education, and substitution of computer networks and electronic bulletin boards for face-to-face conversation were expected to happen and have happened. Some argue that the technology, especially the Internet, is transforming traditional bureaucracy to a new paradigm focusing on "network building, external collaboration, and . . . customer service" (Ho, 2002, p. 440).

E-government refers to production and delivery of public services to citizens through communications technology, especially through the Internet (McNabb, 2009). The goals of e-government include user convenience, operational savings, and increased accessibility to governmental agencies. It provides a whole new dimension for offering some services with 24-hours-a-day convenience (Baker, 2004; Curtin, Sommer, & Vis-Sommer, 2003; Garson, 2006; Heeks, 2005). E-government is viewed as enhancing participation by citizens in decision making (Ho, 2002; Warren & Weschler, 1999; White, 2007). It fosters new types of communities and new roles for government (Kamarck & Nye, 2002). Clearly, citizens have more access and opportunity to participate in decisions affecting them. Many governments, especially local governments, have Web sites where citizens can comment on proposed policies or projects or anything else they wish to. For those who do not have easy access to computers, many governments place computers in libraries, community centers, and kiosks in public places such as shopping malls where citizens can access the information and make their input.

Aside from allowing access to decision making, government agency Web sites are major sources of information. Virtually all governmental jurisdictions and agencies now have Web sites with detailed information about their activities. Sometimes the problem is information overload or difficulty in determining how to get the precise information desired (Ho, 2002). The wealth of information enhances the ability of citizens to know what their government is doing and perhaps to act on it in making election choices. Access to information is a central element of democratic governance. More importantly, citizens can actually conduct business with government online. They can renew auto license plates, get answers to questions on their taxes, file their taxes, and apply for benefits without leaving their homes. They also can vote in some elections. In 2002, residents of New York City could comment on the proposed plans for the rebuilding of the World Trace Center destroyed in the September 11, 2001 terrorist attacks.

Information technology is also expected to reduce costs and help in downsizing (Fountain, 2001). The realization of this promise continues to be debatable (Moon, 2002; Nunn, 2001), (See Garson's *Public Information Technology and E-governance: Managing the Virtual State* [2006] for further discussion on evaluating public information systems.) Although there may be some staffing savings, ancillary costs often increase overall costs. Information technology requires constant updating and constant training of employees as well. Issues of *interoperability,* the ability of different information systems to communicate with one another, also pose problems and consumption costs (Landsbergen & Wolken, 2001). If information is shared, the systems for transferring the information must be compatible.

Less obvious has been the democratization of the workplace through the use of microcomputers. The radical decentralization of data sets and the access to data brought about by microcomputers poses many security and quality control issues, but it has freed individual workers from some of the negative constraints of hierarchy. Freedom of access to and the use of information in an organization are key parts of democratization of administration. The microcomputer has made this literally possible. Privacy concerns and legal issues often arise as a result of the wealth of data available and the number of people who have access to it (Duncan, 1999; Garson, 2006; Prysby & Prysby, 1999; White, 2007).

Combined with computer technology, organizations use other information technology advances to do their work. Meetings can now be conducted with participants from every part of the world connected by voice and video technology. No longer do organizations have to call personnel to a central location to conduct meetings. They can do it with instant communication. Similarly, video displays of ongoing activity can be used to tap into the expertise of people in other locations. An expert in another place can guide the surgeon in the local public hospital, or diagnoses can be made in remote areas through the use of digital technology. Geographic information systems (GIS) provide another tool for public managers. GIS allows public managers to match data about physical, social, and political factors of their jurisdictions to maps (Carr, 1999; Propen, 2007). As such, it is a powerful tool for decision making and studying the consequences of potential decisions about locating a school, routing a light rail system, or rerouting a street. Information technology empowers organizations in ways never thought of a couple of decades ago.

Improving Public Administration Education

One of the secrets of the success of the reformers of the first half of the twentieth century in promoting the public service was the fostering of the development of an administrative class. This had both positive and negative implications. It produced a dedicated group of well-trained professionals. Some of the negative aspects of the growing administrative elite are well known (Lowi, 1979; McConnell, 1966; Thayer, 1981). For a long time, especially in the upper-middle and top echelons, the administrative class has been a very homogeneous white, male, upper-middle-class bastion. It has used its expertise and specialist language to close itself off from the rest of society. It has been a brake against the liberal and conservative reforms and kept many policies from being completely implemented.

Some of the positive accomplishments of this class of administrators are less well acknowledged but in historical perspective, are very important. Overwhelmingly, the American public service is honest and without corruption. The very expertise that has made it arrogant and closed also has permitted remarkable achievements especially, in applied technology and social policy. And finally, much of the burden of humanizing big government has, ironically, been borne by bureaucrats as sort of a modern, late-twentieth-century noblesse oblige.

As pointed out in the earlier discussions of bureaucracy and organization behavior, the report on the net value of bureaucracy and bureaucratic reform is incomplete. However, it is worth considering some of the things that might be done to make the administrative class better at making bureaucracy more democratic and more effective through the improved education and training of administrators.

Efforts to make bureaucracies more diverse through affirmative action has had a mixed history and limited successes (Bayes, 1985; Bonaparth, 1982; Cayer & Schaefer, 1981; Naff, 1998; Thompson & Brown, 1978). Early on, the key problem was that the pool of women and minorities and others in the so-called protected classes was woefully small given the demand for persons from these groups. Concerted efforts to improve the pool by accelerated education and training for members of the protected classes have helped remedy this problem to some extent. Now, for example, women typically make up more than half of the student bodies in master of public administration programs. Likewise, training and cross-training inside agencies and jurisdictions have provided a better pool and some mobility for members of protected classes. Although public agencies are now much more diverse, the gender mix, social demographics, and racial/ethnic distribution of the upper-level administrative class still does not reflect society in general.

The National Association of Schools of Public Affairs and Administration (NASPAA) and the American Society for Public Administration (ASPA) promote diversity. NASPAA encourages "a climate of inclusiveness through its recruitment, admissions practices, and student support services" (National Association of Schools of Public Affairs and Administration Standards, 2009, p. 6). The burden, however, rests with the several hundred undergraduate and graduate programs of public administration and business in the United States. They need to attract, recruit, retain, and graduate a diverse group of students. With challenges to affirmative action at the ballot box (e.g., California, Washington) and the courts, as well as by political leaders, the challenge remains great.

A related issue is change in the curriculum for education for public management. Both NASPAA and ASPA have been increasingly active in pushing for a consistent, rigorous curriculum, especially for the Master of Public Administration, which is becoming the nominal terminal degree in the field. Under the leadership of several deans of schools of public administration, public policy and public affairs, as well as activists in educational reform, affirmative action groups and others, public administration has continued to change its curriculum on a national basis. NASPAA's Commission on Peer Review and Accreditation is the national accrediting body for master's degrees in public administration. The NASPAA standards adopted in July, 2009, require competencies in five domains. These include the following abilities:

(1) To lead and manage in public governance.

(2) To participate in and contribute to the policy process.

(3) To analyze, synthesize, think critically, solve problems and make decisions.

(4) To articulate and apply a public service perspective.

(5) To communicate and interact productively with a diverse and changing workforce and citizenry. (National Association of Schools of Public Affairs and Administration Standards, 2009, p. 7)

The accreditation system used by NASPAA has done much to bring many public administration master's programs into compliance with national standards. Standards adopted by NASPAA continually change to keep up with the times. NASPAA curriculum guidelines try to balance skill development with a broader appreciation of the history of the field, a philosophic understanding of management, and a positive view of the public service.

New Challenges for Public Administration

As public managers navigate the administrative swamp daily, society and public administration continue to undergo immense and rapid change. As different values achieve priority status in society, public administration must adapt as government usually is asked to embody those values. For example, during the 1960s and 1970s, the New Public Administration emphasized social justice. In the late 1970s and early 1980s, there was emphasis on quality-of-life concerns that gave way in the 1980s and 1990s to the New Public Management, with its emphasis on efficiency, entrepreneurship, and privatization. As the 21st century began, *new* concerns for democratic values, responsiveness, and citizenship emerged (Denhardt & Denhardt, 2007; McNabb, 2009). Although all these values seem new, they actually reflect values that have been present in the field of public administration throughout its history. They just ebb and flow in their importance in the public eye or in the way they are labeled. In fact, public bureaucracy is expected to uphold all the values, but at different times, different values are emphasized.

Concerns expressed as new are actually extensions or different interpretations of the fundamental issues public administrators have always been expected to consider. In dealing with social justice, quality of life, responsiveness and the like, public administrators are responding to public interests and concerns. In addition to being responsive to democratic society's values, dealing with these issues also represents some of the basic issues addressed by traditional bureaucracy. The concepts of neutrality and impersonality really presume a sense of equity in treatment. The advocates of social justice ask that bureaucracy provide equal opportunity for all sectors of society to participate. Thus, their demands are partially consistent with the precepts of bureaucratic rationality. In the views of those supporting social equity issues, bureaucracy has always responded to those interests that have the most resources. It now is being asked to respond impartially or to give preference to those who otherwise do not have the resources to participate.

There is yet another way in which the concerns of contemporary bureaucracy can be viewed as a continuation of more traditional issues in public administration. The processes of administration receive much attention in analyses of public administration. Although there were efforts to eliminate the political from the administrative aspects of public affairs in the early development of public administration, it has never been possible to separate the two completely. What has become evident in contemporary public administration is that political processes are important to the administrative process. Those interests that are successful in gaining the attention of public bureaucracy are those that have access. They use their political resources to affect what is going on and use bargaining processes to gain support for their interests.

It is commonplace to speak of specialized interests and single-issue interest groups. These political actors participate in the political process at large, but they also concentrate a lot of attention on the public bureaucracy. The influence such groups have on bureaucracies is significant for the ability of our political system to integrate the varied interests into some form of public interest. If access and influence are too great for narrow interests, the general public may see its interests given short shrift. The implications for the legitimacy of public institutions and confidence in the political system are immense (Catlaw, 2007).

An emphasis on ethics and the moral foundations of bureaucratic behavior also has antecedents in the past. The moral fervor of the reformers of the 19th and early 20th century was clear. During the period in which Scientific Management and managerial efficiency held public administration's greatest attention, the moral and ethical issues were less visible, but they were always a part of the assumptions on which good management was based.

Since the 1970s and the Nixon administration's Watergate scandal, every administration has been plagued with some element of scandal. Though many of the scandals were minor, some were of major consequence for the administrations (e.g., the Reagan administration's Iran arms deal, the Clinton administration's Monica Lewinski scandal, and the Bush administration's Abu Ghraib prison and waterboarding abuses). The media focuses more on misdeeds than ever before making it look as though political leaders are more inept and corrupt than ever. Lapses in judgment among administration officials in the relationship of official and personal business and outright attempts to mislead the public raise ethical questions. People have developed a deep cynicism about the ethics of public officials. Even though these are incidents primarily involving elected political leaders and their political appointees, much of the public does not distinguish them from the career public administrator. The cynicism extends to all of government. Although there are instances of bureaucratic misdeeds, they are much more common among the political officials.

Ethics will continue to be an issue of importance to public administration (Menzel, 2007). There is not likely to be any resolution of the debate as to whether ethical behavior can best be assured through reliance on the character and professionalism of the individual bureaucrat (Friedrich, 1940) or through attempts to regulate behavior through legislation and rules and regulations (Finer, 1941). Certainly the United States uses both approaches, but there is a strong tendency to try to insure against any kind of abuse by developing a prohibition against it. The dilemma is that detailed prohibitions sometimes may make it difficult for the bureaucrat to act creatively and innovatively. Creative and innovative approaches to problems and jobs may be more valuable to the political system than focusing on enacting policies to prevent abuse. The question becomes one of whether the risk inherent in allowing widespread discretion is balanced by the potential for effective solutions to problems or delivery of service.

Conclusion

Public administration will continue to wrestle with competing values and interests. Issues confronting public administrators will continue to change as new concerns face citizens and other actors in the political system. In order to be responsive to elected political leaders, clients, and citizens, adaptive management will remain a hallmark of public administrative behavior.

David McNabb (2009) concurs that the administrative swamp evolves and presents new challenges. He opines that public administrators now deliver services under dramatically different environmental conditions than just a few years ago. He identifies five overarching demands confronting public managers:

(1) learning to cope after decades of pressures to downsize, reorganize, reinvent themselves, and do more with less;

(2) delivering new and expanding services with declining resources for maintenance, repair, and replacement of decaying infrastructure;

(3) seamlessly integrating new technologies alongside aging systems and stovepipe management architectures;

(4) dealing with discrepancies between personnel needs and available staff while capturing and disseminating knowledge being lost because of retiring workers;

(5) finding ways to form and structure new organizations— such as virtual organizations and private-public-sector collaborative units. (McNabb, 2009, pp. 1-2)

Demands for more services will conflict with demands for reducing the size of government and the resources needed by government. In order to serve these conflicting demands, public administrators have to find a way to adapt.

Much has been done recently to bring public administration into closer harmony with its turbulent environment. It remains, however, a stressed profession and a rapidly changing field of study. The swamp is not getting any easier to manage. Crisis management often is the order of the day. Public administrators must be able to make hard choices and provide moral leadership in a time when public regard for the public service has waned.

The issues to be addressed by public administration are the issues that face society. Despite the popularity of those advocating reduction of government intervention in our lives, it is unlikely that such change will occur. Instead, as new problems develop, government is likely to be asked to step in and solve them. We only hope that the fundamental issues of public administration discussed in this book will contribute to an understanding of the way public administration can and is likely to respond. The capacity of bureaucracy to adjust to and embrace change will be important determinants of its effectiveness and ability to emerge from the swamp.

Review and Study Questions

1. What are the tensions between bureaucratic traditions and democratic values? How do contemporary theories attempt to deal with those tensions? How do public bureaucracies adapt to them?

2. Why do differences in production costs and consumption costs lead to public policy debates? What are the issues? Provide an example to illustrate.

3. How does the phenomenon of single interest politics affect the ability of public administrators to do their jobs?

4. What implications does the revitalization of conservatism have for public administration?

5. Why does the rate of economic growth matter to public programs and public agencies?

6. Do you think the welfare state has been successful? Explain why or why not.

7. Why would diversity in public life be considered an opportunity for public administration?

8. Consider your interaction with any government agency or program (e.g., the IRS, drivers' license renewal, vehicle registration). How have changes in information technology affected the way you deal with the agency or program?

9. What does ethics mean to you? Why is it an issue in public administration? Is it possible to assure the ethical behavior of public administrators? Explain.

Exercises

1. Find some recent major ethical dilemma a local public administrator has faced. Use the local newspaper as the main source of your inquiry. Develop a mini-case study of this situation in which you lay out the following:
    a) A short description of the background and setting of the issue.
    b) A short description of the ethical issues.
    c) The contending values and choices confronting the administrator.
    d) The path of action selected by the administrator.
    e) An assessment of the quality of the choice.
    f) A conclusion in which you tell what you would have done if confronted by the same issues and situation.

2. Select a local office of a municipal, state, or federal agency that provides direct services to clients. Study it as an example of the relationship between production and consumption costs. Make some direct observations about the way the office functions, its location, its hours of operation, its publicity, its procedures, and its social climate as a place to visit. Did you observe anything that shows awareness of the trade-offs between consumption and production costs? Does the office and its staff shift costs in ways to increase consumption costs borne by clients? Is this office and its staff making efforts to reduce consumption costs? If so, are they effective? If not, what might the office and its staff do to reduce consumption costs? Overall, what did you learn about making services more consumable?

3. Write a short "profile in courage" about some public official you admire. Pick a real issue that tested that person's resolve, sense of public service, and ethics. What was the issue? What did this person do that is commendable? Why did she or he behave in such a commendable way? What did you learn about public affairs from this profile? Could you have done as well as this person? Why or why not?

4. Write an essay that tells how the personal computer and the Internet have changed your life. What kinds of views, values, skills, and opportunities have these communication technologies offered to you? Which have you taken advantage of? Which remain to be undertaken? In what ways have your electronic communication and computing skills better equipped you to serve the public?

5. Write a short essay on the following topic:

There is an inherent conflict between practical democracy and practical public administration. This conflict means that the earlier dream of a perfectly rational, disinterested administrative state is impossible in the United States. Instead, America always will have a public bureaucracy that is partially ineffective and inefficient as administrators struggle with the swamp.

Take a position on this theme. Develop and support your position carefully, using balanced arguments and information. Come to a definitive conclusion on your agreement or disagreement with this theme.

References

Atkinson, R. D., & Court, R. H. (1998). *The new economy index: Understanding America's economic transformation.* Washington, DC: Progressive Policy Institute.

Baker, D. L. (2004). *E-Government: Website usability of the most populous counties* (Unpublished doctoral dissertation). Arizona State University, Tempe, AZ.

Bayes, J. H. (1985, July). *Women in public administration in the United States: Upward mobility and career advancement.* Paper presented at the XIIIth World Congress of the International Political Science Association, Paris.

Bennis, W. G. (1969). *Organizational development: Its nature, origins, and prospects.* Menlo Park, CA: Addison-Wesley.

Block, P. (1991). *The empowered manager: Positive political skills at work.* San Francisco, CA: Jossey-Bass.

Bluestone, B., & Harrison, B. (1982). *The deindustrialization of America.* New York: Basic Books.

Bonaparth, E. (1982). *Women, power and policy.* New York: Pergamon.

Carr, T. R. (1999). Managing geographic information in the public sector. In G. D. Garson (Ed.), *Information technology and computer applications in public administration: Issues and trends* (pp. 220-230). Hershey, PA: Idea Group.

Catlaw, T. J. (2007). *Fabricating the people: Politics and administration in the biopolitical state.* Tuscaloosa: University of Alabama Press.

Cayer, N. J., & Schaefer, R. C. (1981). Affirmative action and municipal employees. *Social Science Quarterly, 62,* 487-494.

Cayer, N. J., & Sigelman, L. (1980). Minorities and women in state and local government. *Public Administration Review, 40*(5), 443-450.

Choi, S. (2009). Diversity in the US federal government: Diversity management and employee turnover in federal agencies. *Journal of Public Administration Research and Theory, 19,* 603-631.

Conger, J., & Kanungo, R. (1988). The empowerment process: Integrating theory and practice. *Academy of Management Review, 13,* 471-482.

Curtin, G. G., Sommer, M., & Vis-Sommer, V. (2003). *World of e-governance.* London: Haworth Press.

Denhardt, R. B. (2007). *Theories of public organization* (5th ed.). Florence, KY: Cengage Learning.

Denhardt, J. V., & Denhardt, R. B. (2007). *The new public service: Serving, not steering* (expanded ed.). Armonk, NY: M.E. Sharpe.

Denhardt, R. B., Denhardt, J. V., & Aristigueta, M. P. (2009). *Managing human behavior in public and nonprofit organizations* (2nd ed.). Los Angeles: Sage.

Devol, R. C., Klowden, K., Bedroussian, A., & Yeo, B. (2009). *North America's high-tech economy: The geography of knowledge-based industries*. Santa Monica, CA: Milken Institute.

Dolan, J., & Rosenbloom, D. H. (Eds.). (2003). *Representative bureaucracy: Classic readings and continuing controversies*. Armonk, NY: M.E. Sharpe.

Dolbeare, K. M. (1986). *The Politics of Economic Renewal* (rev. ed.). Chatham, NJ: Chatham House.

Dometrius, N. C. (1984). Minorities and women among state agency leaders. *Social Science Quarterly, 65,* 127-137.

Duncan, G. T. (1999). Managing information privacy and information access in the public sector. In G. D. Garson (Ed.), *Information technology and computer applications in public administration: Issues and trends* (pp. 99-117). Hershey, PA: Idea Group.

Finer, H. (1941). Administrative responsibility in democratic government. *Public Administration Review, 1*(3), 335-350.

Fountain, J. E. (2001). *Building the virtual state: Information technology and institutional change*. Washington, DC: Brookings Institution Press.

Friedrich, C. J. (1940). Public policy and the nature of administrative responsibility. *Public Policy, 1,* 3-24.

Frederickson, H. G. (1996). Comparing the reinventing government movement with the New Public Administration. *Public Administration Review, 56*(3), 263-270.

Garson, G. D. (2006). *Public information technology and e-governance: Managing the virtual state*. Sudbury, MA: Jones and Bartlett.

Garson, G. D., & Overman, E. S. (1983). *Public management research in the United States*. New York: Praeger.

Gerber, C. D., & Overman, E. S. (2001). *Stealing the initiative: How state government responds to direct democracy.* Upper Saddle River, NJ: Prentice Hall.

Gulick, L. (1987). Time and public administration. *Public Administration Review, 47*(1), 115-119.

Hall, J. L. (2007). Informing state economic development policy in the new economy: A theoretical foundation and empirical examination of state innovation in the United States. *Public Administration Review, 67,* 630-645.

Hall, R. H. (1999). *Organizations: Structures, processes and outcomes.* Upper Saddle River, NJ: Prentice Hall.

Heeks, R. (2005). *Implementing and managing egovernment: An international text.* Thousand Oaks, CA: Sage.

Heilbrunn, J. (2009). *They knew they were right: The rise of the neocons,* (Reprint ed.). Harpswell, ME: Anchor.

Hill, C. J., & Lynn, L. E., Jr. (2009). *Public management: A three dimensional approach.* Washington, DC: CQ Press.

Ho, A. T. (2002). Reinventing local governments and the e-government initiative. *Public Administration Review, 62*(4), 434-441.

Hsieh, C., & Winslow, E. (2006). Gender representation in the federal workforce. *Review of Public Personnel Administration, 26*(3), 276-294

Huckle, P. (1983). A decade's difference: Mid-level managers and affirmative action. *Public Personnel Management, 12*(3), 249-257.

Kamarck, E. C., & Nye, J. S. (2002). *Governance.com: Democracy in the information age.* Washington, DC: Brookings Institution Press.

Karl, Barry D. (1987). The American bureaucrat: A history of sheep in wolves' clothing. *Public Administration Review, 47*(1), 26-34.

Kettl, D. F. (2005). *The global public management revolution.* Washington, DC: Brookings Institution Press.

Landensbergen, D., Jr., & Wolken, G., Jr. (2001). Realizing the promise: Government information systems and the fourth generation of information technology. *Public Administration Review, 61*(2), 206-220.

Levine, C. H. (1978). Organizational decline and cutback management. *Public Administration Review, 38*(3), 316-325.

Levine, C. (1979). More on cutback management: Hard questions for hard times. *Public Administration Review, 39*(2), 179-189.

Lipset, S. M., & Schneider, W. (1983). *The confidence gap: Business, labor and government in the public mind.* New York: Free Press.

Lowi, T. (1979). *The end of liberalism* (2nd ed.). New York: Norton.

Marini, F., (Ed.). (1971). *Toward a New Public Administration: The Minnowbrook Perspective.* Scranton, PA: Chandler.

McCabe, B. C., & Stream C. (2000). Diversity by the numbers: Changes in state and local workforces 1980-1995. *Public Personnel Management, 29*(1), 93-106.

McConnell, G. (1966). *Private power and American democracy.* New York: Knopf.

McNabb, D. E. (2009). *The new face of government: How public managers are forging a new approach to governance.* Boca Raton, FL: CRC Press.

Menzel, D. C. (2007). *Ethics management for public administrators: Building organizations of integrity.* Armonk, NY: M.E. Sharpe.

Mintzberg, H. (1979). *The structuring of organizations.* Englewood Cliffs, NJ: Prentice Hall.

Moon, M. J. (2002). The evolution of e-government among municipalities: Rhetoric or reality? *Public Administration Review,*
62(4), 424-433.

Mosher, F., (Ed.). (1975). *American public administration: Past,*
present, future. Tuscaloosa: University of Alabama Press.

Murray, D. (2006). *NeoConservatism: Why we need it.* Lanham,
MD: Encounter Books.

Naff, K. C. (1998). Progress toward achieving a representative
federal bureaucracy: The impact of supervisors and their beliefs. *Public Personnel Management, 27*(2), 135-150.

National Association of Schools of Public Affairs and Administration Standards. (2009). National Association of Schools
of Public Affairs and Administration. Retrieved from http://
www.naspaa.org/accreditation/standard2009/main.asp

Nunn, S. (2001). Police information technology: Assessing the
effects of computerization on urban police functions. *Public*
Administration Review, 61(2), 221-234.

Osborne, D., & Hutchinson, P. (2006). *The price of government:*
Getting the results we need in an age of permanent fiscal cri-
sis (new ed.). Jackson, TN: Perseus Distribution.

Ospina, S. (2001). *Managing diversity in the civil service: A con-*
ceptual framework for public organizations, edited by UN-
DESA-IIAS, 5-10. Amsterdam: IOS Press.

Parenti, M. (2007). *Democracy for the few* (8th ed.). Armonk, NY:
Cengage Learning.

Phillips, K. (1982). *Post-Conservatism America.* New York: Random House.

Pollitt, C., & Bouckaert, G. (2004). *Public management reform:*
A comparative analysis (2nd ed.). London Oxford University
Press.

Prewitt, K. (1970). Political ambitions, volunteerism, and electoral accountability. *American Political Science Review, 64*(1),
5-17.

Price, D. K. (1975). 1984 and beyond: Social engineering or political values. In F. C. Mosher (Ed.), *American public administration: Past present, and future* (pp. 233-252). Tuscaloosa: University of Alabama Press.

Propen, A. (2007). Visual communication and the map: How maps as visual objects convey meanings in specific contexts. *Technical Communication Quarterly, 16*(2), 233-254.

Prysby, C., & Prysby, N. (1999). Legal aspects of electronic mail in public organizations. In G. David Garson (Ed.), *Information technology and computer applications in public administration: Issues and trends* (pp. 231-245). Hershey, PA: Idea Group Publishing.

Reich, R. B. (1983). *The next American frontier.* New York: Times Books.

Riccucci, N. M. (2005). *How management matters: Street-level bureaucrats and welfare reform.* Washington, DC: Georgetown University Press.

Riccucci, N. M. (2009). The pursuit of social equity in the federal government: A road less traveled? *Public Administration Review, 69*(3), 373-382.

Rittel, H. W. J., & Webber, M. (1973). Dilemmas in a general theory of planning. *Policy Sciences 4*(1), 155-169.

Rozell, M. J., Wilcox, C., & Madland, D. (2005). *Interest groups in American campaigns: The new face of electioneering* (2nd ed.). Washington, DC: CQ Press.

Rubin, I. S. (1985). *Shrinking the federal government.* New York: Longman.

Seneviratne, S. J. (1999). Information technology and organizational change in the public sector. In G. David Garson (Ed.), *Information technology and computer applications in public administration: Issues and trends* (pp. 41-61). Hershey, PA: Idea Group.

Sigelman, L., & Cayer, N. J. (1986). Minorities, women and public sector jobs: A status report. In M.W. Coombs and J. Gruhl (Eds.), *Affirmative action: Theory, analysis, and prospects* (pp. 91-111). Jefferson, NC: McFarland & Co.

Sirianni, C. (1984). Participation, opportunity, and equality: Toward a pluralist organizational model. In F. Fisher & C. Sirianni (Eds.), *Critical studies in organization and bureaucracy* (pp. 442-503). Philadelphia: Temple University Press.

Slack, J. D. (1997). From affirmative action to full spectrum diversity in the American workplace: Shifting the organizational paradigm. *Review of Public Personnel Administration, 17,* 75-87.

Starks, G. L. (2009). Minority representation in senior positions in U.S. federal agencies: A paradox of underrepresentation. *Public Personnel Management, 38*(1), 79-90.

Thayer, F. C. (1981). *An end to hierarchy and competition.* New York: Franklin Watts.

Thompson, F. J., & Brown, B. (1978). Commitment to the disadvantaged among urban administrators: The case of minority hiring. *Urban Affairs Quarterly, 13,* 355-378.

Tjosvold, D., & Sun, H. (2006). Effects of power concepts and employee performance on managers' empowering. *Leadership & Organization Development Journal, 27*(3), 217-234.

Vinzant, J. C., & Crothers, L. (1998). *Street-level leadership: Discretion and legitimacy in front-line public service.* Washington, DC: Georgetown University Press.

Waldo, D. (1980). *The enterprise of public administration.* Novato, CA: Chandler.

Warren, M. & Weschler, L. (1999). Electronic governance on the Internet. In G. D. Garson (Ed.), *Information technology and computer applications in public administration: Issues and trends* (pp.118-133). Hershey, PA: Idea Group.

Weinstein, D. (1979). *Bureaucratic opposition: Challenging abuses at the workplace.* New York: Pergamon.

White, J. D. (2007). *Managing information in the public sector.* *Armonk,* NY: M.E. Sharpe.

Selected Web Sites

American Political Science Association. (Professional organization for the study of political science).
http://www.apsanet.org/index.cfm

American Society for Public Administration. (Public service organization dedicated to advancing teaching and practice of public and nonprofit administration).
http://www.aspanet.org/scriptcontent/ASPAgeneral.cfm

Center for Technology in Government. (Organization that works with government to develop information strategies that foster innovation and enhance the quality and coordination of public services).
http://www.ctg.albany.edu/

E-Governance Institute. (Organization that explores how the internet and other information technologies impact the public sector).
http://andromeda.rutgers.edu/~egovinst/Website/index.html

IBM Center for the Business of Government. (Organization that connects public management research with practice to improve the effectiveness of government and sponsors independent research).
http://www.businessofgovernment.org/index.asp

National Association of Schools of Public Affairs and Administration. (Accreditation organization for graduate public administration education and training for public service and to promote the ideal of public service).
http://www.naspaa.org/

National Center for Digital Government. (Organization that seeks to advance the use of technology in government).
http://www.umass.edu/digitalcenter/index.html

Public Technology Institute. (Organization created by and for
    cities and counties to identify opportunities for technology
    research).
    http://www.pti.org/index.php

USA.gov. (Official information and services from the U.S. govern-
    ment).
    http://www.usa.gov/index.shtml

Index